PHILHARMONIA ORCHESTRA

A Record of Achievement

1945–1985

By the same author

Dennis Brain: A Biography

Philharmonia Orchestra

A Record of Achievement
1945–1985

by

STEPHEN J. PETTITT

ROBERT HALE · LONDON

First published in Great Britain 1985

Robert Hale Limited
Clerkenwell House
Clerkenwell Green
London EC1R 0HT

British Library Cataloguing in Publication Data

Pettitt, Stephen J.
Philharmonia Orchestra: a record of achievement
1945–1985.
1. Philharmonia Orchestra—History
I. Title
785'.06'2421 ML123/

ISBN 0-7090-2371-5

Photoset in North Wales by
Derek Doyle & Associates, Mold, Clwyd.
Printed in Great Britain by
St Edmundsbury Press, Bury St Edmunds, Suffolk.
Bound by Hunter & Foulis Ltd.

Contents

Illustrations

Between pages 64 and 65

Between pages 128 and 129

Between pages 160 and 161

ACKNOWLEDGEMENTS

The following pictures have been reproduced by kind permission of : DGG/Barda, 1, 43, 47; Sophie Baker, 34; Barcelo, 36, 37; Columbia Gramophone Co Ltd., 9; *Daily Express*, 25; Bill Duxbury, 23; Gerald Drucker, 35, 41; EMI, 4, 5, 7, 8, 12, 18; Mike Evans, 39; Fayer, Vienna, 19, 20; David Farrell, 29; P. Freyham, 30; Douglas Glass, 2; General News Features, 11; Keystone, 28; G. Macdomnic, 10, 24, 26, 31, 32, 33, 42; Doug McKenzie, 44; Gerald Murray, 38; Press Illustrations, 6, 45; Jean Schneider, 13; Teatro Alla, Scala, 46; *The Times*, 22; Paul Weber, 21; Roger Wood, 15; Franz Votava, 16

For M.

KENSINGTON PALACE

I am delighted to have this opportunity of joining the Philharmonia Orchestra in their celebration of forty years of making music. This book chronicles the fascinating story of their growth and development; a story of which they can be justly proud.

Since I became Patron of the Orchestra in May 1980 I have attended several of their excellent concerts. They have all been very enjoyable occasions and I am constantly reminded of the Philharmonia's outstanding contribution to the musical heritage of our nation, as well as the players' hard work as ambassadors of their art abroad. I shall always be ever-lastingly grateful to the orchestra for the way in which its members responded to my request for some assistance at our wedding. It was a great example of British music-making at its best.

Music has been a source of much joy in my own life and the Philharmonia are to be admired for their continuing efforts to share their high cultural achievements with others. This they do through concerts and recordings, through the admirable regional projects and youth schemes which they have pioneered so enthusiastically, and by a courageous promotion of new music.

I wish them every success and good fortune in the years to come.

Charles.

Introduction and Acknowledgements

Although my name appears on the cover of this book, the task of compiling it has been very much a team effort. It speaks volumes for the esteem in which the Philharmonia Orchestra is held that all those I approached for help gave their time and whole-hearted co-operation most generously.

Christopher Bishop, Managing Director of the Philharmonia, invited me in 1983 to make this book a fortieth anniversary tribute. Not only has he given me hours of his time but he has also given me unlimited access to every nook and cranny of the orchestra's offices, for which I am deeply grateful to him and all the staff at New Cavendish Street. Christopher has also given me a great deal of helpful advice and information, and I thank him most sincerely. I should, however, point out that any opinions expressed are my own and that errors of fact or emphasis are to be laid at my door.

Others have read sections of the text and made very helpful suggestions or corrections: Barrie Iliffe, Gareth Morris, Nick Tschaikov, Gavin Henderson and Stephen Gray all deserve my deep thanks for this. Within the orchestra itself I must especially thank Chairman Martin Jones for his unstinting help, Clem Relf, Vivienne Dimant, Julia Hirst, Lucy Breaks and the late J.R. Mead. Ronald Archer and Joyce Reah have offered much advice and information on the activities of the Philharmonia Chorus.

The staff of EMI have been most co-operative at every stage of the book, and I want to thank Ruth Edge of the EMI Archives at Hayes, Joan Coulson at Manchester Square, and Peter Andry, Richard Bradburn, Anthony Locantro, John Mordler, Charles Rodier and John Watson of the International Classical Division at Gloucester Place.

The rest of my helpers all deserve individual thanks but I hope they will not mind if I list them below in alphabetical order – to all of them I am equally grateful: John Amis, BBC Written Archives, Hugh Bean and his wife Mary, the late T.E. Bean, Ian Beers, David Bicknell, George Boxall, Gwydion Brooke, Jack Brymer, Eric Caller, Tom Carter, Alan Civil, Gillian Eastwood, Vernon Elliott, Tony Farnell, Fiona Grant, Lord

Harewood, Dr Harriet Harvey-Wood, Peter Heyworth, Jessie Hinchliffe, Leonard Hirsch, Joan Ingpen, Harold Jackson, Cecil James, Philip Jones, Jack Kessler, Lotte Klemperer, Lawrie Lea, the late Walter Legge, Robert Leslie, Mary Jo Little, Gerald McDonald, Denis Matthews, Harry Mortimer, Riccardo Muti, Manoug Parikian, Jasper Parrott, Anthony Pini, Shirley Rees, Frederick Riddle, Max Salpeter, Alan Sanders, Elisabeth Schwarzkopf, Ian Stoutzker, Ursula Strebi-Jones, Patrick Strevens, George Stringer, Sidney Sutcliffe, Christopher Warren-Green, Jane Withers.

Finally, I must thank my wife and children who must have wondered over the past two years who the stranger was about the house who sat pored over the typewriter and occasionally took meals.

I sincerely hope this volume will be a fitting tribute to a great orchestra and one of our finest national assets. If it also informs and entertains its readers, I will be more than happy.

Whitley Bay, February 1985 — Stephen J. Pettitt

1. *Walter Legge*

The history of the Philharmonia Orchestra is a remarkable one. Within months of its foundation in the summer of 1945 there began to pour from it a stream of recordings that grew to a tidal wave in the mid-1950s. Many of those recordings are classics of the gramophone and have remained in the catalogues despite the developments of stereophony, quadraphony and digital techniques, and the Philharmonia is still among the world's most recorded orchestras. The list of artists who have appeared with it, on record and in the concert hall, is a glittering one. Within three years of its foundation the Philharmonia was at the Edinburgh Festival; after only seven years it toured Europe, and in its tenth anniversary year it astonished the United States with its first tour there. It soon became a regular visitor to the great international festivals, has toured South America and Poland, Iceland and Australia, and regularly fills the Royal Festival Hall in London for concerts that are highlights of the musical year.

In the first twenty years of its existence the Philharmonia was the personal property of the man who had conceived the idea of the orchestra, founded it, nourished its growth and ruthlessly guarded its quality. That man was Walter Legge, one of the most influential figures on the British musical scene of the last fifty years, a kind of 'musical midwife' responsible for the birth of some of the greatest musical achievements of his time, from the Philharmonia itself through his recordings to the artists he 'spotted' with his uncanny ear for real potential and its realization in performance. He had enemies: no one could work in the way he did and not incur enmity, and yet men of the calibre of Furtwängler, Lipatti and Karajan said of him that there was no one from whom they could learn more, and the directors of opera houses from Vienna to San Francisco relied implicitly on his judgement and advice.

To study Walter Legge's early life before and during the Second World War is to gain an understanding of his unique position in the world of music, and of his ability to draw together the elements that made possible the creation of the Philharmonia Orchestra.

Walter Legge was born in London on 1 June 1906. His parents had married in their mid-thirties: his mother had the literary talent; father and son shared a mutual love of music, and Walter himself claimed he learned to read from record labels! He learned the piano sufficiently to 'get by' and then studied music from records, books and concert-going. In Walter's early teens his father bought him a record collection to which he began adding with his pocket money. Even at this age he began to be discriminating, choosing new additions to his collection after careful listening to all the different versions available. So began a quest for perfection, or as near perfection as he could approach. This same quest he applied to his concert-going. In the early 1920s he had the opportunity of hearing the great conductors of the day both in concert and in rehearsal, and from 1924 he attended nearly every international performance at Covent Garden.

When he left Latimer Upper School at the age of sixteen, he had only one ambition – to join a record company and pursue in a practical way the ideals of performance and criticism he had already formulated. His father wanted him to join the family tailoring business but in 1927 he joined HMV as a lecturer, travelling round Britain giving talks with musical illustrations. Later he became a writer in the artists' department, reviewing the famous Cortot-Thibaud-Casals recording of Beethoven's *Archduke* Trio so well that he was given the task of writing analytical notes for record albums and sales literature; he was the head of a department of one, a position he enjoyed as often as he could for the rest of his life.

Once inside the HMV organization, Legge looked around for ways of widening his interests. For a while he edited the 'house' magazine, *The Voice*, which was circulated around the company; he also gained access to the studios. Then, in 1931, came an impressive series of subscription recordings of Wolf *Lieder* – it is not clear whose was the initial inspiration, but the idea put Legge on the musical map of HMV. By the time the last songs had been recorded, in December 1931, enough subscribers had been found, and the first volume was issued in April 1932.

The first Society album undoubtedly marked an important stage in Legge's career. He supervised many of the subsequent Wolf sessions himself in London and Berlin, trying out his forward-looking ideas. He also aroused resentment: officially he was only a music copywriter and had no right to a recording position but the Wolf albums were an undoubted success. He was also associated with the international artists he began to record; Albert Schweitzer, Wanda Landowska, John McCormack – all of them worked with him, and from them he learned the art of music. The success of the subscription idea induced HMV to expand it.

Early in 1934 Legge went to Manchester to discuss with Sir Thomas Beecham plans for an International Music Society, and after a day with Beecham he had the support he needed. It matters little that the International Music Society never came into existence, for Legge was soon producing nearly all Beecham's recordings with the London Philharmonic Orchestra. This meant more than a foot in the door of the recording studio: he had so charmed Beecham that the latter refused to record unless Legge was the producer, despite the fact that Beecham was a Columbia artist and Legge was from the HMV 'stable'. Beecham and Legge made a fashionable pair, for they shared a passion for excellence in performance both live and recorded.

Legge also built up a fund of experience in recording the human voice, learning the art of the record producer from the inside and with artists who were in the 'luxury' class – Flagstad, Thorborg, Melchior, Janssen, Weber, Lemnitz. About the same time the Glyndebourne Mozart Opera Society sets, conducted by Fritz Busch, were appearing on the market and receiving wide acclaim. They had been shrewd business ventures. As well as the subscription idea, HMV got excellently rehearsed recordings from a small number of sessions and thus quite cheaply. Legge, with Beecham's support, knew something better could be done, given a free hand in the choice of artists. He pounced. With Beecham on his side he feared no real opposition from his HMV colleagues, and after checking availability he proposed, at a repertoire meeting early in 1937, a recording of Mozart's *Magic Flute* with Beecham conducting the Berlin Philharmonic and the best all-German cast available. It was an outstanding success. Recorded in just over a week in November 1937 in the Beethovensaal in Berlin, it is still regarded as *musically* one of the best versions on record and is still available, nearly fifty years later. Legge's first complete opera recording demonstrated the qualities that were to make him world-famous in this field: the choice of the best artists available in their respective roles; patient hours of coaching and preparation before a single note was recorded; and skilful use of the studio and equipment (the 1937 *Magic Flute* was recorded on 78s but is still musically highly satisfying – the artistic result transcends the primitive means).

Such was Beecham's delight at the success of the *Magic Flute* – it was *his* first complete opera recording abroad – that over Christmas 1937 he invited Legge to become his assistant artistic director at Covent Garden. It was a significant step in Legge's career. Hitherto he had largely been involved in the literature of music, only recently coming to and gaining experience in the recording of it. Now, at Covent Garden, he was an administrator. Beecham was to agree the repertoire and the operas he wished to conduct himself. The rest was up to Legge.

It was a daunting task but Legge tackled it with enthusiasm and skill. The seasons of 1938 and 1939 were outstanding for the calibre of artists engaged and the artistic standards achieved. Furtwängler, Gui, Kleiber and Weingartner all conducted, and the singers included Leider, Melchior, Janssen, Gigli, Berger, Konetzni, with débuts for Fritz Krenn, Richard Tauber and Jussi Björling.

The outbreak of war in September 1939 was no more a bolt from the blue to the musical world than it was to the ordinary citizens of Britain. For the duration of the 'phoney' war Covent Garden, like most theatres, remained closed, and when it did reopen it was as a Palais de Danse, leased from the management by Mecca Cafés. Legge and Beecham had to content themselves with shelving their plans for 1940 which had promised such luxurious novelties as Gluck's *Iphigénie*, Berlioz's *Les Troyens* and *Boris Godunov*.

Legge was still employed by HMV and soon found that he was the only record producer left in the company. The recording of most foreign artists was either impossible or impractical, so he was given the responsibility for all new classical recordings within a much-reduced EMI structure, using British artists for the most part. The BBC Symphony Orchestra was an obvious target for his activities, and he began with two days of recording in April 1940 in the Colston Hall, Bristol.

After the Munich crisis of 1938, Sir Adrian Boult and the BBC Orchestral Manager had been given the unenviable task of drawing up a contingency list 'in the event of war' of ninety essential players for a balanced symphony orchestra and thirty 'dispensable' players. Plans were laid for evacuation from London as soon as war was eventually declared, the orchestra itself to be sent to Bristol, where it had the excellent facilities of the BBC West Region's headquarters, the rest of the Music Division, with Boult's deputy Musical Director R.S. Thatcher, to go to Evesham. In a rather underhand manner the BBC also signed contracts with a number of 'star' musicians, not all of them BBC players, to form a new combination to play high-quality light music. This became the BBC Salon Orchestra. Throughout the winter of 1939-40 conditions in Bristol seemed almost attractive. Concerts began again, and so did even some short tours. In this period of calm it was decided to record the orchestra, and hence the arrival of Walter Legge and his HMV engineers in the Colston Hall. He went from Bristol to record the Liverpool, Birmingham and Hallé Orchestras. From the early days of the War he had Britain's post-war music foremost in his mind, and these recording trips made useful contacts with the players and enabled him to keep track of where the best of them were.

When the BBC Salon Orchestra was moved to Evesham in January 1941, Legge seized the opportunity, with so many good chamber players on hand, to record some chamber works, particularly featuring the clarinettist Reginald Kell. In January and February 1941 Kell recorded the Mozart Clarinet Trio with Frederick Riddle and Louis Kentner, and the Brahms Trio with Anthony Pini and Kentner.

Legge had Riddle and Pini in mind to form a first-rate string quartet, and also the ideal leader, Henry Holst, formerly leader of Furtwängler's Berlin Philharmonic from 1923–31, who was now leader of the Liverpool Philharmonic; Legge had already met him before the Cheltenham recordings, and Holst was willing to come to Evesham on a regular basis. So, in the early days of 1941, Henry Holst, Jean Pougnet, Frederick Riddle and Anthony Pini became the Philharmonia Quartet. (The name came from the title of the miniature score Legge used for the first work they recorded – Mozart's B flat *Hunt* Quartet.) The work was recorded in Cheltenham in August 1941. Again, Legge's ability to spot real talent and prepare it meticulously paid off, for the records were well reviewed. A second quartet, Beethoven's First *Rasumovsky*, was prepared. Jean Pougnet had not been over-enthusiastic about playing second violin, even to Henry Holst whom he respected and liked, and so for the Beethoven his place was taken by David Wise. It was recorded in January 1942 and was followed by Schubert's *Death and the Maiden* Quartet in July 1942. In *The Gramophone* for November 1942 Compton Mackenzie wrote: 'With this performance of *Death and the Maiden* of Schubert I have no hesitation in acclaiming the Philharmonia as the best string quartet in the country.'

Events in 1942 made some changes to the Philharmonia Quartet necessary. The Salon Orchestra, while keeping a group of outstanding players on reserve, had not proved a musical success. Legge made attempts to record some light music repertoire with them during the summer and autumn of 1941 but failed to reach agreement with the players and the idea was dropped. Frederick Riddle was then called up into the Army, and Jean Pougnet went to lead the London Philharmonic Orchestra. With little to hold them together as a viable musical unit and with the BBC Symphony Orchestra, together with Thatcher, now in Bedford, the BBC disbanded the Salon Orchestra with effect from 11 July 1942. Players like David Wise, Reginald Kell, Anthony Pini and John Cockerill found posts in the Liverpool Philharmonic Orchestra; Herbert Downes now replaced Riddle as the Philharmonia's viola player, and Ernest Element took over second violin late in 1944, when David Wise became leader of the Liverpool Philharmonic. In Liverpool the Philharmonia Quartet continued to meet, if somewhat sporadically, with some concerts in late 1942 and early 1943, but the important thing was that the players were known to Legge and in the company of other notable instrumentalists of the calibre of Arthur Ackroyd (flute) and John Alexandra (bassoon).

Not all the best wind and string players in Britain had avoided call-up, and many of the younger generation of instrumentalists had found their way into the RAF at Uxbridge through the persuasive influence of Squadron Leader R.P. O'Donnell. So persuasive was he that O'Donnell found himself with over nine hundred players but they included wind players such as Dennis and Leonard Brain, Gareth Morris, Cecil James and Harold Jackson, as well as string players such as Harry Blech, Leonard Hirsch and the Griller Quartet. The formation of a symphony orchestra soon followed, and at its nucleus were thirty-two strings, led by David Martin.

The impression may be that Legge led a life of comparative inactivity during the War years. Far from it. At the outbreak of war he knew he would be automatically excluded from military service for he had the most appalling eyesight. In September 1939 he therefore applied for a job with ENSA (Entertainment National Service Association), and within a few months he was put in charge of Contracts 'A', an office on the NAAFI (Navy, Army and Air Force Institutes) side of the organization that dealt exclusively with artists' contracts.

ENSA had been an active force in the 1914–18 War but now it had assumed a much more prominent and highly organized role, wrestling with the problem of getting performances of the best music to the Forces and factories in Britain. As time passed, its organizer, Basil Dean, became increasingly worried that the standard of music being promoted appealed to the lowest common denominator, and sounded like it. Then, as he put it, 'Providence blew a stormy petrel into my office, with a cigarette drooping from its mouth and waving a walking-stick, a creature of uncertain temper with a supreme indifference to the feelings of those who sought to hinder its unerring flight towards that rarified upper air where only the finest music can be heard. This was Walter Legge, the recording manager of the Gramophone Company (HMV).'

Within a few weeks the ENSA Advisory Music Council was formed, as a result of Dean's meeting with Sir Victor Schuster, Bart., who was attached to the Ministry of Information, to discuss the future promotion of good music for the Forces. Sir Victor Schuster was Chairman, William Walton was Vice-Chairman and Walter Legge was Liaison Officer. Within a year the work had become so extensive that Legge was transferred from the Contracts Branch to take charge of the newly formed Music Division.

The Council was probably one of the most representative bodies of musical opinion ever assembled in Britain and ensured the support of all the leading conductors and soloists in the land. Apart from the immediate gain this brought to war-torn Britain in terms of high standards of performance, it also put Legge in touch with influential people in the highest echelons of music, with colleagues who would work tirelessly and enthusiastically for him; for the future gain of post-war music, it also widened his contacts with the best players in the country. His work with Sir Victor Schuster, for example, stood him in good stead for the early Philharmonia Concert Society days. The two of them co-operated so well that at first their plans were merely rubber-stamped by the Council – but this soon had to stop: monthly meetings were held and minutes kept, much to Legge's annoyance, whose contempt for the routine of organization was well known.

The achievements of Legge's ENSA Music Division were outstanding in their diversity and their quality. Each of the Military Command Areas was assigned a musical adviser by the Council. Their appointment often invoked a mixed, even cool reception, but with men of the calibre of Dr W.G. Whittaker, Boyd Neel, Richard Austin and Herbert Lodge occupying these posts, such scorn was misplaced and short-lived. Herbert Lodge had formed a Southern Command Symphony Orchestra in the autumn of 1940, and others followed suit. Artists such as Moiseiwitsch, Solomon and Barbirolli were regularly engaged; Walter Süsskind joined the Symphonic Division of ENSA, conducting three concerts a week, and Vilem Tausky joined in the uniform of a Czech soldier and later conducted at Covent Garden; George Weldon started a conducting career through ENSA that took him on to the Hallé and the City of Birmingham Orchestras.

The autumn of 1943 also saw the first of the concert tours abroad. In October Solomon and Herbert Lodge toured the Middle East and found not just receptive audiences but orchestras too, made up entirely of Servicemen, who accompanied them in Malta and Cairo.

Legge kept his finger very much on the pulse of British musical talent. In three years he took ENSA from one experimental concert to being one of the largest concert-giving organizations in the country. With auditions, rehearsals and concerts he knew where all the best players were. He was highly respected by musicians and singers in the recording studio and even in the conference room, where his sweeping judgements carried an authority that was borne out by events. His colleagues did not always go along with these tactics, and in May 1944 Basil Dean was irritated but not a little surprised to receive a memorandum from the Music Council, asking for Legge's removal. They saw the organization at headquarters as faulty and felt that too little consultation was being sought from the regional advisers. Basil Dean had lived for four years with Legge's contempt for routine; now that it undermined the allegiance and co-operation of the regions, it had to be brought under tighter control, and this Dean did. The memorandum implied that standards were too high and that concessions should be made to more popular taste. Here was Legge's greatest tenet – that only the best is good enough – under direct attack, and Dean was not prepared to allow such an attack. Both ENSA and Legge survived the storm, but it was not the last time that his ruthlessness and obstinacy in the pursuit of excellence were to ruffle the feathers of his professional colleagues.

The liberation of Paris was the beginning of ENSA's last significant contribution to wartime music and Legge's first opportunity, wearing his HMV hat, to take up the links again with artists who had been unable to record during the War. As the troops advanced, the musicians followed. In Paris, too, Legge made many discoveries for HMV through his friend Jacques Thibaud. Soon he had signed contracts with Ginette Neveu, Samson François and Dinu Lipatti. In Brussels he found the young violinist Arthur Grumiaux, and in Germany the tenor Rudolf Schock.

During the War years Legge had kept in regular touch with John Barbirolli. Particularly after Barbirolli took over the Hallé in 1943 and began to revitalize it. Legge began to see in him the kind of conductor with whom he would like to work after the War, and the two of them discussed the possibility frequently. Barbirolli, however, was committed to building the Hallé into a first-class orchestra again, and everything else would have to go by the board until that had been achieved.

As 1944 wore on, Legge started to formulate the plans he had made in the early War years to form his own first-class orchestra of the best musicians in the country. He revived the Philharmonia Quartet and presented very successful series of the complete Beethoven Quartets in Liverpool in May and June 1944 and in Birmingham from May to September 1944. He had the name for his orchestra, and he had seen and heard the best players in Britain. Now they were to be brought together into one orchestra – the Philharmonia.

2. *Philharmonia – Birth and Infancy, 1945-7*

Almost since the beginning of the War Walter Legge had been preoccupied with the problems that would surround the resumption of music in Britain when hostilities ceased. He was in a unique position in this respect: he had assumed almost total control of EMI's wartime recording activities, building up an enviable reputation and experience as a record producer; in ENSA his administrative work had brought him into contact with every type of artist and orchestra. Closest to his heart, however, was the human voice in opera, and throughout the War he cherished the ambition to resume control of Covent Garden, with Beecham, as soon as opera started again. Rightly, he felt that every good opera house needed a first-class pit orchestra, and he saw it as one of his first tasks to establish at Covent Garden an orchestra which, on the lines of the present Vienna Philharmonic, would be for most of the time the opera house orchestra but would also be available for some concerts and for recording. The War years had shown him that there were in Britain enough first-class players to form such an orchestra; many then in the Forces would thus be assured of regular work when they were demobbed; others were playing in the established London and provincial orchestras and had made it clear that they would welcome the chance of higher standards than they were at present enjoying.

Even in Walter Legge's own writings there is some confusion between his early ambitions, undoubtedly connected with Covent Garden, and the first gathering of the players for recordings in July 1945. Posterity has made much of the recording connection with EMI – *too* much at this early stage, when it says that the Philharmonia was formed primarily for recording and even though its recording début preceded its first public concert by nearly four months. By the end of 1944, however, Legge knew that the administration of Covent Garden after the War would be very different from that in 1939 and that it would include neither him nor Beecham. The committee formed to administer the opera house, chaired by Lord Keynes, was anxious to employ as the new manager a businessman with a deep feeling for the Arts, not someone who was a musician first and foremost. When Beecham realized that Covent Garden had fallen into the hands of those who disliked him and whom he despised, he protested, through the medium of the Press, but failed to gain his own way. For Walter Legge, any hopes of managing Covent Garden and giving it a world-class orchestra vanished at a stroke.

Legge now seems to have decided to form an orchestra anyway, but he badly needed an initial outlet for it, a *raison d'être*. An opportunity came with a projected complete recording of Purcell's *Dido and Aeneas* for the British Council, conducted by Constant Lambert. Legge was setting this up early in 1945, and on 2 February he wrote to the British Council to say that the only outstanding obstacle to recording before mid-May was the return to Britain of the RAF Orchestra, 'whose strings I regard as the best in the country for this purpose'. By June 1945 the orchestra was described in correspondence as the 'Philharmonia String Orchestra'; Legge had asked James Whitehead, principal cellist of the RAF Orchestra, to engage twenty-four string players for this and some other recordings. The twenty-four strings and a few wind players met in EMI's Abbey Road studios on 2 July 1945, to record a J.C. Bach Sinfonia and the Hugo Wolf *Italian Serenade*, both conducted by Walter Süsskind. The Purcell *Dido and Aeneas* was recorded from 4 to 6 July, also in Abbey Road studios.

At much the same time, Legge and Sir Victor Schuster formed the Philharmonia Concert Society to promote the Philharmonia Quartet's first London concerts, in July 1945 at the Wigmore Hall. The Quartet, Henry Holst, Ernest Element, Herbert Downes and Anthony Pini, had recorded the Mozart Clarinet Quintet in February 1945 with Reginald Kell, and the success of this and their earlier records gave Legge the confidence to launch the London series. The Philharmonia Concert Society's prospectus for the summer of 1945 promised further chamber concerts, and the July Wigmore Hall series was all that Legge hoped for. Despite some last-minute changes in programme and personnel, because of the RAF Orchestra players' absence in Potsdam for the peace conferences, there was no compromise in quality. *The Times* spoke of 'rare excellence', 'sensitive delicacy and aristocratic polish' and 'the quality we must now associate with the title Philharmonia'.

It was now time for the threads of the orchestra's organization to be drawn together. As a result of the *Dido and Aeneas* recording, EMI were interested, for the orchestras they had hitherto supported were no longer adequate. The BBC Symphony Orchestra had lost a number of eminent players on their return to London and were preoccupied with reorganization; the London Philharmonic were very undistinguished and soon signed exclusively for Decca; the London Symphony were even poorer, so it seemed a practical proposition to carry on the process of consolidating the Philharmonia Orchestra now there was promise of regular recording work.

The summer of 1945 was spent collecting the remaining wind players necessary for a full complement. Reginald Kell was already committed and was soon joined by Arthur Gleghorn (flute) and Jack Alexandra (bassoon), both colleagues from the Liverpool Philharmonic. Alec Whittaker, principal oboist in the London Symphony during the War, now joined the Philharmonia. Legge had kept these players' interest by some solo recordings with the new orchestra: the J.C. Bach Sinfonia had featured Alec Whittaker as soloist, and later in August the Bach B minor Suite was recorded with Arthur Gleghorn, and a Tartini Concerto with Reginald Kell. Heddle Nash was the first singer to be invited, and he recorded some Handel arias; the strings alone recorded the Purcell *Chaconne* and Bartók's *Rumanian Dances.* Finally, on the last two days in August 1945, a full orchestra of fifty-one players recorded the Tchaikovsky First Piano Concerto, with Moiseiwitsch as soloist and George Weldon conducting.

It was now time to present the Philharmonia Orchestra before the public. The autumn season of concerts would soon begin, and more players were available as they were demobbed. When Legge returned from Germany in late September, the Philharmonia Concert Society prospectus announced, in addition to a further series of chamber concerts, the public début of the Philharmonia Orchestra in Kingsway Hall for the afternoon of 27 October 1945. Beecham had been invited to conduct an all-Mozart programme, a sensible choice for an orchestra which was still of modest size and in a building which, ideal for recording, was rather too resonant as a concert hall. The programme for the concert carried no personnel list, but Legge had already made public the list of principal players. There were the original twenty-four strings from the RAF, with leader Leonard Hirsch, and other section principals Gerald Emms, Max Gilbert, James Whitehead and James W. Merrett. The woodwind players were Arthur Gleghorn, Alec Whittaker, Reginald Kell and Jack Alexandra; horns Dennis Brain, Norman Del Mar, Alan Hyde and Frank Probyn; timpani James Bradshaw and first trumpet Harry Mortimer.

A full Kingsway Hall heard the Overture to *Don Giovanni*, the G Minor Symphony, Reginald Kell in the Clarinet Concerto, the D Major Divertimento and *Five German Dances.* The critics were quick to notice Beecham's magic with Mozart but were equally quick to pick out the qualities of the new orchestra: 'hand-picked players' wrote one paper 'whose execution of the notes was beyond normal professional competence'. The same paper suggested a longer association between the Philharmonia and Beecham, and perhaps with that in mind Sir Victor

Schuster invited Beecham and Legge to lunch the following Monday, to hold a post-mortem and to lay plans for the future.

It was at this lunch that Beecham accepted his famous box of cigars, the only fee he would take for 'the privilege of directing this magnificent consort of artists'. It was at the same lunch that he offered his services as musical director of the new orchestra: he had access to the Royal Philharmonic name as well as substantial financial resources, but Legge clung to his independence and his principles. The Philharmonia would have no permanent conductor, and he told Beecham politely but firmly that he had no intention of making him a present of the orchestra. Beecham left angrily, scoffing as he went: 'The name Philharmonia is ridiculous, anyway; no one will ever remember it.'

It seems strange to anyone who knew both men that Legge ever imagined he could achieve Beecham's co-operation with the Philharmonia and not lose control over it, for both were men who did not take kindly to being told what to do by others, especially in the fields in which they were both eminent. Beecham's name had given a useful fillip to the orchestra's public début but the price of his permanent association was too high. The whole episode led the London Philharmonic Orchestra to review its attitude to Beecham and try to get a contract out of him, but the breach made by his flirtation with the Philharmonia was already too wide and their failure was a major factor in the founding, a year later in the autumn of 1946, of the Royal Philharmonic Orchestra. Legge, meanwhile, was left with fifty-two hand-picked players and conductors such as Walter Süsskind, George Weldon, Maurice Miles, Warwick Braithwaite and Constant Lambert who would undertake recordings, for the most part accompanying singers and a few instrumentalists. It was not enough work to hold them together and give him time to build.

The Philharmonia players were paid by the session or by concert and rehearsal, and consequently the personnel in those early days was variable in identity, though rarely variable in quality. Many new chamber orchestras were springing up around London, and the same players were to be found in most of them, including the Philharmonia players. The first leader of the Philharmonia was Leonard Hirsch. Born in Dublin (though his father was Russian), he was a gentle-mannered and dapper man of great charm. Ex-leader of the second violins in the Hallé before the War, he brought a great deal of experience to the Philharmonia. He also had his own quartet, two of them members of the original Philharmonia Orchestra – Gerald Emms, Max Gilbert and Harvey Philips – and this took him away from the Philharmonia quite frequently. On these occasions Thomas Carter led: equally experienced, he had led the Scottish Orchestra under Barbirolli and Szell, led the second violins for Beecham's pre-war London Philharmonic and then spent five years in the RAF. Even at this early stage Legge was attracted by the idea of the Continental use of joint leaders, or concert-masters, but throughout the orchestra's life he had the utmost difficulty in convincing the leaders of the scheme's viability. Leonard Hirsch frankly disliked the system, and so Tom Carter was always 'deputy leader'; Carter liked the idea but was perhaps more of a 'session' man anyway and less likely to find it irritating. The arrangement kept the loyalty of the two men for three crucial years in the growth of the Philharmonia Orchestra.

Before the euphoria of the October concert could die away, the orchestra was engaged to make its first big recording, of the Sibelius Violin Concerto with Ginette Neveu and conducted by Walter Süsskind. Neveu had been one of Legge's discoveries in liberated France and had signed a contract for EMI in September 1945. Now, two months later, and with fifty strings in the Abbey Road studio, the first of her (tragically) few recordings was put on disc in two intense sessions. London was fog-bound; even the Abbey Road studio was fog-bound. Neveu had just one day available to record, and by 10.30 p.m., with half an hour's overtime from an exhausted orchestra and recording team, the Sibelius was completed. No more recordings or concerts were planned for the Philharmonia that year.

In January 1946 Legge and his HMV colleague David Bicknell left for the Continent on a trip that was to net for EMI a glittering array of artists with whom they could rebuild a sadly depleted catalogue: Furtwängler, Josef Krips, the Vienna Philharmonic Orchestra, de Sabata, Alceo Galliera, Hans Hotter, Dinu Lipatti, von Karajan, Irmgard Seefried and Elisabeth Schwarzkopf. Most of these were sooner or later to record with the Philharmonia regularly, but for the moment home-grown talent had to suffice.

In the studios in early 1946 the Philharmonia were kept reasonably busy, mostly with an assortment of accompanying records but also with some purely orchestral items. Further British Council recordings with Constant Lambert were a helpful boost and stimulating to the players whose ranks were being swelled gradually as servicemen continued to be demobbed. The film studios were interested in a high-quality body of players who needed work, and both Denham Studios, with Muir Mathieson, and Ealing Studios, under Ernest Irving, began to employ the Philharmonia Orchestra regularly during the early part of 1946. For the players, film sessions were highly enjoyable. They were paid good rates, in cash, and by tortuous movements could spin out the music to fill as many sessions as possible. Denham's distance from the centre of London meant an early start for a morning session but its canteen offered bacon and eggs for a late breakfast, a positive luxury in the austerity post-war days. During these early months the film sessions were a lifeline to the orchestra's finances and kept the allegiance of the players.

With this mounting tide of fortune Legge now had the confidence to present a series of concerts at the Royal Albert Hall featuring Arthur Schnabel and the Philharmonia. They would be followed, in early June, by some recordings with Schnabel, the first under the Philharmonia's new exclusive recording contract with EMI.

The securing of a recording contract was a major achievement; the Philharmonia had existed for only eleven months when it was signed. Since the beginning Legge had run it personally, but it would clearly not be right for him to be instrumental in securing for the orchestra a recording contract with the company of which he was an employee. Legge turned to a former ENSA colleague, Joan Ingpen, for help. She was already helping with the hiring of wind players for the Philharmonia and for some months had been operating a concert agency of her own in London. She agreed to help form a company to run the Philharmonia, and on 14 January 1946 Philharmonia Limited was officially incorporated; the major shareholders were Joan Ingpen herself and Irene Seymour, with whom she ran her agency. Both ladies were directors, and Sir Victor Schuster became a shareholder and director; secretary of the company was Frank Sykes, partner in the firm of Sykes & Carley who acted as subscribers to the formation of Philharmonia Limited, and the registered office was their Clarges Street office. Joan Ingpen ran the Philharmonia from her own Clarges Street office. She had already secured many of the film sessions for the orchestra and now she began to negotiate a recording contract with EMI. This was duly signed by her and Leonard Smith of Columbia on 7 June 1946 and was to run initially for one year from 3 June 1946.

The contract was for only twenty sessions per annum, but EMI had access at this time to both the American RCA-Victor and US Columbia catalogues. It was not usual for orchestras to receive royalties on the sales of their records, but right from the start Joan Ingpen made it her ambition to secure this for the Philharmonia. The rate was five per cent per 78 rpm record on eighty-five per cent of the gross sales (i.e. the wholesale price) for recordings without a soloist; with instrumental soloists it dropped to 2½ per cent, and to nothing with a vocalist, but this was protected by a guarantee that at least half the annual sessions would be for orchestra alone. EMI found it difficult to refuse a royalty: Decca paid it, as well as extra payments to certain 'star' players. Joan Ingpen pursued this latter facility as well and she got her way. EMI wanted the Philharmonia and they were now under exclusive contract to Columbia with the right to record for HMV under the same terms.

The Schnabel concerts, in late May 1946, and his sessions, were a delight, for the orchestra loved him. They covered all the Beethoven piano concertos and brought two new conductors before the Philharmonia: the Russian-born Issay Dobrowen, from the Stockholm Opera, and from Italy Alceo Galliera. Galliera began his recordings with some orchestral works, and then two of the Beethoven piano concertos were successfully put on disc by Schnabel and Dobrowen. Dobrowen went on to record three complete symphonies, the first for the Philharmonia; the only one of the three not issued was Beethoven's Fifth. The concert season might have ended but EMI pushed ahead with recordings so that by the end of August the minimum twenty sessions required by the contract had already been well exceeded. One of the summer sessions was for RCA-Victor, with Leonard Bernstein playing and conducting the Ravel *Concerto for Left Hand.* Newly appointed conductor of this New York State Symphony Orchestra, Bernstein was making his London début in June 1946, and RCA arranged for him to record with HMV at Abbey Road on 1 July.

With the significant upturn in the number of recording sessions and film work and the security of a recording contract, the Philharmonia was now attracting more good string players to its ranks. Some came from the National Symphony Orchestra which, despite a successful European tour in May 1946, seemed to be on the wane. Several fine players came from the BBC, which was finding difficulty in keeping the loyalty of players in the face of one successful freelance orchestra – two, when Beecham formed the Royal Philharmonic Orchestra in September 1946. Players such as Jessie Hinchliffe (violin), Anne Wolfe and Lindo Southworth (violas) and Raymond Clark (cello) gave the rank-and-file desks of the Philharmonia a new injection of quality. There is no doubt that Walter Legge would have liked to fill the woodwind desks with talented young players of the calibre of Dennis Brain, but the majority of them, as they left the Services, preferred to play freelance and not commit themselves wholly to one orchestra. Apart from the BBC, the London Symphony and the London Philharmonic, no orchestra in London could yet offer a player enough work to secure that total commitment. There were very many chamber orchestras – the Boyd Neel, Jacques, New London, London Chamber – which offered a variety of high-quality work, and woodwind principals could play in most of them, since dates rarely clashed. It left room, too, for solo and chamber engagements, and the result was that the same nucleus of players freelanced for most of the chamber orchestras – only the rank-and-file differed from orchestra to orchestra. Certainly neither the Philharmonia nor the Royal Philharmonic was able to offer a full engagement book for some time, and players like Dennis Brain, James Bradshaw and Jack Brymer could play in both.

The principals Legge did have in the Philharmonia at this time were thus older men of experience who preferred a slightly less demanding schedule of work but who gave a prestige look and sound to the Philharmonia. The 'Royal Family' in 1946 was Arthur Gleghorn (flute), Alec Whittaker (oboe), Reginald Kell (clarinet) and Jack Alexandra (bassoon).

Arthur Gleghorn was a flautist of great natural musicality with a lovely style and intonation. Technically, he seemed to know no limits; he preferred sessions to symphony concerts and was infinitely happier, on his own admission, playing the lighter classics. Oboist Alec Whittaker was equally talented but far less predictable. BBC and London Symphony by background, he *was* a concert man with a magic sound that could bring tears to the eyes. That plaintive magic came from his unusually short reed, but it had its perils: as soon as the reed was pulled out just a little, the oboe went sharp, which was anathema to Whittaker's excellent ear. He was a concert man, too, in the sense that the occasion brought out the best in him, superb playing of the big solos.

Reginald Kell had been at the birth of the Philharmonia with his recording of the Mozart Clarinet Quintet. A veteran of the London Philharmonic and the London Symphony, he had been the first clarinettist to use *vibrato* freely to match the style of his oboe and flute colleagues. Players even now would claim it was sometimes excessive but few would deny his effortless ease of tone production and impeccable intonation. Also from the pre-War London Philharmonic came bassoonist Jack Alexandra. A player of vast experience, like Kell he had spent the War years with the Liverpool Philharmonic Orchestra, and he completed a woodwind section with gave the Philharmonia's early years a 'star quality' and individuality.

For the growing Philharmonia in the autumn of 1946 Legge brought a third conductor of international repute to nurture its development: Paul Kletzki. His greatest impact was on the strings of the Philharmonia. A solo violinist himself at the age of thirteen, he was leader of the Philharmonic Orchestra in Lodz, Poland, three years later. He had studied conducting in Berlin (where he admitted he was much influenced by Furtwängler) and followed a prestigious career in Russia. As a Pole he had to leave Russia in 1938, and as a Jew he was excluded from middle Europe, so he settled in Switzerland where from 1943 he conducted at all the Lucerne Festivals; he was signed up for Columbia by Legge in May 1946.

Kletzki's experience as a player made his conducting gestures particularly sympathetic to the strings of the Philharmonia Orchestra, to whose tone he brought a bloom – 'the burning sound!' as he demanded from them. He was a very emotional conductor, too; his desire for a warmth of string sound came from this emotionalism. 'Cry it!' he would beg, tears rolling down his cheeks as if in sympathy, and the tone came. From his earliest recordings with the Philharmonia, of well-tried classics like Schubert's *Unfinished* Symphony and Tchaikovsky's Fifth Symphony, to his later essays in Sibelius and Mahler there runs a thread of professionalism in his meticulous knowledge of scores and sheer panache in works like the *Bartered Bride* Overture and Berlioz's *Les Francs Juges*.

For the rest of 1946 the Philharmonia used smaller concert halls, such as Watford Town Hall and Central Hall, Westminster. The cost of the Royal Albert Hall could be justified only by full attendances. Exception was made for popular works with popular soloists, such as Eileen Joyce the pianist, who appeared regularly with the Philharmonia over the next ten years.

One of the new generation of pianists to become associated with the Philharmonia for all too tragically a brief period was Dinu Lipatti. Already stricken with the leukaemia that was to kill him, he had to cancel his Royal Albert Hall début with the Philharmonia on 28 February 1947 when he was due to play the Grieg Concerto with Alceo Galliera. He did succeed in getting to London a few days later, to make some recordings, and was able to play a concert with the Philharmonia, in Walthamstow Assembly Hall on 3 March, where he played Mozart's C major Concerto K.467 with Karl Rankl. Fortunately for posterity Lipatti returned in September 1947 to record the Grieg with Galliera and the Philharmonia.

One of Legge's unwritten rules for the Philharmonia was that a work, however familiar, would not be performed or recorded after just one rehearsal. British players were noted for their ability to sight-read, and this led many a promoter to rely on one rehearsal per concert. More than this was an expensive luxury few orchestras could afford, but the Philharmonia's recording links made it possible to rehearse concert programmes that included at least one or two items that were to be recorded within the next few days. The Schnabel Beethoven concerts in May 1946 were among the first examples of this procedure, and Kletzki's début with Schubert's *Unfinished* Symphony and Tchaikovsky's Fifth coincided with recordings of the same works.

Some conductors, however, made their gramophone début with the Philharmonia long before they conducted them in public. One such was Nicolai Malko, who had signed for EMI in December 1946 and began to record a series of popular Russian works in March 1947, when his concert début was still several years away. This man, who had studied with Rimsky-Korsakov and Glazunov, conducted for such artists as Chaliapin, Pavlova and Nijinsky, and had a command of many contemporary works as well as the standard Russian repertoire, was very much a conductor of the old school, and Philharmonia loved him with his cries for '*Ee*ntonation!' and his old-fashioned style.

The Russian composer Medtner, who was living in exile in London, had already written a couple of times to Walter Legge trying to interest him in recording his larger works, but the market was not really ready, and Legge could not foresee any public interest except, possibly, through a revival of the 'Society' edition idea. The proposal seemed doomed to failure. But also in London was the representative of the Maharaja of Mysore, Captain Sidney Binstead, who was responsible for paying Medtner a modest pension through the Maharaja's generosity and genuine interest in his music. Now the Maharaja offered to pay for the recording of a range of Medtner's works, and they began in May 1947, with Dobrowen conducting Medtner and the Philharmonia in the second of the piano concertos. The Third Concerto followed immediately, and the First (with George Weldon conducting) in October of the same year. Each concerto did in fact become the nucleus of a 'Medtner Society' album which also contained piano solos and songs.

The success of the 1946 Schnabel concerts led to another series in the Royal Albert Hall in May 1947, this time with a mixture of composers rather than all-Beethoven. Dobrowen and Galliera again conducted, and Sir Adrian Boult conducted the last, on 8 June. Two Beethoven concertos were recorded with Dobrowen, but there were signs of Schnabel's age in the playing of the Third Concerto in particular. One trill had been mistimed, and Schnabel asked for the recording to remain unpublished until he could re-record it. This never proved possible, and the recording was in fact issued many years later in the Long Playing *Great Recording* series. The rapport between pianist and orchestra remained undimmed, Schnabel suggesting phrasing to Leonard Hirsch in a gentle whisper – 'Not too staccato' for the beginning of the Finale to the Fourth Beethoven Concerto, for example.

There was great excitement throughout the spring of 1947 as plans were made for Richard Strauss to come to London. Now aged eighty-three, he was to attend the Strauss Festival in October planned for him by Beecham with the Royal Philharmonic Orchestra. Strauss and his wife were living in Switzerland, exiles in the wake of war. His music seemed unpopular and he stubbornly refused to make any public statement to dispel the taint of Nazism which his wartime associations seemed to have pinned on him. Money was short, and not the least of his reasons for coming to London was to collect some of the royalties on his music due to him and hitherto unavailable because of a ban on payments to 'aliens'. For the Philharmonia Orchestra the visit was a real scoop, since Strauss was to conduct only one complete concert himself, and

Joan Ingpen had arranged that it would be on an exclusive basis with the Philharmonia, although he did also conduct just one item in a subsequent BBC Symphony Orchestra concert.

Strauss wanted his *Alpine Symphony* to be the centrepiece of his Philharmonia programme in the Royal Albert Hall but was eventually persuaded to substitute the *Sinfonia Domestica.* He was not happy at the change but could see the difficulties posed by the scoring of the *Alpine Symphony* which needs (among much else) a heckelphone and twenty horns! Even the *Sinfonia Domestica* calls for a rather sizeable orchestra, and extra players were engaged so that the orchestra which took its place on the Albert Hall platform was the Philharmonia *plus* many 'star extras'. The clarinet section alone had Reginald Kell, Frederick Thurston, Walter Lear and Jack Brymer in its ranks.

Josef Krips wrote the following in the Strauss concert programme, after only three weeks with the Philharmonia:

> The Philharmonia orchestra is the first English orchestra with which I have worked and I can only say it is a first-class body of musicians. The strings, like the wind, are artists of the highest class, who naturally fulfil the desires of the most exacting conductors.
>
> Most of all, this orchestra has heart: heart combined with ability, talent and discipline, are the essential qualities of this orchestra.
>
> London should be proud of its Philharmonia Orchestra.

The Philharmonia looked forward apprehensively to its first meeting with Strauss. Many of them also played in the Royal Philharmonic and had met him at the rehearsals for the Beecham concerts in the Drury Lane Theatre, prowling around the orchestra in his shabby raincoat, a word here, a gesture there. When he first met the assembled Philharmonia, he began with *Don Juan.* 'Do they know it?' he asked Tom Carter, who was leading; when he learned they had recorded it with Galliera the previous summer, he played it straight through and left it at that. The *Sinfonia Domestica* was totally unknown to most of the orchestra. Strauss took this through, too, but then spent the best part of his three rehearsals patiently teaching them the work. He had included the *Burlesque* for Piano and Orchestra to ensure a good fee for Alfred Blumen, who had given the work its première and had toured twice with Strauss and the Vienna Philharmonic. Rehearsals for the *Burlesque* were more tense, with Strauss accusing Blumen of playing too fast and Blumen muttering to the orchestra that in the 1930s he had found difficulty in keeping up.

At the dress rehearsal on the Sunday morning, 19 October, Strauss had one more word on *Don Juan*, aware that the time he had spent on it had been brief. To Tom Carter he said just: 'Watch me tonight!' That evening seven thousand people in the Royal Albert Hall rose to their feet as he shuffled onto the platform through the vast orchestra, muttering the now famous phrase: 'Well, the old horse leaves the stable again.' He insisted on conducting standing up, with his usual small, firm gestures and almost solely with his right hand. He always maintained that the left hand was for resting in the waistcoat pocket and nothing more. At the end the audience cheered until long after he and the orchestra had left the platform.

For the Philharmonia it had been a unique experience and had brought undoubted prestige to its name; for the audience it was a unique opportunity to catch a last glimpse of one of the great composers of the twentieth century, conducting his own music. One suspects that many of them were surprised to see him alive at all, let alone drawing from the vast orchestra his precise intentions with an apparent minimum of effort.

Important though the Strauss concert was, it had been an isolated event and it was difficult to fill the vast Royal Albert Hall unless a Schnabel or a Strauss was appearing. It was almost as difficult to attract audiences to smaller halls like Kingsway Hall or Westminster Central Hall. A small boost came in January 1948 when the newly-formed New Era Concert Society chose the Philharmonia as its permanent orchestra. Formed by Richard Austin in 1947 on the lines of the pre-war Sargent-Courtauld concerts, the New Era Concert Society invariably included a new or rarely-performed work at each concert. In March 1948 Otto Klemperer made his first post-war London appearance at a New Era concert, at the age of sixty-two. He directed Bach's Third Suite from the harpsichord but a latecomer caused him to start the second movement again. Klemperer fixed the unfortunate man with an angry stare and followed him all the way to his seat. The concert finished with Beethoven's *Eroica*, a performance which hinted at the excellence of his concerts in the late 1950s. Sandwiched between these two works was Stravinsky's *Symphony in Three Movements* – a test of any conductor – but Klemperer coped with its intricacies with little or no problem.

3. *Karajan and Mysore, 1948-51*

It was April 1948 when Walter Legge brought Herbert von Karajan to London to conduct the Philharmonia for the first time. Little known outside Germany, he had remarkable abilities coupled with relentless ambition and had found a formidable ally in Legge, who had supported him through the long, sordid process of 'denazification' by securing for him a contract with EMI to record with the Vienna Philharmonic Orchestra.

By an ironic coincidence Karajan's rival, Wilhelm Furtwängler, conducted the Philharmonia for the first time on Good Friday, 26 March 1948, just two weeks before Karajan's London début. Furtwängler was recording, with Kirsten Flagstad, the 'Immolation' scene from Wagner's *Götterdämmerung*; Flagstad was making her first post-war appearances at Covent Garden in *Die Walküre* and *Tristan*, and she recorded some scenes from the latter a week later with Dobrowen.

Furtwängler was conductor-for-life of the Berlin Philharmonic and had the allegiance of the Vienna Philharmonic and a virtual monopoly of the Salzburg Festival; he had also been free to conduct in public since the end of the War, which Karajan had not. Furtwängler's jealousy of the young Karajan dated from before the War, from 1938 to be precise, when Karajan made a guest appearance at the Berlin State Opera, conducting *Fidelio* and *Tristan*. The Press were astonished: *Das Wunder Karajan* ('The Karajan miracle') was the headline in the *Berliner Zeitung* after the first *Tristan* performance, an epithet which aroused the jealousy of Furtwängler and the interest of some high-ranking Nazis, who decided to play off the two conductors against each other. From that point the rivalry and mutual antipathy had developed until, to Furtwängler at least, it became obsessive.

The programme that Karajan was to conduct with the Philharmonia, on 11 April 1948 in the Royal Albert Hall, was conventional: Strauss's *Don Juan*, Schumann's Piano Concerto, with Dinu Lipatti, and Beethoven's Fifth Symphony. Karajan arrived a week before the concert to rehearse the concert and prepare to record the Schumann, on 9 and 10 April, at Abbey Road. This was to be Lipatti's last appearance in

London: leukaemia was tightening its grip, but he still had a beauty of touch and sensitivity of phrasing that made the recording and the concert performance memorable. Karajan's economy of gesture was coupled with an unerring ability to accompany him sympathetically. One critic described Lipatti's playing as 'very good, bringing a masculine approach to a concerto that seems to suit women best'. The same critic described Karajan's 'new German technique of making the strong beat by an upward movement, like a woman shooing hens in a farmyard'.

The concert was an occasion, in several senses. Some Londoners obviously had longer memories than others, for Leonard Hirsch was telephoned by the *Jewish Chronicle* and asked if he 'really intended leading for *that* man'. The Nazi stigma was to prove very difficult to throw off.

Karajan and Legge got together after the concert and compared notes. It was too soon to woo Karajan away from the Vienna Philharmonic completely, but Legge could see that he was more than mildly interested in the Philharmonia. The woodwind and brass had impressed him but the strings were still on the light, rather anaemic side; also the finances of the Philharmonia were still precarious. Legge was now determined to spend the immediate future building up both the musical and financial resources of the Philharmonia sufficiently to interest Karajan in a more permanent association.

Recording continued in September 1948 with a new EMI contract, under virtually the same terms as the 1946 contract, twenty sessions per annum and with the same royalty but to be paid only on purely orchestral recordings. In practice the number of sessions now regularly exceeded the contractual minimum, and some recordings were now being made for Parlophone.

By now the Philharmonia's personnel was being strengthened and reshaped almost daily. String players such as Marie Wilson (who after over twelve years as No. 2 First Violin and Deputy Leader in the BBC Symphony Orchestra had spent the post-war years in solo work) now occupied rank-and-file desks in the Philharmonia. Legge had also started moves to put the leadership of the Philharmonia firmly on the Continental pattern of two joint leaders, though the one player who really approved of the idea, Thomas Carter, left the Philharmonia in October 1948 after a minor disagreement. (Carter was attracted by the offer of the leadership of the London Chamber Orchestra and, despite attempts by Legge to get him to stay, he remained determined to go.) Leonard Hirsch would not accept the joint leadership idea, and for a while he remained sole leader, with three associate leaders: two very experienced players, Jessie Hinchliffe who had come from the BBC, and Jack Kessler, a former member of the Hungarian Quartet who had played for Toscanini at Lucerne before the War, and a young newcomer who had led the Liverpool Philharmonic for a season, Manoug Parikian.

Parikian, born in Turkey of Armenian parents, was an outstandingly talented violinist. He had been in London since June 1948 where he freelanced for Boyd Neel and some other orchestras. Within a few months he had been invited to lead a couple of Kingsway Hall sessions for the Philharmonia. The position as one of three associate leaders suited him for the winter months of 1948–9 but it soon became apparent that his interest lay in leading and only the hope of this would keep him permanently with the Philharmonia.

Some reshaping of the Philharmonia was also taking place in the wind sections. Beecham had been putting pressure on some players to choose between his Royal Philharmonic and the Philharmonia as sessions and concerts became more numerous and there were clashes of dates. Dennis Brain, later in 1949, left the Royal Philharmonic for a whole year but as an exceptional case was allowed back under a special arrangement for nearly four more years, but his horn-playing colleagues Ian Beers and Frank Probyn left for the Royal Philharmonic. Principal flautist Arthur Gleghorn emigrated to the United States in 1948 to play for the film industry; he had become less happy in the Philharmonia as it grew into a big symphony orchestra, and for a while his place was taken by Arthur Ackroyd. Craggy-faced, with a mischievous sense of humour, Ackroyd had been first flute in the Liverpool Philharmonic during the War. He had a formidable technique which made him also about the best piccolo player in Britain. Most sessions and rehearsals were played with a cigarette held between his fingers that seemed not to make one iota of difference to his agility. To replace Gleghorn, Legge asked Gareth Morris, one of the ex-RAF young freelance players who since the War had been leading flute sections in no fewer than six London chamber orchestras as well as playing a good deal of solo and chamber work. Morris was a pupil of Robert Murchie; like Murchie, he played on a wooden flute (the same instrument, eventually, left to him by Murchie) and used the same tight embouchure with the flute player's 'smile'. Offers had come from most of the big London symphony orchestras but Morris, naturally, wanted to play only for the best and under the best conditions. Legge and the Philharmonia interested him with the promise of great international conductors and plans for the expansion of the Philharmonia into a world-class orchestra.

During this period, mid-1948 to mid-1949, more international conductors became involved with the Philharmonia. In October 1948 Rafael Kubelik recorded Dvořák's Eighth Symphony. Son of the famous violinist, Jan Kubelik, Rafael's talent for conducting became apparent before he was out of his teens, and from 1942 he had been chief conductor of the Czech Philharmonic Orchestra. The Communist take-over of his native Czechoslovakia in 1948 forced him to emigrate, and he made a strong impression in Britain with his conducting of *Don Giovanni* at the 1948 Edinburgh Festival.

Karl Böhm first conducted the Philharmonia in June 1949. His strength lay in the Viennese repertoire but he began with Wagner, excerpts from *Die Walküre* and *Tristan*, with Flagstad and Svanholm, who were appearing at Covent Garden. The Russian repertoire, already well served by Dobrowen, was now complemented by Igor Markevich, who in the 1930s had been one of the leading lights in Franco-Prussian composition, but in 1941 he gave up composing for conducting. No one could equal him for his ability to teach the Philharmonia works like Stravinsky's *Rite of Spring*, a new and challenging work to many of the players which in concerts he conducted without a score.

As the summer of 1949 approached, the last of the changes were made in the ranks of the woodwind. Late in 1948 Reginald Kell had toured the United States with the Busch Quartet, and Bernard Walton had played first clarinet in his absence. Kell had become somewhat disenchanted with British orchestral life, and the USA tour opened his eyes to new and more tempting possibilities. During his time with the Philharmonia he had not only brought a high standard of artistry to its performances but also cared for its welfare as an active Union man; notably, he had insisted on the same rates of pay for all the principal wind players. For a while Bernard Walton occupied his place. He and his brother, the trumpeter Richard 'Bob' Walton, came from a strong north-country musical family. Bernard was already established as an outstanding chamber player, with a similar technique and tone to Kell. Walter Legge had, however, been promised the services of Frederick 'Jack' Thurston, one of the most highly respected clarinettists of his generation who had left the BBC in 1946 and now, in mid-1949, found himself able to keep that promise. Walton stayed, sometimes as co-principal, sometimes doubling first clarinet when a conductor required double woodwind for a work.

Only the principal oboe chair remained unchanged but, Alec Whittaker's reliability was not absolute, and as the amount of recording grew, so did the problem. An outstanding player whom Legge coveted was Sidney 'Jock' Sutcliffe, then principal oboist of the London Philharmonic Orchestra. He had already been invited to join the Philharmonia when he played extra second oboe for Karajan's début and when he was asked again in the spring of 1949, Alec Whittaker's advice was to 'take it'. Sutcliffe finished the London Philharmonic season and joined the Philharmonia in time for Solomon's recordings of the Scriabin and Tchaikovsky piano concertos, in the last week of May 1949.

There remained two questions to be resolved – the dual leadership and finance for the future – and both were solved almost at a stroke. Especially now Karajan was in the offing, Legge was resolved to press for the dual leadership, although he knew Leonard Hirsch would resign rather than go along with the idea. Hirsch was too experienced a player and too nice a man to turn nasty over it, and his excellent quartet was flourishing so well that he had ample work to turn to. In the meantime, Legge had gained the interest of Max Salpeter, then leader of the New London Orchestra, who had already played for some very early Philharmonia sessions; in fact he had been one of the original twenty-four strings in July 1945. Manoug Parikian was now earnestly pressing his interest in leading, and the two of them seemed suitable and quite willing to agree to joint leadership. Only sufficient financial resources would allow Legge to go out on a limb over it, and in the summer of 1949 the Maharaja of Mysore came to the rescue.

The Maharaja had already financed the Medtner Society recordings in 1947, and when Legge agreed to help him widen his interests by recording some of the more neglected works in the orchestral repertoire, he was invited to Mysore in July 1949 to discuss the details. Useful though the recording work would be to the Philharmonia, the real excitement of the visit was the Maharaja's offer of £10,000 annual grant for three years to the Philharmonia Concert Society. Legge gratefully made the Maharaja President of the Philharmonia Concert Society, but one of the conditions placed on his money was that it should be administered by a committee of non-performing musical personalities, a prospect that Legge faced with some trepidation since he had a fear of committees composed of more than one member. The timely offer enabled Legge to complete his reorganization of the Philharmonia personnel and bring Karajan more closely into co-operation with its development. It came at a time when there was still not enough recording work to keep the Philharmonia together on a more permanent basis.

On 30 August 1950 Joan Ingpen sold Philharmonia Limited to Walter Legge in its entirety. For five years it had been convenient to run the orchestra through Ingpen & Williams but Legge's growing links with Karajan and the quite significant influence effected by the Mysore money meant that overall control of the Philharmonia was becoming somewhat diffused. But the orchestra could not live on concerts alone, even with the Mysore money, and even that was becoming difficult to guarantee as sterling became less easily transferred from India to Great Britain; the subvention was to drop to £5,000 for the 1950–1 season, half the original guarantee offered by the Maharaja.

One immediate result of the Mysore money was the appointment in

October 1949 of Manoug Parikian and Max Salpeter as joint leaders. They would arrange between them at the beginning of each season who would lead for each concert or group of sessions. Leonard Hirsch was not bitter, just a little sorry to leave an orchestra in which he had been very happy.

There were still some arrangements to fulfil before the new arrangement came into effect on 1 October, notably the Philharmonia's first Edinburgh Festival. Still in its infancy as an international festival, Edinburgh nevertheless offered a shop-window for British orchestral wares and the chance for soloists and ensembles of world repute to come together. Rafael Kubelik conducted both concerts, on 1 and 2 September, but did not receive unreserved acclaim. *The Scotsman*'s critic found his accompaniment of Rudolf Serkin in Beethoven's *Emperor* concerto 'unpredictable' and in Dvořák's Eighth Symphony 'indulging in meaningless pieces of legerdemain with his stick'. The occasion, for all that, was a gala one, given as it was before the Queen and Princess Margaret and followed by a long reception, given by the Lord Provost of Edinburgh.

Edinburgh in 1949 was undoubtedly an important 'first' for the Philharmonia, and it was followed by a tour back to London with concerts in York, Sheffield, Nottingham, Leeds, Liverpool, Manchester and Birmingham, conducted by Eugene Goossens. The combined events of the first ten days of September brought the Philharmonia before the public just as it was embarking on a new stage in its life.

The Philharmonia Concert Society, which had hitherto promoted mostly chamber music and *Lieder* recitals, now assumed a leading role in the promotion of orchestral concerts by the Philharmonia Orchestra. A brochure was produced for the 1949–50 season promising conductors such as Karajan, Furtwängler, Edwin Fischer and Kletzki, singers who included Kirsten Flagstad, Boris Christoff and Elisabeth Schwarzkopf, and soloists from Cortot to Serkin. Subscription tickets for the concerts, which could now be held regularly at the Royal Albert Hall, worked out at under five shillings per concert if booked in advance, and they were available more than a month ahead of the single tickets.

The first major orchestral concert promoted by the Philharmonia Concert Society and financed by the Mysore money brought Karajan back to London to conduct Beethoven's Ninth Symphony. He was also in London to record with the Philharmonia a series of works for the Mysore Foundation. These began on 18 November 1949 with Balakirev's First Symphony and, spread over three days, the sessions enabled the orchestra to get to know Karajan and his ways of working. There were the minor difficulties posed by his command of English which was good but not always infallible. He always referred to the fingerboard of the violins as 'fingerbowl' but no one had any problem understanding what he *meant*. In the Balakirev at one point he wanted a particular phrase to 'sound like a whip' and he stamped his foot to emphasize the point: this elicited an immediate 'tut-tut' from the orchestra. It was all quite good-humoured but it was the beginning of a relationship by which Karajan, patiently but insistently, got precisely what he wanted from the Philharmonia while they could occasionally pull in the bridle a little and assert *their* wishes, too, without a clash of wills or temperament.

After completion of the Balakirev recording, Karajan opened the Philharmonia Concert Society series with a memorable Beethoven Ninth Symphony. Unfortunately, it followed hard on the heels of another very good Beethoven Ninth by Nicolai Malko and the London Philharmonic, with the result that there were almost as many performers as audience in the Royal Albert Hall. It was a pity, for the critics spoke highly of the concert. There was high praise for the chorus and orchestra for 'their lightning response to the conductor's demands' and for Karajan's 'firm but modest action of presence'. The latter's control did not extend to quite all the orchestra. At least the first two desks of first violins found Karajan's tempo for the slow movement too hurried to give full weight to the phrasing and conspired to pull it back at the concert to a more comfortable pace. A small example, but one that underlines the two-way control that was possible from time to time.

A Royal Albert Hall concert in May 1950 was presented by Victor Hochhauser and used the Philharmonia's own leader, Manoug Parikian, as soloist; such a suggestion would not have come from Legge, who, for some reason, did not like him to play solo engagements, at least with the Philharmonia. Many of the other first-desk men in the Philharmonia, such as Gareth Morris and Dennis Brain, did this regularly. Perhaps Legge feared he would lose Parikian to a solo career just when he was giving the Philharmonia a stylish and authoritative leadership.

The climax of the month was undoubtedly the return of Furtwängler on 22 May to conduct a programme of Wagner and Richard Strauss, including the first performance of Strauss's *Four Last Songs*. Kirsten Flagstad sang them in the original order (i.e. *Frühling* first in the set instead of third) and with the manuscript in her hands. As *Im Abendrot* came to a close, the audience were silent for several moving seconds, in hushed reverence for the composer who had died just eight months before and who had poured such loving care into these masterpieces.

Much to the delight of the string players in the Philharmonia, Heifetz had spent a week recording with them in June 1950. With Walter Süsskind he recorded the Tchaikovsky Concerto, Lalo's *Symphonie Espagnole* and the two Beethoven Romances, and the Walton Concerto with the composer. Walton was one of the leading British composers of the day included in Walter Legge's circle of friends, and the results were some fine recordings of good contemporary music. Bliss and Rawsthorne were others whose works were similarly promoted by the Philharmonia. But such endorsements were rare, for Legge was highly selective in his appreciation of modern composers. Richard Strauss, Elgar, Sibelius and Stravinsky were among the 'chosen few' and with the possible exception of Elgar got a fair hearing at Philharmonia concerts.

In July 1950 Lipatti made an outstanding batch of solo piano recordings with Legge in Geneva, during a brief respite from his leukaemia afforded by a two-month course of cortisone. The doctors could not risk more, the drug was too new, and Lipatti played the Chopin E minor concerto in Lucerne in August with Karajan conducting and with Schnabel ready to step in at a moment's notice; a whole battery of medicines were also to hand. He was then scheduled to appear in October at the Royal Albert Hall to play the same concerto with Galliera and the Philharmonia and record it, but he was by then far too ill. Claudio Arrau stood in at the concert, and Galliera recorded Respighi's *Brazilian Impressions* a year earlier than planned as a substitute. On 2 December 1950 Lipatti died, aged thirty-three.

Not a great number of recordings were made by the Philharmonia during late 1950, for Beecham was touring the United States with the Royal Philharmonic and had taken with him quite a few Philharmonia players, including Dennis Brain and James Bradshaw. By now, though, the system of doubling between the orchestras was proving not just difficult for the players as the work grew but irritating to Beecham and Legge, who quite naturally wanted to keep the best players for themselves. In the woodwind sections the two orchestras had acquired almost totally separate personalities by now: the Royal Philharmonic had Gerald Jackson, Terence McDonagh, Jack Brymer and Gwydion Brooke, the Philharmonia had Gareth Morris, Sidney Sutcliffe and Frederick Thurston. To replace an ageing Jack Alexandra, Legge undoubtedly coveted Brooke, but he was firmly committed to the Royal Philharmonic, and the Philharmonia players had already recommended Cecil James, a superbly competent player with a warm, majestic sound.

One of Cecil James's first engagements was an Albert Hall concert with Edwin Fischer and Furtwängler in Beethoven's *Emperor* concerto which they had just recorded. This was February 1951, and the year was to prove one of the busiest so far in terms of concerts and recordings. One reason was the opening of the Royal Festival Hall, which provided a new outlet for concert-giving in London. Dubbed a 'chicken-coop' by Beecham, it was at least a realistically sized hall compared with the Royal

Albert Hall's nine thousand seats. By no means acoustically perfect, despite being designed and advertised as such, it offered an infinitely less diffuse, if rather dry, sound which the players found unnerving at first but eventually seemed more responsive as they got used to it. The LCC's Music Adviser, Owen Mase, had negotiated with Toscanini to come to London to conduct three concerts to open the new Hall, finishing with Beethoven's Ninth Symphony, but the eighty-three-year-old composer was not well and regretfully had to cancel, promising to come again as soon as he could. The concerts had been planned with the BBC Symphony Orchestra, and Sargent conducted the three programmes almost without change. The inaugural concert itself, on 3 May 1951, was a gala occasion and included a significant number of the Philharmonia players in a composite orchestra which Sargent, Dykes Bower and Boult each conducted.

The flurry of music-making that followed to celebrate the Festival of Britain included two appearances by Otto Klemperer, a conductor who was to play a major part in the Philharmonia's later history. His concerts were specific invitations to the Philharmonia to play for the Festival of Britain, for which Legge had engaged Schnabel as soloist. Legge also invited Szell to conduct, but he was not available, and both he and Schnabel suggested to Legge that Klemperer be engaged. Legge had serious reservations: Klemperer's previous appearance with the Philharmonia in November 1949 had produced an erratic Brahms First Symphony, a complete contrast to his earlier success with Beethoven's *Eroica* Symphony in March 1948. Now Legge took a gamble on the unpredictability of the ageing German, and in the event it paid off. *The Times* wrote of the first concert: 'Here indeed is a musician whose emotional intensity is wonderfully matched by an impressive intellectual force – the very combination which the classical Beethoven demands of his interpreter ... the orchestra met every demand of its inspired and inspiring conductor.' Of the second, it deprecated the loss of a chance to hear Klemperer's reading of the *Enigma Variations* but in the *Jupiter* which replaced them it praised his performance which with 'dignified proportions, glowed with exhilarating vigour'. The success of these two concerts was the beginning of Klemperer's long association with EMI and the Philharmonia, although it would be three more years before Legge could achieve the contract he wanted and provide Klemperer with a real niche again in European music.

If there had been worries about adequate work for the Philharmonia in the late 1940s, 1951 dispelled these with a heavy workload. It was just as well, for the orchestra could no longer rely on the money from the Maharaja of Mysore to sustain its financial stability. As it happened, the £5,000 for the 1951–2 season was to be the last sum that could be made available despite efforts in Mysore and London, but the subventions had nicely tided the Philharmonia over a critical period until it could now begin to stand on its own feet.

Legge had bought out the Philharmonia Company, and now in 1951 he put the Philharmonia Concert Society on a more commercial footing. In February 1951 he negotiated to make it a company, and on 7 March it was incorporated as such, with Jane Withers (Legge's former ENSA colleague and secretary at EMI) as Secretary, running the orchestra from offices on part of the top floor of the Ibbs & Tillett building in Wigmore Street. One of her greatest assets was her almost total lack of any musical knowledge. In running an orchestra a little learning can be a highly dangerous thing, but Jane Withers had no such hindrance. She could concentrate her skills and energy on administration, which she handled imperturbably well, and leave those who *were* concerned with the musical side to get on without interference. Her musical ignorance could be a frequent source of amusement, such as her complaint that 'They've changed the programme again! We asked for the *Nutcracker* and they've sent us *Casse-Noisette*!' Her unique quality in the Philharmonia position was the combination of a very clever mind with total loyalty to Walter Legge. He had no time for 'yes-men' (or women) but, equally, he could not tolerate persistent, even intermittent, opposition to his ideas, and Jane Withers had the brilliance to manage the Philharmonia and the willingness to do it as Legge wanted. There were, naturally, times when she did not agree, but she had the diplomacy and tact to go quietly on her own way until Legge had either forgotten or the issue had resolved itself.

By late 1952 Jane Withers appeared on the Philharmonia letterheads as 'Managing Director'. Walter Legge still retained his anonymity as the major shareholder in the Philharmonia, although the world in general and EMI in particular must have been aware of it.

In simple terms, the running of the Philharmonia went thus. For a recording session, for example, EMI would write specifying the works to be recorded and the numbers of strings required by the conductor concerned. This information would be passed on to the fixers, who then telephoned or spoke to the players and booked them for the dates. Clem Relf would arrange for the correct music to be available and returned after the session; EMI paid the costs of collection and return. The fixers also paid the players at the recording sessions or rehearsals, and the royalties earned on the recordings were made up half-yearly by EMI and sent on to the Philharmonia. The players did not receive the royalties. They were paid into the company, Philharmonia Limited, which of course was Walter Legge himself. In practice, of course, the system was a good deal more complicated. The fixers could not always get all the players for a session and had to resort to strange tactics. After ringing round all the possible players a second or third time, some extra enticement could sometimes be offered.

The Philharmonia players, being freelance, were paid by the session or rehearsal plus concert. Rates were standard Musicians' Union rates: in 1953, for example, this was £4 per three-hour session for a principal player, £3.15.0 for sub-principals and £3.10.0 for rank-and-file. These were the *basic* rates, with the addition of porterage for the heavy instruments and 'doubling' fees where a player played oboe and cor anglais, for example. Both represented about twenty-five per cent on top of basic fees. Where the Philharmonia players gained financially was on two counts. They were now getting many more recording sessions per annum than any other London orchestra, which meant regular work without the bother of dressing up for a concert and the tension of a live performance. Certain 'star' players, too, were paid higher rates to keep their loyalty; their identity was meant to be secret, but in fact most people knew who they were. Dennis Brain was a prime example, and even in 1953 he was the highest paid player in the Philharmonia Orchestra. There were at this time in fact twelve other 'star' players who were paid one guinea above the session rates: the five string principals, principal flute, oboe, clarinet, bassoon, trombone, tuba and timpani.

In fact, in all fairness to Walter Legge, the Philharmonia players were well looked after financially. One third fees were soon paid to the trombones and harpist when the scoring of a work did not require them, and this was soon extended to third and fourth horns, tuba, the percussionists and the trumpets. It was also increased very quickly to half fees for sessions when they were not required since these players were receiving comparatively so much less work that it was becoming difficult to keep first call on their services.

An orchestral librarian's job is not one to be envied, and Clem Relf, for all his long experience, found the Philharmonia had its fair share of panics and incidents. In his early Philharmonia days one or two sets of music were bought, but the majority had to be hired and this meant hurried marking and sometimes a lot of copying. For a vocal recital record the task could be frightening, with perhaps six or seven short arias to be checked for the correct number of parts, numbering against the conductor's score (if there was a score) and pencilling in alterations to begin and end the aria satisfactorily out of context of the opera concerned.

Conductors varied considerably in their attitude to bowing, as did the leaders themselves. Leonard Hirsch had been happy for the bowing to be left at least until after the first play-through, so that he could get an idea of what the conductor had in mind. The rest of the strings would pick up the bowing by watching Leonard Hirsch, but as the orchestra grew in size this became less easy. Few conductors bothered with bowing – Karajan and Furtwängler notably – and Manoug Parikian found it hard work in the early days to sort it out in time for it to be transferred to all the copies. Cantelli often brought his own NBC Symphony Orchestra parts to use which were pre-marked and would spend some time with Clem Relf going through it, saving untold time and trouble. At least few players took the parts home to practice, so it was easy to keep track of them all.

Legge rarely interfered directly with the running of the Philharmonia but, like the players, the office staff knew that his word was law and diverged from it at their peril. He was a dictator, and his dictates came to the players and staff through Jane Withers, particularly if it was bad news. Sometimes when the Philharmonia played out of town or a Sunday afternoon 'pops' concert, the better players cried off and poorer extras were engaged as substitutes. Next day Legge would appear in the office to ask 'Why wasn't so-and-so playing?' If it was not a good reason, the fixers made sure 'so-and-so' was there next time. Solo engagements constituted good reasons, and the orchestra's principal players were often so engaged. The fixers' books contained a list of absent players for each engagement and their reasons for absence.

Such dictatorship demanded fierce loyalty from the Philharmonia staff, who worked long hours at high pressure. Demarcation lines of responsibility broke down in a crisis: if someone was free, they did the job. At such times Legge could make a tactless remark, but the staff were not afraid to tell him that they were doing their best. Then he would smile sweetly, put his hands on the person's shoulders and say: 'My dear, I know you are.' They worked so hard because they knew where they stood with such an organization and because they knew, even at the time, that history was being made with a great orchestra. They certainly did not do it for the money. In those days a typist in the Philharmonia earned £3.10.0 per week, a sum which a rank-and-file violinist could earn in one three-hour session in the recording studio.

The office staff became well known to the orchestra as time went by. The fixers were the bearers of good tidings in the form of pay cheques and further engagements. Two of them in fact became so well known that they later married members of the orchestra: Mary Harrow eventually became Mrs Hugh Bean, and Marian Inglefield became Mrs Charles Verney. Jane Withers and one or two staff usually went with the orchestra on tour and so, little by little, began to understand some of the excitement of playing with conductors like Karajan. One poor girl found herself trapped amongst the orchestra when the red light went on for the beginning of a recording session and, not daring to move, spent the next twenty minutes caught up in the pulse-racing excitement that such a session generated.

There were many lighter moments to alleviate the tension of recording difficult music, the strain of coping with a temperamental conductor or just the draughts in Kingsway Hall. Someone has credited Beecham with the discovery of Kingsway Hall as one of the best recording halls in Europe. Whoever deserves the credit, the Hall is hard to equal for sound, despite its drawbacks. John Culshaw, Decca's dowager producer, rather ironically described it as the only Methodist church to make a profit, referring to the large retainers paid by EMI and Decca, who have used it almost exclusively for nearly fifty years. Its qualities are a mixture of the measurable and the indefinable. Many players will tell you it is a comfortable place (in the acoustic sense): the sound 'feels' right as it leaves the player, particularly from the strings. The acoustics were expertly analysed by Denis Vaughan in *Wireless World* (May 1982) where he points out two significant factors: the horseshoe balcony surrounding the main auditorium gives a quick response to the players' initial sound which then has time and space to gain warmth and depth, and the large storerooms and basements below them give a bass response that is resonant and full.

EMI's own Abbey Road No. 1 studio in St. John's Wood is not so generally acceptable for recording, although a few conductors prefer it for certain types of work. Over the years there have been a number of experiments to improve the sound: new baffles on the walls, small speakers at strategic points to assist the reverberation, and large cloths draped from the walls, but none have given the same feeling of 'human presence' that can be felt in Kingsway Hall. It has two choices of seating for an orchestral recording, on the stage or down on the main floor, and in general the preference is the same as has to be followed in Abbey Road – for the floor, where there is more room and better acoustics. The disadvantage of the floor in Kingsway Hall is the slope towards the middle so that the strings, in particular, feel as if they are playing downhill. In winter the draughts from the side doors of Kingsway Hall are something not shared by the purpose-built Abbey Road.

Abbey Road has its own control room with a proper studio double-glass panel so that the recording producer can both hear and see the session in progress. Kingsway Hall has no such facility: three rooms behind the stage are used, one for the conductor and soloist, one for the tape machines, and a spare, for when there is a large cast for operas. As at Abbey Road, the link between control room and studio is the telephone, buzzer and red light. In 78 rpm recording days, when recording was directly onto wax, the buzzer was a vital link, as timing was crucial. The fourteen-inch translucent amber waxes were kept in a glass-fronted cabinet at 100°F and put on the cutting lathe one at a time when the conductor and producer were ready to record. The breaks between the four-minute sides were pre-arranged and marked in the score. Rehearsal took place in the studio as they went along and gave the engineers the chance to check balance between microphones and levels of volume generally. A single buzz would signal the players to be quiet and sometimes had to be held on for some time until there was silence. Then two buzzes would indicate that the 'run-in' groove had started, and a second or two later the red light would go on and the recording had to begin immediately.

In pre-tape days it was possible to hear a playback from one of these waxes but it was then useless for further processing and it might have been the best of a series of takes. The role of the producer was important not only in deciding when a good take had been obtained but in recalling which was the best. Frequently, if the replay wax was a good take, Walter Legge would say 'Leave it!', knowing that it was not worth the risk of spoiling the take in order to hear it. With the introduction of tape, the ability to play back was the first advantage to be treasured by artist and producer alike, and indeed, in the early days of tape it was used almost solely for this purpose, as a back-up in case none of the waxes could be used. After a couple of years, and with the advent of LPs, the use of tape for editing was realized, and short passages could be spliced in to replace takes that were marred by faulty intonation or mistakes.

The Musicians' Union regulations governing recording covered both the amount that could be recorded and the length of break in a session. In 78 rpm days the maximum amount of music that could be recorded in one three-hour session was four 78 sides; this became twenty minutes of music when tape was used. The stipulation referred to the amount of music not the number of times it was recorded, so there was the strange anomaly that a session could consist of fifteen takes of the same four-minute passage but not fifteen single takes of different passages. The interval was laid down as a minimum of five minutes per hour, which usually meant a quarter-hour break about halfway through the session.

From 5 to 16 June 1951 the Philharmonia was recording every day, usually two sessions per day and occasionally three. The variety of work within such concentrated spells brought its own special difficulties. Karajan and Gieseking recorded five piano concertos in as many days, and then Stokowski came to record *Scheherazade* just three days later.

The last day of the Karajan-Gieseking sessions was also the day of a concert in the Festival Hall that included Britten's *Les Illuminations* and the first London performance of Orff's *Carmina Burana*, conducted by

Walter Goehr. The contemporary music flavour was taken up again in mid-October 1951 when William Walton recorded his First Symphony in Kingsway Hall.

On 30 September 1951 the thirty-one-year-old Italian Guido Cantelli conducted his first Philharmonia concert. His impact on the orchestra was interesting. In their seven years of playing they had been subjected to every grade of conductor from the inspired to the indifferent and had reacted accordingly. For conductors they respected, they played supremely well; those who were second-rate and put on an 'act' were given a rough ride, while the mediocre were just ignored. They had acquired some of their wisdom in spotting the difference the hard way. When the eleven-year-old Pierino Gamba conducted them at Earl's Court in January 1949, his presence seemed to annoy some of the older and tougher players until they realized he knew his scores. He stopped the trombones from playing inaccurate parts in a Rossini overture, and when a woodwind player tried a deliberately awkward question, he was met with a very confident and knowledgeable answer. In Cantelli they had the precision and the emotionalism of an Italian, a whole world apart from the cold steel of Karajan and the swaying warmth of Furtwängler, but not so far removed from men like Kletzki who would often ask the players to 'Cry it!' The real difference lay in Cantelli's self-criticism with which he almost tore himself apart and to which the Philharmonia players took a long while to adapt. From the start, however, they admired his very expressive conducting, long lines of movement which were beautiful to watch and, more important, effective in their results.

Cantelli's first concert, on 30 September, opened with Mendelssohn's *Italian* Symphony, which he and the Philharmonia recorded two weeks later – his first recording with them. It was not a happy group of sessions: in the studio Cantelli seemed unable to make his arms do what his mind wanted. Repeatedly he slapped his right wrist, as if reproving it for its stupidity, each time looking back at the orchestra and apologizing 'My fault! My fault!' Then, at the interval, hearing the playbacks in the Abbey Road control room, he was almost in tears, unable to believe that what he was hearing was what he had just recorded. The Mendelssohn was completed but never issued, and yet it had not all been wasted time. The Philharmonia were getting to know this young man – 'the little boy' as they soon dubbed him – so emotional, sweat pouring from him and often near to tears but so clearly certain in his mind of his intentions. They in turn caught some of his frustration and anxiety and tried to help him along, although there were some who found it all a bit too histrionic. In the five short years they knew him, the Philharmonia grew to love or hate Cantelli, but either way they produced some magical recordings.

Cantelli later told one reporter, 'I like to conduct the Philharmonia. Except for the NBC Symphony it is the only orchestra that makes me feel completely secure.'

The day following the Mendelssohn, Cantelli recorded Tchaikovsky's *Romeo and Juliet* Overture; despite the rather muddy HMV reproduction, there is captured a performance that is at times frankly shattering. The sound of principal trumpet Harold Jackson in full flight is just one facet of what he, the Philharmonia and Cantelli could do. The care he took is seen in his sending the strings away for half a session to concentrate on the wind tuning at the beginning.

The Tchaikovsky compensated a little for the abortive *Italian* Symphony, but there was more trouble ahead. The third work scheduled to be recorded, which like the previous two, had formed part of that first Festival Hall concert, was Ravel's *La Valse*, for which a huge orchestra was packed into Abbey Road. For nearly an hour Cantelli rehearsed and then began to record, but by now he was so overwound that it needed only a minor upset to unbalance him. Sure enough it happened: after all the painstaking rehearsal the intonation was insecure, largely through one player who had arrived late, an incident in itself not calculated to fill Cantelli with joy. Without a word he rushed out of the studio, and five minutes later the session was abandoned. By an inspired piece of psychology, David Bicknell allowed Cantelli to unwind and then gently suggested he tried Wagner's *Siegfried Idyll*, a work that had gone supremely well at a subsequent concert and which, in its tranquillity and chamber-music delicacy, was the ideal antidote to the Ravel. The ploy worked, although it was hard on the Philharmonia. Take after take went into Cantelli's search for a perfect performance, and Dennis Brain, for one, was heard to mutter as he left that afternoon, 'Never again!'

The idea of re-recording even familiar pieces of music was new to orchestras at that time. Since 1948 tape had been used in parallel with wax recordings but only as a back-up and in four to five minute lengths like the 78 rpm sides. In 1951 the long-playing disc was new and as yet unadopted by EMI, who came rather late into the LP market, but the idea of using tape to edit longer 'takes' was a possibility that was becoming more familiar. Some conductors picked it up more quickly than others. Cantelli's repetitions were an extension of his personality, and he knew little of the mechanics of the end result. Karajan's were the product of careful study of the possibilities presented by tape editing, and he approached it with all the enthusiasm of a child with a new toy.

Karajan had finally decided to record principally with the Philharmonia, and he began, on 28 November 1951, with Beethoven's Seventh Symphony. He promptly spent a whole session on the opening few bars of the slow introduction to the first movement. When he started on Handel's *Water Music,* two days later, he began a series of sessions on that work which were to become spread over the next six months. Not every work Karajan recorded with the Philharmonia came under this kind of treatment, however. Strauss's *Don Juan* and *Till Eulenspiegel* were recorded complete on consecutive days at the beginning of that December. It is significant that, from the players' point of view, the detailed approach did not always have the result one might expect; the Philharmonia learned Bartók's *Concerto for Orchestra,* for example, from Cantelli's concert rehearsals rather than Karajan's recording sessions, and much of this may be attributed to Cantelli's phenomenal memory, which extended far beyond the notes themselves. He knew every player's individual line by heart and could even pinpoint, from memory, how many bars after D a certain passage appeared. His memory was perhaps less visual and more aural, more general in application and designed to capture the structural balance.

Karajan had a great ear for getting the right sound from the Philharmonia. When he returned to them after six months of absence, they would sound different within ten minutes. Part of this success was technique: he could time the entry of orchestral sections to a split second, merely by gesture – a gesture that was a beat that nearly always flowed, but he could also tell them how to achieve the sound he wanted. Violin bows moving smoothly onto strings that were already vibrating produced the glossy string sound that became his hallmark, and he asked for brass chords to come in just after the beat so that the sound of the tongues could not be heard. When he recorded Mozart's *Così fan tutte* in July 1954, two whole sessions were spent trying to achieve the right sound in Kingsway Hall. Karajan was not convinced that the orchestra's Mozart playing was coming across with sufficient clarity. He and Legge spent much of that night listening to various tests. Next day, at the beginning of the third session, they announced that they were transferring to Abbey Road. The whole orchestra, with double basses, drums and smaller instruments, was bundled into a fleet of cars and taxis and within an hour Karajan was making his first test for a recording that is still a classic, over thirty years later.

For all Karajan's sometimes inhuman zeal, the majority of the Philharmonia admired him. Even in their cattiest moments they had to admit he had ability and was successful with audiences. The criticisms that his tempi were sometimes a little eccentric or his performances were brilliant but unsmiling are perhaps valid, but what endeared him to the Philharmonia in those days was his knowledge of the psychology of the orchestra. A session or a rehearsal rarely ended later than five minutes before the official finishing time, and although Legge might have been his 'alter ego' Karajan refused to be dictated to, much to the delight of the Philharmonia. While recording Sibelius's Fifth Symphony, Legge came through on the telephone from the control room for the umpteenth time with some comment on the balance. Karajan listened for a while and then, with a wink at the orchestra, held the receiver at arm's length. 'His master's voice,' he whispered, and dropped the receiver on the floor. There was also the time when buzzers, telephones, shouts, all failed to bring Legge into the studio: Karajan simply put two fingers in his mouth and produced a whistle that any newspaper boy would be proud of. Legge soon appeared.

Karajan was also impervious to tantrums, by singers and players alike, and so they simply did not bother. They valued his ability to follow them, to give time for breathing and phrasing comfortably and yet never spoiling the flow of the music. Ask any singer who has worked with him and they will tell you that he is the ideal accompanist. You can hurry, you can drag, he seems to know you are going to do it before you do it. Like a piece of chewing-gum stuck to the heel, it is impossible to shake him off.

Karajan was also considerate to the moods and mischances of the Philharmonia in a way that Cantelli, for example, never was. If a player, particularly a principal wind player, was having an 'off' day, Karajan would concentrate on another section of the orchestra, letting the player find his form without feeling he was under pressure. He never picked on players unless he knew they were just being slack. Cantelli, on the other hand, picked on Renata Scheffel-Stein, Gareth Morris, Bernard Walton, players whose temperaments did not match his own. Karajan, like Cantelli, had a great respect for most of the players but was always tolerant of their human weaknesses. The orchestra responded to this humanity by adopting Karajan into the 'family', as it were.

4. *On Tour and Toscanini, 1952-3*

Few would dispute that the Karajan years with the Philharmonia Orchestra were mutually beneficial. For their part, the Philharmonia had a regular (not 'permanent') conductor who knew the psychology of an orchestra as well as anyone, rather better than most, and who made them sound different within minutes of rehearsing them. For the next eight years he was to be able to conduct them for long spells two or three times a year; in between, they could still enjoy the diversity of such outstanding conductors as Furtwängler, Markevich, Kletzki and Malko. With such an orchestra, Karajan was able to record, and thus absorb, an enormous repertoire and perform it both in London and abroad.

Karajan's reward, over and above the experience, was a platform through his recordings and concerts from which he could stake his claims to the other musical prizes he coveted. Through the help of de Sabata he had conducted regularly at La Scala since 1948, and when Bayreuth was reopened in the summer of 1951, he conducted there, too. Salzburg was to elude him until 1956: Furtwängler had ensured that, after a couple of operas and concerts in 1948 and 1949, Karajan would not be allowed to conduct at Salzburg so long as he, Furtwängler, was alive. His continued presence in this world also prevented Karajan's designs on the Berlin Philharmonic Orchestra from being realized. Karajan's reaction to all this, however, was an almost relentless patience. He knew full well that Berlin and Salzburg would not be his while Furtwängler lived, but he said many times: 'We can wait; we have time.' He still had the Philharmonia and an EMI recording contract which he could use systematically to promote his future career.

A European tour with Karajan had been talked of for some time. Walter Legge knew that Karajan was somewhat disenchanted with the Vienna Philharmonic, who still had more sympathy with Furtwängler, and now that he was more permanently associated with the Philharmonia such a tour would enhance his European reputation without his having to make any concessions to his enemies. It would be of great benefit to the Philharmonia, too. The financial risk was substantial, especially now that the Mysore money had virtually dried up. Fortunately for the Philharmonia, the number of recordings had grown sufficiently to guarantee the orchestra a good regular income. When David Bicknell renewed the Philharmonia contract in June 1952, the minimum number of sessions was raised from twenty to thirty per annum, although the actual number in 1952, for example, was more than five times that amount. The royalties payable no longer applied to records accompanying singers *or* instrumentalists, which is indicative of the marked increase in the purely orchestral items that were being recorded. Concertos and vocal recitals were still featured, and regularly, but the orchestra now commanded the reputation to record the symphonic repertoire and fear no serious competition. Igor Markevich recorded Stravinsky's *Rite of Spring* in November 1951, a work that was still an adventure for an orchestra to record at all, let alone on an expensive HMV label.

For Karajan now, however, the repertoire needed to be focused on a few works that would be good 'box-office' but also showpieces for orchestra and conductor. In April and early May 1952, the Beethoven Seventh Symphony and Handel's *Water Music* recordings were completed, and starts were made on Brahms First Symphony and Tchaikovsky's Fifth. These formed the basis for the planned European tour programmes, together with the Mozart B flat Divertimento K.287 for two horns and strings which Karajan also began to record with the Philharmonia. As well as making high demands on the horns, which were brilliantly met by Dennis Brain and Neill Sanders, it also allowed the strings no room for error. From the first sessions the strings complained that they would never manage it but Karajan sensed a challenge. It took ten sessions to complete, and the finished product was immaculate, but Karajan achieved much more. The Mozart featured in many of the concerts on his foreign tours with the Philharmonia, and in this there was not just the satisfaction of a work well played in public but also the success of a piece that had defeated many of the great conductors, among them Toscanini.

Jane Withers spent the winter of 1951–2 planning the details for the European tour which was to take place in May. The cities to be visited were Paris, Berne, Turin, Geneva, Basle, Zürich, Milan, Vienna, Linz, Munich, Hamburg and Berlin. To make the task of organization easier, the booking of halls and local publicity was handled by various agents in the countries concerned. With five countries involved, there was the task of organizing cash facilities to pay subsistence for players' day-to-day expenses and then the booking of hotels, planes, trains and coaches. The Philharmonia reserves would just take the costs involved when ticket sales were taken into account, and several of the concerts were sold out before they left Britain. EMI were in fact eventually persuaded to pay £250 towards the tour as it would undoubtedly enhance their record sales of Karajan and the Philharmonia. No other financial help was forthcoming.

Legge and Karajan had individual and common interests in the tour's success. For Karajan, there was the furtherance of his own career by successful concerts with a first-rate orchestra in some of the prestige musical cities of Europe; it would also be his one chance to play in Berlin again. Legge had designs on Toscanini with the Italian concerts. The maestro's failure to get to London for the Festival of Britain in 1951 had been followed by a promise to come when he could.

Involvement with Toscanini came sooner than Walter Legge expected: after concerts in Paris and Berne, the Philharmonia were in Turin on 15 May for a concert that was to be broadcast. An hour before the concert, Legge was telephoned by Toscanini's daughter, who explained that her father would not be able to be at the forthcoming Milan concert as anticipated but would be listening to the Turin broadcast. Legge quickly relayed this to Karajan and the orchestra, imploring them to play as they had never played before. Psychologically, it was not a very wise ploy: the Turin concert was not one of the best of the tour, but Toscanini was intrigued. Four days later, when the Philharmonia arrived in Milan, Walter Legge and Elisabeth Schwarzkopf were invited to tea with Toscanini. He immediately told them he was too old to start work with a new orchestra and turned the conversation to Legge's recording work and grilled him on his views of his own latest recordings, on which Legge gave him his usual candid opinions.

The next concert took place on 19 May with a rapturous welcome by the La Scala audience. Karajan they knew already from his opera performances, but the Philharmonia was new to them, and its ninety-two players drew rave notices from the Press next day. After the concert they were treated to a lavish reception by de Sabata, who expressed *his* interest in conducting the Philharmonia at the earliest opportunity. On the 20th there was a second concert, again at the late hour of 9.15 p.m.; immediately it was over, preparations were made for the journey over the Alps and on to the first Vienna concert. As he was packing, Walter Legge was telephoned by Toscanini's daughter: 'Father wants to see you immediately – it's urgent!'

At Toscanini's villa, Legge found a sight he would never forget. With the maestro were ten or twelve very old men, some even older than Toscanini himself. In an intuitive flash he realized who they were: the people who had been in Toscanini's La Scala orchestra in the great days, men who had probably played in the first performances of Verdi's *Otello* and *Falstaff*, and Toscanini had sent them in to report in detail on the Philharmonia. Without more than a cursory 'Good evening,' he said. 'I will come to London – what programmes should I conduct?'

What Walter Legge did not know, or had overlooked in his excitement, was that the LCC, in the persons of Festical Hall Manager T.E. Bean and Concerts Adviser Owen Mase, had been in negotiation with Toscanini since 1950 to come to London to conduct. They had a promise from the maestro, after his disappointment at not being available to conduct the Festival Hall inaugural concerts in 1951, that he would repair the omission as soon as possible. The original idea had been that he should conduct the BBC Symphony Orchestra, but after the success of the Cantelli concerts the discussions had continued with the Philharmonia very much in mind. The London impresario S.A. Gorlinsky had already been to Italy to discuss terms with Toscanini and suggest he take the opportunity to hear the Philharmonia while they were in Milan before giving his decision. Toscanini now felt he could come to Britain to conduct an orchestra of whose playing he had been able to form an opinion. This was the scoop of Walter Legge and the Philharmonia's life. With the confidence that he had the situation firmly in his hands, Legge immediately began to discuss with Toscanini the programmes for six concerts later that year, to include a collection of what he conducted best plus a few pieces which Legge knew he could do supremely well, such as Sibelius' Fourth Symphony.

From Zürich, Legge telephoned Jane Withers, asking her to book six dates in late summer at the Festival Hall, six dates with four or five days between each as Toscanini would need rest and there would be many rehearsals. Jane Withers rang Legge back in Vienna that evening to tell him that six dates were not possible, especially during the Promenade Concert season. After consulting Toscanini's daughter, Legge flew back to London: he found he had stirred up a hornet's nest that nearly wrecked any chance of Toscanini's coming to London at all. Apparently in ignorance of the LCC's negotiations, he had cabled Toscanini's manager (his son, Walter Toscanini) in New York to tell him of the proposed six concerts. This was considerably more than his advisers had suggested to the LCC would be wise to accept on Toscanini's behalf, and Walter Toscanini was now strongly opposed to the visit in any form. Only after careful discussion between Owen Mase and Walter Toscanini was it finally agreed that *two* concerts would be reasonable, and two – 29 September and 1 October – were booked at the Festival Hall. Toscanini himself suggested that the major orchestral works of Brahms would be suitable programmes; Legge was not happy, but Toscanini's enthusiasm was undeniable and so he agreed. He little knew how nearly his personal intervention had nearly wrecked the whole enterprise.

Meanwhile the Philharmonia's tour continued through Austria and then back through Germany. Berlin was the last stop, and the timing of the two Berlin concerts was, by chance, bound up with Furtwängler who was also conducting in the Titania Palast in the same week. The Senate had arranged the Philharmonia concerts, and the critics merely highlighted the fact that this was Karajan's first appearance in Britain for ten years and that after Furtwängler's concert this seemed a more festive occasion. Comparisons were also drawn with the Boston Symphony Orchestra, that the Philharmonia was more direct, more sensitive and expressive.

The tour brought untold dividends to the Philharmonia. It was now acclaimed throughout Europe as an orchestra in the world class, fulfilling the expectations aroused by the records that were becoming more widely known and appreciated. It had induced Toscanini to come to London, an event that was now eagerly awaited, and for Karajan it had given an international orchestral dimension to his already formidable operatic reputation. Josef Szigeti summed up the 1952 tour when he said: 'The Philharmonia showed the Continent for the first time all the qualities of perfect chamber-music playing raised to the power of a great symphonic orchestra.'

The tour had lasted just three weeks. After an Albert Hall concert, a start was made on a recording of Vaughan Williams's Oboe Concerto. Written for the present soloist, Leon Goossens, it was recorded under the advice of the composer himself. The presence of Vaughan Williams was very helpful, advising and commenting where he could, and this contrasted sharply with Legge's sessions, where no one got in the way of running of the recording, not even composers. Legge's presence at recordings was rather like that of a headmaster. It was a *presence*, and the players, although used to it, found themselves always on their guard. However unnerving, it did make each session an occasion, and the results on tape or wax reflected that. Players and conductors alike ignored Legge's advice at their peril, for he had an uncanny ear for potential ability and for all the nuances of balance in recording.

One conductor who was not always ready to follow Legge's advice was Furtwängler, and yet, over three weeks in June 1952, he recorded with Legge the Philharmonia first complete opera, Wagner's *Tristan und Isolde*, still arguably one of the great opera recordings of all time, with Flagstad and Suthaus in the title roles. The three weeks were hot and sunny and there were two sessions per day in Kingsway Hall, ten till one in the morning and six to nine in the evening. Some heat went into both the preparation and the production of the recording. As late as April 1952 it was certain neither that Flagstad would sing the title role nor that Legge would produce the recording. Flagstad was still singing regularly at Covent Garden and elsewhere, but she was not too happy about the top Cs she would have to sing in Act Two and readily agreed to let Elisabeth Schwarzkopf sing them in for her, for the two singers were great friends. Flagstad had the utmost confidence in Legge, but Furtwängler felt otherwise: it was just a year since he had last recorded with Legge, at the re-opening of the Bayreuth Festspielhaus, and since then, both at Bayreuth and with the Philharmonia, Legge had made his association with Karajan so public and so close that the old rivalry flared up again. Furtwängler refused to record *Tristan* if Legge was to be producer, and attempted to have him replaced.

Legge succeeded in calling both Furtwängler and EMI's bluff, and on 9 June 1952 cast and orchestra assembled in Kingsway Hall, with Flagstad, with Furtwängler and with Legge. Ever since they had first worked with him, the Philharmonia had found Furtwängler remote and austere but always to be respected. The Philharmonia players' only reservation was that they wished Furtwängler would trust them more. Sensing something of the pressure of overwork and ill-health on the conductor, they certainly played their best for him, even when, sometimes, he was not on top form.

Despite all the problems of temperament, *Tristan* was finished with time to spare, and the last two days were spent recording the Mahler *'Lieder eines fahrenden Gesellen'* with the young Dietrich Fischer-Dieskau and Brunnhilde's 'Immolation' from *Götterdämmerung* with Flagstad. When Legge played Furtwängler the proof pressings of *Tristan*, he received probably the only kind remark from him that he had ever had, and, in the circumstances, a surprising one. 'You know,' said Furtwängler after a while, 'We have done this together: my name will go on the label but yours deserves to – that is *our* work.'

Soon after recording *Tristan* with the Philharmonia, Furtwängler worried and overworked, collapsed with pneumonia that turned to meningitis. His hearing was impaired and gave him much trouble, and the strain was taking its toll. The day when Karajan would succeed Furtwängler in Berlin was coming nearer. Legge knew that when Karajan went to Berlin he would virtually lose him from the Philharmonia, so he turned his time and energies to engaging new conductors who might replace him, both as a first-class orchestral trainer and as a box-office draw. For the moment, as Karajan frequently reminded him, they had time, and that time was now filled with prestigious engagements at home and abroad.

For the Toscanini concerts, Legge tried to get the Festival Hall at the straight £200 minimum rental but to no avail. The Manager had every right to let the Hall on the terms he thought were in the best interests of the LCC, and he was unlikely to agree to the minimum rental for a function which promised the promoter(s) a handsome profit of some thousands of pounds. The sense of a major scoop for London's music was soon sensed by the public, over sixty thousand of whom applied by ballot for the 6,500 seats for the two concerts.

Toscanini was on his way to America, and the two Philharmonia concerts would form part of a two-week stopover. Rehearsal began on 26 September, and the orchestra arrived nervous of the man who, according to legend, broke batons and players' wills alike in terrible tantrums that came out of the blue and, apparently, at the smallest provocation. Before he arrived in the Festival Hall on the 26th, the orchestra were in their seats, ready and tuned long before 2 p.m. – a novelty for the Philharmonia. Owen Mase came onto the platform to make sure everyone was quiet. But to everybody's surprise Toscanini was very gentle throughout the rehearsals. He spoke little, smiling occasionally as certain passages pleased him. He spent a long time on the Third Symphony, especially the cello passages and their bowing. It is in many ways the most difficult of the four Brahms symphonies, and Toscanini admitted to Legge that he was still wrestling with it. 'It is still not right,' he confided to him. 'I once heard Steinbach conduct it in the late '90s – he knew how to do it and I have never been able to recapture what Steinbach did.' As well as the symphonies there were the Haydn Variations, in which he asked the Philharmonia to play the fifth variation again, purely for the pleasure of it.

Throughout the rehearsals, in the Festival Hall and in the BBC's Maida Vale No.1 Studio, Toscanini was helped about by Cantelli. Toscanini had both affection and admiration for the young conductor, and Cantelli took every opportunity to learn from the maestro, watching his rehearsals, discussing points of interpretation with him.

The programmes for the two concerts were also to include the *Tragic* and *Academic Festival* Overtures: this was at the suggestion of S.A. Gorlinsky, the impresario who with the LCC and the Philharmonia Concert Society was promoting the concerts. In the event only the *Tragic* was included. Toscanini was so delighted with the Philharmonia's playing that he dispensed with two of the six scheduled rehearsals and rested, ready for the first concert.

On 29 September every seat in the Festival Hall was filled: hundreds more had queued outside for up to forty-eight hours for the three hundred standing places available on the night. Thousands more were listening in on the BBC's Home Service. A special ramp had been constructed so that the eighty-five-year-old conductor could reach the podium with ease. The platform itself was fuller than usual, as some extra strings had been brought in at the last minute to strengthen the sound which Toscanini had felt was rather dry. The back desks had players such as Hugh Maguire, Felix Kok and Neville Marriner, and the cello section included Ambrose Gauntlett, Raymond Clark's former principal in the pre-war BBC Symphony Orchestra and who had played for Toscanini in the 1930s. In the green room, Parikian was taking Toscanini through the National Anthem, then they made their entrance.

The National Anthem was electrifying, and the audience settled back in their places for the *Tragic* Overture. In the heat of the moment Toscanini brought his hands down slowly to start the First Symphony and was almost knocked off the podium by the two quick chords that followed. There was a split-second's unease and then all was well as the cellos and basses launched into the main theme. It was not the last anxious moment of the night: after sitting through three movements of the First Symphony, the trombones suddenly found themselves paralysed when they came to play the chorale melody in the Finale. In a live concert which had already produced mistakes from conductor and players alike, the audience soon forgot, but Legge felt he had been 'crucified' by his trombones and took his anger out on the unfortunate principal later.

At the end of the Second Symphony that night, the audience exploded. Rising to its feet, it cheered and cheered. Toscanini would not turn to acknowledge the ovation until he had motioned to the Philharmonia to stand. Three times he came back to take a call, and then he signalled to Manoug Parikian to lead the players off. He was happy, as he told Legge later, 'Not a conductor, but making music with musicians.'

For the second concert, on the 1 October, both Toscanini and the Philharmonia seemed more at ease. Toscanini himself seemed to be in a vein of mellowness which allowed none of the unyielding, uncompromising discipline of approach which had been evident in the First Symphony. There was more flexibility of flow and change of tone colour in the orchestral playing, which seemed to look beyond the small, effortless gestures of the conductor. Even the fireworks let off by hooligans on the roof of the Festival Hall during the second half did nothing to disturb London's farewell to this wonderful old man. At the end he was presented with a laurel wreath wound round the Italian flag, on behalf of the standees who had subscribed to make the present. He was genuinely moved and asked them to come backstage afterwards so that he could thank them. As he made his farewells to Walter Legge after the concerts, Toscanini paid the highest tribute to the Philharmonia and to Legge himself. As soon as he could, he would come back to conduct them again, and if only he were ten years younger he would have dearly wished to record with them and Legge. They seemed the one orchestra who could play his repertoire *his* way, and Legge was the one man not afraid to tell him the truth about his work.

Toscanini remained in London for several more days before flying on to New York, and he spent some time at the Philharmonia rehearsals for the forthcoming Cantelli concerts. From his seat ten rows back in the Festival Hall stalls he took a keen interest in all that was going on. Cantelli was rehearsing Beethoven's Seventh Symphony and was grateful for the maestro's comments in the intervals, but more than once the old man, in his black coat, was to be seen chatting to members of the orchestra, telling them excitedly of his own plans to record some works again, works that he had known for much of his life but which in his humility he still wanted to perfect.

In December 1952 EMI issued their first long-playing records – nearly a year later than their rivals. The advent of tape recording had already paved the way for the editing of longer works and much of what the Philharmonia had recorded during the latter part of 1951 and during 1952 had been very much with the LP in mind. Many of the first issues were of works that had already appeared in 78 format, but now the way was open for a planned programme of recording for the new format which offered an orchestra like the Philharmonia a rich future, since it made its living principally through its recordings.

Walter Legge took an early, if unusual, opportunity to use the new long-playing format to record a work which had certain intrinsic difficulties that tape made it possible to overcome. Bach's B minor Mass relies for its success or failure on a good chorus, and Legge felt that as yet Britain had no chorus in the class of the Vienna Musikverein. The work also requires a team of first-class *obbligato* soloists, and the Philharmonia could offer these – Manoug Parikian, Sidney Sutcliffe and Dennis Brain, for example – but at this stage costs were too large to contemplate bringing the Vienna chorus to London or taking the Philharmonia to Vienna for what could be nearly two weeks recording. Legge thus contrived a plan that was unusual in its conception and produced a result that was adequate but too much of a patchwork to put it into the world-beating class. Karajan recorded the choruses in Vienna with the chorus and orchestra of the Musikfreunde during early November 1952. Legge supervised the sessions, and then, during the winter and spring of 1952-3, the solo sections with their instrumental accompaniments were recorded at Abbey Road with the Philharmonia, again supervised by Legge to ensure a good match in sound. The two separate tapes were then spliced together. Karajan found this kind of work intriguing. His ability to pick up a tempo after a long period of time was already legendary: in Brahms' First Symphony he restarted a section where he had left it nearly three months before, at precisely the same speed. The Bach had the same continuity both musically and acoustically but was less successful.

Although Karajan was now firmly established as the Philharmonia's regular conductor, Legge never lost sight of the fact that his eyes were firmly turned towards Berlin and the Philharmonic. He therefore continually sought to maintain the Philharmonia's work with a wide variety of conductors, each specialists in their own line. During the winter of 1952-3 there was something of a 'Russian crisis'. Issay Dobrowen, who had been with the Philharmonia since their first season, made a superb recording of *Sheherazade* at the end of December 1952 and then was too ill to take any more sessions. (He died the following December.) His only real successor, Igor Markevich, had become increasingly discontented with HMV since he had been under contract and in January 1953 ended his collaboration with them. Legge was on friendly terms with him and, after some persuasion of both parties, arranged for the company to re-engage him on more favourable terms on the Columbia label. This served the interests of Russian opera in particular, for which there was no other obvious successor to Dobrowen. Markevich began recording again in early 1954; the Russian repertoire was safe again, at least for the Columbia label.

Legge wanted to begin recording the Strauss and Lehar operettas with high-quality singers and using the Philharmonia. At that stage Karajan was not interested, although he did later record *Die Fledermaus*, but Otto Ackermann was ideal for the job. He was an absolute gentleman in front of an orchestra, one of the greatest conductors of the Viennese repertoire, and the Philharmonia found him delightful to work with. The *Merry Widow* sessions in April 1953 were utterly relaxed but totally effective, held in a kind of party atmosphere. The series of operettas were outright successes for they had all the ingredients one wished but could never find together in one live performance. Singers like Schwarzkopf, Kunz and Gedda, and the Philharmonia Orchestra conducted by a specialist in his field, all were combined in *productions* which were coached to perfection and recorded with loving care.

The operettas were among the first Philharmonia recordings to be marketed in the United States on the new 'Angel' label. Karajan, in particular, was anxious for more publicity through recordings in the States, and the existing outlets through RCA and American Columbia were promoting only a tiny proportion of the British catalogue and with poor presentation. In 1952 Legge had started negotiations with Dorle and Dario Soria who at that time ran their own Cetra-Soria Company in New York, selling principally operatic recordings. They had a unique flair for marketing records as a 'product', and in Legge they found a

Giuseppe Sinopoli, Principal Conductor of the Philharmonia Orchestra from 1 January 1984.

left Walter Legge (1906–79) – founder and artistic director of the Philharmonia from 1945–64.

bottom left Leonard Hirsch, the first leader of the Philharmonia from 1945–9.

bottom right Walter Süsskind, who conducted the very first recording of the Philharmonia and was virtually 'house' conductor for EMI recordings.

One of the earliest photographs of the Philharmonia, recording in Kingsway Hall and conducted by Walter Süsskind in 1946.

The composer Richard Strauss rehearsing the Philharmonia for the Royal Albert Hall concert 19 October 1947.

Four conductors who were responsible for the early development of the Philharmonia in the 1940s. *Top left* Issay Dobrowen; *top right* Wilhelm Furtwängler; *bottom left* Alceo Galliera; *bottom right* Paul Kletzki.

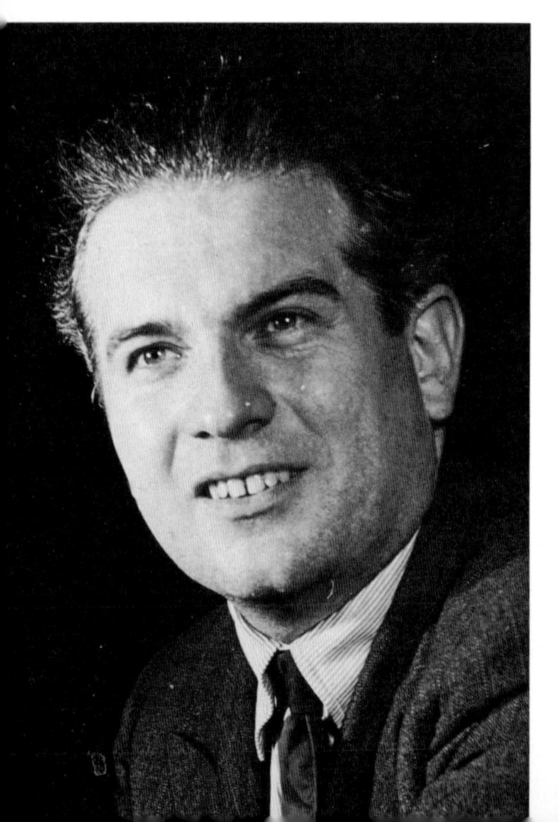

The Philharmonia and Toscanini take their bow at the opening of the first of the Toscanini concerts held in the Festival Hall in the autumn of 1952.

Sir William Walton and the Philharmonia recording Walton's own music in Kingsway Hall, 18 March 1953.

At the 1954 Lucerne Festival the Philharmonia was the resident orchestra. This picture shows the 8 August concert conducted by Karajan.

Furtwängler conducts Beethoven's Ninth Symphony at Lucerne.

Aram Khachaturian rehearses with David Oistrakh for a performance of Khachaturian's violin concerto in the Royal Albert Hall on 25 November 1954. Centre is Manoug Parikian, leader of the Philharmonia at the time.

Karajan recording Beethoven's Ninth Symphony in Vienna in July 1955. With him are (hidden) Marga Höffgen, Elisabeth Schwarzkopf, Otto Edelmann and Ernst Haefliger.

The Philharmonia's 10th birthday in New York, October 1955. Left to right are Karajan, Marie Wilson (from the first violins), Jane Withers (Managing Director of the Philharmonia) and Walter Legge.

Hugh Bean's first recording as leader of the Philharmonia in December 1957. In EMI's Abbey Road No. 1 Studio Elaine Schaffer records Mozart flute concertos with her husband, Efrem Kurtz, conducting.

kindred spirit. By the autumn of 1953 Legge and EMI had wooed them away from Cetra to start up a new label, Angel Records, to market EMI's quality LPs. It was a timely venture, for the LP industry was now booming, and now came the operettas, packaged by the Sorias as *Champagne Operettas*. The Philharmonia's reputation was well known throughout America long before they were able to tour there.

Two Karajan recordings made in the summer of 1953 illustrate the kind of search for perfection that went into the preparation for the Philharmonia's recordings and why it acquired such a formidable reputation on disc. The opening of Tchaikovsky's Fourth Symphony, recorded in Kingsway Hall in July 1953, requires a heroic, open-tone quality from the horns, and Karajan, unsatisfied with the results from their normal position in the orchestra, made a number of tests with the players in other positions, even standing on their chairs. Finally, it was found that the sound Karajan wanted would be achieved only by placing them with their backs to him and the bells of their instruments facing towards the microphones instead of towards the back of the hall as normal. The orchestra's response was typical of the rapport that existed between them and Karajan. When Karajan returned from the control room after hearing the sixth or seventh play-back of the problem passage he could not see the horns at all. Suddenly, into the expectant silence came the *fortissimo* strains of the opening – from the organ-gallery, where the players had hidden themselves. Amid general merriment, not least from Karajan himself, they climbed down to try yet another placing. In complete contrast to this frustrated experimenting, the recording of Humperdinck's *Hansel and Gretel* a week or two earlier seemed to float onto tape with effortless ease. In those pre-stereo days effects such as the children wandering lost in the forest were effectively captured by clever microphone placing alone. Towards the end of the sessions Karajan made a test of the overture, the orchestra playing it straight through at sight, and at the play-back it was found to be so good that it was left untouched for the master tape.

After a four-year absence, the Philharmonia Orchestra was invited to appear at the 1953 Edinburgh Festival to give four concerts, three were with Karajan, on 1, 2 and 4 September, one on 3 September with Sir Adrian Boult. Karajan's programmes were, as for his tours abroad, rather on the conservative side, with Handel's *Water Music*, Beethoven's Seventh Symphony, Tchaikovsky's Fifth and Bartók's *Concerto for Orchestra* prominent among works that had been recorded. The critics spoke of the Philharmonia as 'passing for the finest in the land', when welcoming them back to Edinburgh, and found Karajan at his best in the Beethoven Seventh Symphony for the opening concert. At the last of the Karajan concerts it was difficult to fault the

Philharmonia strings in their performance of the Mozart K287 Divertimento, and the critics found his Tchaikovsky 'an honest and impeccable reading which overcame the pretentiousness of the work'.

If the Karajan concerts had been unadventurous, Boult's was more varied and contained a novelty in the world première of Fricker's Viola Concerto by its dedicatee, William Primrose. Boult was an infrequent visitor to the Philharmonia, and it seems he under-estimated the two extroverts of the orchestra, Harold Jackson on trumpet and Jimmy Bradshaw on timpani, for in Walton's *Orb and Sceptre* and Elgar's *Enigma Variations* he allowed them to drown playing of 'the rarest and most loving perception'. Perhaps the finest feature of the concert was Mozart's *Sinfonia Concertante* K364, where Isaac Stern and William Primrose collaborated with 'unanimity of style and beauty of sound'. It is a pity that the Philharmonia never recorded the work in those early days. Nevertheless, they left Edinburgh well content with the comment that they 'can fear no rival'.

The use of Philharmonia players as soloists was a practice continued on record as well as in concert. Many of them had been well-known soloists in their own right before joining the Philharmonia, and men such as Gareth Morris, 'Jack' Thurston and Dennis Brain played solos regularly both with the Philharmonia and outside. Dennis Brain and Harold Jackson had both recorded concertos with the Philharmonia, and Fischer's Brandenburg recording had featured Gareth Morris, Manoug Parikian and Harold Jackson. In November 1953, during a batch of Karajan's Kingsway Hall sessions, Philharmonia principals were again featured in two Mozart recordings. Dennis Brain recorded the four Mozart horn concertos and in doing so produced one of EMI and the Philharmonia's best sellers of all time.

During the same fortnight the *Sinfonia Concertante for Wind* K297b was also recorded. It was marred by the illness of Frederick Thurston, who was scheduled, with Sidney Sutcliffe, Dennis Brain and Cecil James, to begin recording on 17 November, but he was already too ill with lung cancer to take part. He had missed many engagements during the last year but had recently rallied enough to play again regularly. Now, as earlier, Bernard Walton stepped in and acquitted himself nobly. It was a fitting tribute to his co-principal, for just a month later Thurston was dead, aged only fifty-two.

When Toscanini had taken the first Philharmonia rehearsal in September 1952, he had said to Walter Legge: 'That first clarinet – *that* is a great artist! He plays with the accents of a human voice.' Such was the calibre of the musician the Philharmonia had now lost. Principal clarinet of the BBC Symphony Orchestra since its inception, Thurston had succeeded Reginald Kell in the Philharmonia in 1948 and been very much the senior player amongst the woodwind principals. He followed in the tradition of Charles Draper, producing a firm, clear sound by using a medium length of lay with a medium-hard reed. As a teacher he had a unique gift of passing on his own selfless devotion to his pupils, and as a man was loved by all. Despite his rich experience and authority, he also had great humility: if his intonation was ever suspect, he was the first to whisper to his neighbour, 'Am I bit too sharp?' and immediately make the necessary adjustment. It would take the Philharmonia some some while to make *their* necessary adjustment to the loss of a great player.

But 1953 did not close on an entirely unhappy note. That October Walter Legge had married Elisabeth Schwarzkopf. Their professional relationship remained unchanged, with Walter acting as coach, agent and critic of Elisabeth's operatic and *Lieder* career. He had found in her the perfect interpreter of his beloved Hugo Wolf as well as a superb Fiordiligi, Donna Elvira, Countess Almaviva, Marschallin and Alice (in *Falstaff*). Now they found in each other a happiness and companionship that was to last a lifetime.

5. *Festival Years 1954-5*

Since the summer of 1953 the idea of joint leadership of the Philharmonia Orchestra had been abandoned. For the two individuals concerned it had never really worked. The plan had been that Manoug Parikian would lead for certain conductors, for Karajan and Cantelli for example, and Max Salpeter for Furtwängler, and this would be by mutual agreement at the start of each season. In practice the conductors often took the initiative and asked for a particular leader, but in any event Manoug Parikian invariably came in for a bigger share of the best sessions. It was unwise to prolong a system that put a strain on two players working so closely together, and neither of them felt that the idea was a particularly good one. Indeed, Parikian threatened to leave if Legge persisted with it. Legge had felt that the joint leadership gave the Philharmonia a European flavour, perhaps even the foreignness of their names giving added credence to the idea, but the position of the Philharmonia in the musical world no longer needed such aids.

1954 started with an interesting bout of recordings involving both old and new artists. One of the new was the young Hungarian pianist Geza Anda. Only thirty-two, he promised to succeed Lipatti as one of the most remarkable young pianists of his day. Members of the Philharmonia, with whom he had already recorded two concertos, compared his authority and brilliance of playing with Horowitz's and his profound musicianship with that of Lipatti. His Royal Festival Hall début with the Philharmonia was on 19 March 1954, playing the Brahms Second Concerto, conducted by Klemperer, who was with the Philharmonia again for the first time since his Festival of Britain concerts.

Klemperer was one conductor whom Legge saw as a possible successor to Karajan when the latter eventually went to Berlin, but his path to the Philharmonia was a stony one. In the autumn of 1951, when Legge had finally persuaded Klemperer and EMI to agree to a recording contract, Klemperer promptly broke his hip in a fall and was out of action for nearly a year. He had retained his American citizenship and under the terms of the McCarren Act had to return regularly to the

United States. It also meant, unfortunately, that he was forbidden to record in Europe, and so the contract with EMI, signed in May 1951, was terminated without a single note being recorded. The same McCarren Act limited his concert-giving outside the USA and prevented a proposed European tour with the Philharmonia late in 1952. Legge was persistent, however: two concerts with the Philharmonia in early 1954 and some persuasive talking led to a new recording contract with EMI. Klemperer settled in Zürich and reclaimed his German citizenship.

A second conductor to be introduced to the Philharmonia in 1954 was Wolfgang Sawallisch. In Legge's words, he was 'a better pianist than any greatly gifted conductor had the right to be', and indeed he made his London début in 1957 as accompanist to Elisabeth Schwarzkopf in a *Lieder* recital, nearly a year before he was to make his London conducting début. Legge had high hopes of Sawallisch at this stage, as he did of Lovro von Matačić, who had conducted in Cologne and Salzburg before the War and then in his native Yugoslavia. A chance meeting between Legge and Matačić led to an EMI contract and some fine recordings.

When Karajan came to London in July 1954 for a month's recording, the first plans were already being laid for a tour to the United States by the Philharmonia. For the furtherance of his own career, Karajan needed to go to the USA, where memories of his wartime associations were even keener than in Europe. The work of the Sorias with EMI's 'Angel' label was beginning to overcome this by promoting his recordings with the Philharmonia as high-quality products, but these were still early days. A tour would benefit the Philharmonia, too, and they were keen to follow Beecham's example in his 1950 USA tour with the Royal Philharmonic. But Beecham had had access to money for that tour, and herein lay the major obstacle to the Philharmonia's own plans. Legge was working on this. He needed to convince EMI that it was in their interest to put up enough money to cover any loss.

However, EMI delayed their decision over financing the USA tour until after the summer of 1954, while the Philharmonia were involved in three major European festivals – Aix-en-Provence, Lucerne and Edinburgh.

Aix-en-Provence is an open-air festival, and the Philharmonia and Karajan had been engaged to give the last two concerts of the festival on 28 and 30 July. The first was enlivened with a mistral which blew several players' music away, leaving them to play from memory; the second evening proved so hot that at least one player had to leave the stage for revival in the First Aid tent. But the Philharmonia were well received. A French critic wrote: 'It is said that Herbert von Karajan conducts only these orchestras – the Vienna Philharmonic, La Scala, Milan, and the Philharmonia. This is not true in the case of the Philharmonia, as he showed us last night, he only stands and listens with closed eyes to their magical playing.'

There was nearly a week after the Aix concerts for the players to get home and pack for their three weeks stay in Lucerne. The invitation was a little unusual in that Legge had succeeded in getting the Philharmonia invited to play all the orchestral concerts of the 1954 Festival, an arrangement that caused some stir amongst the Swiss musicians, who were accustomed to providing the regular Festival Orchestra. Lucerne had one of the greatest traditions of European festivals, inaugurated shortly before the War by Toscanini and Fritz Busch.

The concerts were an interesting mixture. Karajan opened with his favourite Mozart Divertimento K287; Kubelik conducted Gioconda de Vito in the Brahms Violin Concerto; Walter Gieseking and Clara Haskil, two renowned pianists, appeared as soloists, and the young Hungarian Ferenc Fricsay conducted the Philharmonia for the first time, in one the fastest performances of Tchaikovsky's Fifth Symphony that they could remember.

One highlight was on 18 August, when Edwin Fischer directed Mozart's E flat Concerto K482 from the keyboard and a performance of Bach's Second Brandenburg Concerto with the Philharmonia soloists who had recorded it with him just over a year before – Manoug Parikian, Sidney Sutcliffe, Gareth Morris and Harold Jackson.

Wilhelm Furtwängler, a local resident, conducted what were to be his last concerts with the Philharmonia, two performances of Beethoven's *Choral* Symphony and one featuring Haydn's Symphony No 88 and Bruckner's Symphony No 7. The Beethoven performances were very moving, with the Festival Chorus and soloists Elisabeth Schwarzkopf, Elsa Cavelti, Ernst Haefliger and Otto Edelmann. A recording exists of the second performance and gives some indication of the power still available to the ailing conductor; the cello and bass unison theme in the last movement sounds particularly compelling. One of the great strengths, still, of Furtwängler's performances was a sense of unity. His rehearsals, particularly in the last years, were concentrated almost entirely on the transition passages, and he would study the scores of even very familiar works right up to the last minute, looking for something that had perhaps missed his attention or some new way of making a passage more meaningful, more beautiful.

For the final concert, on Sunday 28 August, the conductor was the Belgian André Cluytens. The soloist was the young Igor Oistrakh in Khachaturian's Violin Concerto, a work the young Russian had recorded with the Philharmonia the previous December and which was dedicated to his father, David. In the audience was Otto Klemperer, and after the concert Manoug Parikian asked him his opinion of Igor

Oistrakh's performance. Klemperer's eyes twinkled: 'Why did he not play the Beethoven? Then I could judge!'

After Lucerne the Philharmonia was booked to play six consecutive concerts at the 1954 Edinburgh Festival, from 6 to 11 September. The Edinburgh critics knew that the orchestra was glowing with its success in Lucerne, and they would give no quarter. The first three concerts were conducted by Karajan, and he opened the first with the Berlioz *Symphonie Fantastique*. As the papers remarked, it was a sort of 'insolence of virtuosity that the orchestra is so sure of itself that it can dispense with the usual warming-up process'. The following night was all-Beethoven and evoked comparisons with Furtwängler's pre-war Berlin Philharmonic and Mengelberg's Concertgebouw – tribute indeed for an orchestra not yet ten years old. In this, and in Karajan's third concert, the orchestra's principals were singled out for mention as 'players who are the envy of Europe'. The 'delicate artistry of Dennis Brain's horn-playing', the 'filigree delicacy and perfection' of Gareth Morris's flute-playing and the 'refined sensibility' of Manoug Parikian all came in for praise, together with less poetic but equally complimentary praise for the trombones 'rich and strident in their dramatic entries, but smooth as toothpaste in their pianissimo passages'.

Cantelli was to conduct the next three concerts, and his was the unenviable task of following the glamorous welcome given to Karajan. This he undoubtedly succeeded in doing: Karajan was in the audience and went round to congratulate him afterwards. 'There is room for both of us!' he said generously. The Press certainly found his performances at once different but of equally outstanding virtuosity to those of Karajan. They noted that Cantelli conducted from memory, not just as a gimmick but leaving himself free to interpret. 'This is one of the reasons why he is a great and not a star conductor,' wrote one critic. Familiar works such as Debussy's *La Mer* and Beethoven's *Pastoral* Symphony were given performances that were some of the best at the Festival, and for some the best ever. The last concert, also the last of that year's Edinburgh Festival, echoed to a tumultuous reception of Mussorgsky's *Pictures at an Exhibition*, paying tribute to a great conductor and to the Philharmonia, 'an orchestra without a peer in Europe'.

If the Philharmonia felt a rest was long overdue, it was disappointed. Seven weeks had gone by since they were last in the recording studio, and there was a backlog of work. Cantelli recorded *La Mer* while it was still 'fresh' from Edinburgh, and then the orchestra spent a week at Watford Town Hall, recording arias with Maria Callas and Tullio Serafin. Callas had been under contract to EMI since 1952 and had recorded a classic *Tosca, Norma, I Pagliacci* and Rossini's *Il Turco in Italia*, all at La Scala under Legge and three of them with Serafin.

On 5 October 1954 Otto Klemperer began his recording career with the Philharmonia, with Mozart's *Jupiter* Symphony, the work with which he had convinced the London audiences and the Philharmonia that he had something to offer. Before the War, Klemperer had been a successful champion of contemporary German music and now, in deference to that, Legge persuaded him to record Hindemith's Horn Concerto with Dennis Brain, who had given the first performance of the work just four years previously, with the composer conducting, and had been given free rein to interpret the tempi as he thought fit. In Klemperer, though, he found an accompanist who stubbornly refused to budge from his own, rather deliberate conception of the work. Klemperer's tempi were often on the slow side, sometimes eccentrically so, but chosen in the interest of clarity of texture even if at the cost of a progressive pace. Dennis Brain saw that the collaboration was not going to work and told Legge so at the interval of the first session. He would not labour on for something which would be published. In a lightning face-saving exercise Legge changed the evening session to another Hindemith work – *Nobilissima Visione* – and warned Brain to act as if nothing had happened. The first Klemperer crisis was over.

As if 1954 had not been busy enough, a fortnight's tour for the Philharmonia had been arranged for the second half of October, with Karajan again. There were visits to new cities – Antwerp and Brussels, for instance – and a return to places visited on the 1952 tour – Berne, Milan, Turin and Paris. This time, the Italian leg of the tour included Rome and Naples and even Sicily, where in the Teatro Mazzino in Palermo the reception was so great that two encores had to be played, Wagner's overture *Die Meistersinger* and Verdi's overture *The Force of Destiny*. In Brussels, the Queen of the Belgians went backstage to meet Karajan and congratulate him, and at the second of the Milan concerts both Cantelli and Toscanini were in the audience and, as the critics were quick to notice, were the first to join in the tumultuous applause.

Back in Britain, a significant recording was made with David Oistrakh. Since 1946 Legge and Oistrakh had been friends, and Legge had tried, unsuccessfully, to record with him. Too many restrictions were placed on his activities by the Russians, and from the time he first became available to record, in early 1954, the sessions had to be hastily improvised because Oistrakh could never be certain he could get the necessary visas. On 13 and 14 November he recorded the Lalo *Symphonie Espagnole*, with Jean Martinon conducting, and then, a fortnight later, he was able to link a Royal Albert Hall concert with Khachaturian and a recording of the composer's own concerto. Legge was particularly pleased, as he had heard an earlier recording of Oistrakh in the work and desperately wanted him to record it with the

Philharmonia. The orchestra found Oistrakh patient and gentle. His first recording sessions were besieged by armed Russian bodyguards, who found every recording lead suspicious, but Oistrakh shrugged them off, mixing with the string players in the Philharmonia during breaks in the sessions, comparing instruments and exchanging ideas. The Albert Hall concert, on 25 November, was conducted by Norman Del Mar for the Brahms Concerto but Khachaturian, who was visiting Britain with a delegation of Russian artists and scientists, conducted his own work.

During May 1954 David Bicknell had written to ask if the Philharmonia had two or three weeks available in which they could record with Furtwängler a complete *Die Walküre* but the following months were far too hectic. Furtwängler used the Vienna Philharmonic, and the Philharmonia missed a chance to make a second great Wagner recording.

On 30 November 1954 Wilhelm Furtwängler died after another attack of pneumonia, opening the way for Karajan's transition to Berlin. The timing was unfortunate, right in the middle of preparations of the Philharmonia's USA tour, planned for late 1955. In September 1954 EMI had discussed the tour and agreed with Legge that it would be difficult to sell the Philharmonia in the USA unless it was with their own conductor, and so Karajan should go with them. His fee of $1,000 per concert and the cost of transporting over one hundred players with instruments and baggage would lead to a loss of at least £15,000: this EMI agreed to underwrite. Karajan also insisted on a maximum of two hundred miles between stops and that the halls used would be those normally taken by the major orchestras. The same day that Furtwängler died, EMI wrote to the Philharmonia explaining that Angel Records had been granted exclusive use of the name 'Philharmonia' in America and offering to renew the orchestra's contract for a further five years from June 1955. EMI also proposed to extend Karajan's contract for a minimum of two years from August 1957, although this now proved a risky venture.

Furtwängler's death created a difficulty just then, as he had been scheduled to tour the USA himself with the Berlin Philharmonic from February to 1 April 1955, and it was a certainty that Karajan would be invited to replace him. If Karajan went with the Berlin Philharmonic and Legge went on with plans for the Philharmonia's tour, as he fully intended to, EMI would be reluctant to pay the losses now that some of the limelight would be stolen by the earlier tour. Legge was quick to put pressure on EMI to continue their support for the Philharmonia tour. In a memo in December, he claimed that there was a real danger that Karajan could be persuaded to go with the Berlin Philharmonic and sign for Deutsche Grammophon. Moreover, two leading concert agents in the USA were interested in Karajan touring with the Philharmonia on the strength of reports they had received of the successes in Aix and Lucerne earlier in 1954. Legge pushed still further: Karajan, he said, had seen all the correspondence relating to the Philharmonia tour, and EMI could in no way consider withdrawing their support, or they would need several conductors to replace him.

It was a threat, and there was undoubtedly some wheeling and dealing in all this, but an element of truth, too. EMI could *not* afford to back out of supporting Karajan's Philharmonia tour of America even if he did go with the Berlin Philharmonic first; they had in the Sorias at Angel Records an outlet in the USA for Karajan's recordings, and that was something Karajan valued very highly. His records sold well in the United Kingdom, too, and EMI could not at this delicate stage afford the risk of losing him to a rival recording company. So they agreed, and plans went ahead.

As it transpired, Karajan went to America with the Berlin Philharmonic and was offered the conductorship actually on the US tour itself, the result of election by the players on 5 March in Pittsburgh and confirmed by the Senate in Berlin a few days after their return.

The protection of the Philharmonia's name and work with EMI was quite fiercely championed by Legge. As early as August 1953 a request had come from Kurt Woess, chief conductor of the Nippon Philharmonic Orchestra in Tokyo, for eighteen members of the Philharmonia to record Mozart's *Eine Kleine Nachtmusik* for the Nippon Polydor Company, but Jane Withers declined in the orchestra's interests and David Bicknell supported this as being outside the contract with EMI. In the USA, efforts had been made to protect the use of the Philharmonia's name ever since Angel Records had been set up in the autumn of 1953, despite attempts by RCA Victor to use it for their cheaper 'Bluebird' label. The name 'Philharmonia Promenade Orchestra' was suggested as an alternative, but this was a title already reserved (for their own cheaper labels) by EMI, and therefore Angel. It was a struggle that was to continue and to the casual observer might seem a slight issue but one must remember that at this time the Philharmonia was establishing an association with the highest musical standards, at home and abroad; anything that threatened to undermine this was to be discouraged before any real damage could be done.

In June 1955 the Philharmonia's recording contract came up for renewal. EMI had already guaranteed this, but it is a reflection of the growth in recording work that the new five-year contract now stipulated a minimum of 150 sessions per annum, of which 75 were to be without instrumental or vocal soloist. In practice, the first year of the new contract produced a total of 276 sessions.

The recording sessions provided not only a regular source of income for the Philharmonia players but the widest variety of music, and this was a major attraction for the players. The concerts during the months leading up to the USA tour used mostly standard repertoire. Indeed, many were deliberately 'popular' in appeal: Tchaikovsky Ballet Suites, Dvořák's *New World* Symphony, Beethoven and Mozart programmes were regularly featured. There were the occasional novelties, with items such as *München* by Richard Strauss and conducted by Norman Del Mar, Ghedini's *Battle* and Casella's *Paganiniana* both conducted by Cantelli, as well as an American evening in April 1955, with music by Gershwin.

Since the transfer of Igor Markevich to the Columbia label, HMV needed a replacement conductor for the Russian repertoire, although it still had Nicolai Malko. In March 1955 Efrem Kurtz began to record for HMV with the Philharmonia. He had signed for EMI in January 1955 and now began with a recording of Shostakovich Symphony No.10, a work still less than two years old. Kurtz had worked for many years with the Russian Ballet and the Anna Pavlova Company, and as 23 January 1956 would be the twenty-fifth anniversary of the death of Pavlova, a record was planned to be issued as a tribute to her art. Kurtz was the natural choice, and in June 1955 he began recording with the Philharmonia a collection of short pieces particularly associated with Pavlova and chosen in close collaboration with the Anna Pavlova Committee in London.

Walter Legge had been instrumental in introducing Karajan to Sibelius' music by recording the Fifth Symphony with him in 1952, following it a year later with the Fourth. In July 1955 Karajan recorded the Sixth and Seventh Symphonies, the latter obviously new to him and which he appeared to learn as he went along. The first three symphonies Legge had promised to Kletzki, whose work with the Philharmonia strings was equally astounding. Kletzki, however, worked less happily with Legge, who perhaps found it difficult to make the necessary mental adjustment after the Karajan sessions. The sessions in Kingsway Hall with Kletzki were tense, with the phone ringing every few minutes from the control room with comments or suggestions. Kletzki eventually lost his temper and suggested with some heat: 'You had better put *your* name on the record label!' It was a long time before he and Legge were able to work harmoniously in the studio again.

Karajan had been steadily working his way through the Beethoven symphonies, and when it came to recording the Ninth there was the eternal problem of finding a suitable chorus. Karajan and Legge agreed that there was no choir in Britain to match the quality of the

Philharmonia. Legge had the seeds of an idea sown, in his own mind at least, to form his own chorus, but that was a year away yet. Although Karajan did not get on well with the Vienna Philharmonic Orchestra, he had done marvellous work with the choir of the Musikverein, transforming them into a first-class chorus, ridding them of the rather soggy, beer-garden quality they had when he took them over. They seemed the ideal choice for the Beethoven Ninth, and in practice it proved cheaper to fly the orchestra out to Vienna to record than to bring the Singverein to London. It was, even so, a large undertaking to transport and house a hundred players in Vienna during the last week of July.

The Philharmonia now had extra help in the form of an Orchestral Manager, Barrie Iliffe. He had just finished a period of similar work with the Liverpool Philharmonic and had written to the Philharmonia in the hope that he could obtain a post with them. As it happened, Legge wanted this new post to be created. The Vienna recording would certainly benefit, but he had more than half an eye towards the USA tour, and the new man could take a lot of work from the shoulders of the office staff and Clem Relf, the librarian.

The Vienna Beethoven Ninth went well, but the orchestra was a little irked at recording in tiny bits a work that depends on an overall line for maximum effect. Karajan worked on the patchwork principle more and more, and the Beethoven Ninth had been no exception. The result perhaps justified the means but the minor irritation of working that way was there and at a time when Karajan's relationship with the Philharmonia was coming under some strain with his increased interest in Berlin.

In the three months left before the USA tour and while the preparations for it were in full progress, there was a heavy programme of recording still to be completed. A new conductor appeared on the Philharmonia scene whom Legge and Karajan had spotted in Milan. He was Carlo Maria Giulini, de Sabata's assistant at La Scala, and had been signed up by Legge after watching just one rehearsal. Now, after a successful début in Edinburgh, conducting *Falstaff* at the Festival with the Glyndebourne Company and the Royal Philharmonic Orchestra, he spent a week with the Philharmonia recording just two works, Vivaldi's *Four Seasons* and Bizet's *Jeux d'Enfants*. Manoug Parikian played the solo violin for the Vivaldi, as he had for the 1951 Cantelli concerts. Legge's resistance to Parikian's solo work was perhaps part nervousness that he would lose him to a solo career and part meanness at having to dip into the Philharmonia's own pocket. With the latter consideration in mind, he offered Parikian a solo fee per session, fully expecting Giulini to complete the work in a day or two. It took four days and involved nearly six sessions! In fairness to all parties, some of the delay was due to the music coming late from Italy. It arrived after the first session was over, and the Philharmonia's own set of *Spring* copies had to be used. Legge was sure that Parikian was responsible for the larger number of sessions, but Giulini wanted to make a success with his first recordings – he had a self-critical dedication similar to that of Cantelli, and the strings of the Philharmonia loved working with him. The woodwind were less enthusiastic about the young Italian, perhaps because he sent the strings away for much of the time allotted to the Bizet and concentrated on them. Legge was well satisfied, anyway; he regarded Giulini as the best conductor Italy had produced since Cantelli and he was good for the Philharmonia.

Klemperer then recorded the Beethoven Third, Fifth and Seventh Symphonies in the first week in October. The start of the USA tour was now just two weeks away, and the countdown was beginning. William Walton had made new arrangements of the 'Star-Spangled Banner' and the British National Anthem for use on the tour. The latter, a flamboyant setting, received its première at the 'eve of departure' concert on 18 October. It featured the horn section very prominently, and at a signal from Dennis Brain they raised the bells of their instruments in the air for maximum effect. It was a popular arrangement and was still pasted inside the music folders ten years later.

The Philharmonia now had the reputation of being the leading orchestra in Europe, a reputation enhanced by their recordings. With a series of twenty-four concerts in the major concert halls of America, they must offer a limited repertoire, dazzlingly played. They were also touring with a conductor who now held the most prestigious post in European music and who was making his second visit to the USA in less than twelve months.

The personnel for the tour totalled a hundred players and included some minor changes. Alan Civil, principal horn of the RPO since Dennis Brain had left them in April 1954, came in as third horn and was to stay with the Philharmonia after the tour, for some time as co-principal. The celeste player was Raymond Leppard, now a famous conductor, then a twenty-eight-year-old *répétiteur* at Glyndebourne and who had already played some concerts with the Philharmonia. Violinist Kathleen Tierney was mortally ill and her place had been taken at the last minute by Peter Gibbs.

The first concert was not until the orchestra's second day in the USA, Sunday 23 October, in Washington, and so there was time to settle in and rehearse for the début in Constitution Hall. True to form, but still taking something of a calculated risk, Karajan opened the programme with the Mozart K287 Divertimento. With a reduced string section the critics could admire the 'brightness of the slender-bored horns' and the 'perfect sheen of the strings who played ... as the polished Kreisler might once have done'. At the opposite end of the musical spectrum, Berlioz's *Symphonie Fantastique* evoked the comment that the Philharmonia 'can give its fullest effort without the slightest sense of over-producing'. A capacity audience reassured all concerned that the Philharmonia had taken the US by storm, and Verdi's overture *Force of Destiny* had to be played as an encore.

The total programme, as for all Philharmonia tours, was small – fourteen works that could be 'permed' to provide consistency of standard with variety of content. The Verdi overture was a standard encore: it had been used frequently as such on previous tours and was now actually scheduled for three of the small-town concerts.

The next concert, in Carnegie Hall on 25 October, was to be a twofold celebration, for as well as marking the Philharmonia's New York début it was to coincide with the orchestra's tenth birthday celebrations. Although the 25 October was two days short of the exact ten years, it was a decision of convenience, for the 27th itself was to be spent at Yale for a much less glamorous concert. The programme in Carnegie Hall on the night of 25 October was a repeat of the Washington concert, and so was the reception given the ten-year-old orchestra by the audience. Again, strings and horns were singled out in the Mozart: 'The two horns must have come from another planet,' quipped the *Tribune*'s writer, while for one critic the orchestra proved itself 'the most brilliant orchestra in the world'. The tenth birthday celebrations took place after the Carnegie Hall concert. At the Lotus Club a sumptuous party had been arranged and a magnificent cake prepared. The American musical world was somewhat shaken, not least by the fact that the majority of the Philharmonia players were native British as compared with the high percentage of European immigrants that made up most of the American orchestras. The average age of the players was also barely thirty-five.

There were three New York concerts, on 25, 26 and 28 October, and then a second Washington concert, followed by a group of concerts in a tour that took in Huntington and Charleston (West Virginia), Columbus and Toledo. The weather was beginning to turn colder, and as they headed back north to Chicago it began to snow. Instruments were starting to suffer in the extremes of temperature from icy cold to full central heating.

The Philharmonia found Karajan increasingly aloof on the tour, and while he kept in close touch musically, getting the six first violins together before each concert when the Mozart was being performed, for example, to go over some of the tricky passages, yet his personal contacts were few to the point of remoteness. As well as dashing from concert to concert, his curtain-calls became fewer and more perfunctory, despite the size of the acclamation; he seemed always to be in a hurry. This haste crept into the music, too: in Beethoven's *Pastoral* Symphony he seemed to be hurrying the slow movement, and Gareth Morris, sensing this, played Karajan at his own game by deliberately holding back. Karajan's eyes opened momentarily, acknowledging the duel, and then closed again!

After Grand Rapids, Detroit and Toronto, Philadelphia played host with a sumptuous lunch reception given by the Philadelphia Orchestra and Eugene Ormandy, who had already conducted them in Britain. One Philadelphia critic started by asserting that 'any orchestra that has the temerity to invade the Academy of Music must stand comparison with the world's best' and went on to allow that, 'Choir for choir, soloist for soloist, the Philharmonia can hold its own.' That was Tuesday and when the Philharmonia completed the tour on Saturday 19 November, with its Boston début, the reviews were no less lavish in their praise; the standard had been upheld to the end of four gruelling weeks. *The Globe* described them as 'assuredly one of the great orchestras of the world', and the *Post*, describing the frenzied ovation given by the two-thousand-strong audience in Symphony Hall, noted the 'incredible integrated sound ... like none I have heard so far, though through the orchestra's many superb recordings I had long suspected this was true, but recording engineers can do wondrous things in control rooms'.

The Boston concert was undoubtedly a fitting climax, but there was a price. That final week of the tour brought to a head a crisis which rocked the orchestra, although it was not truly of their own making, and which terrified Legge because it jeopardized a number of important forthcoming engagements; doubtless it also worried EMI, who stood to lose an important conductor already in the process of transferring his allegiance elsewhere. The whole affair grew out of Karajan's rather perfunctory and off-hand manner over curtain-calls which often left the orchestra feeling a little silly, sitting in front of an audience that was still applauding madly. Karajan's aloofness could be put down to his somewhat neurotic sensitivity over the Americans' attitude towards him; he sensed, or thought he sensed, that the wild acclaim was for the Philharmonia, not for him personally, although the Press reviews do not bear this out. The last week of the tour included several 'small' dates, and it was more in the small towns that Karajan seemed to sense most antipathy. The Baltimore audience was rather small and somewhat cool in its enthusiasm. At the University of Massachusetts the roof leaked, chiefly during the *Water Music*. Most of the orchestra found this at least mildly funny, but during the week small irritations were beginning to assume unusual proportions; there is no doubt that Karajan's rapid disappearance at the end of concerts were becoming an embarrassment and soon downright annoying. Many wanted to say something privately, as it reflected on the orchestra's public image. Sadly, when the eruption came, it was ill-timed and tactless.

Peter Gibbs was a back-desk violinist who had been brought in at the last minute to replace a regular player who was ill, and so was not in the strict sense a member of the Philharmonia. At the seating rehearsal in Boston's Symphony Hall he stood up and demanded an apology from Karajan for his inconsiderate behaviour towards the orchestra, Karajan ignored him, but Legge, who was sitting in the hall with some of the Boston Symphony players, called to him to sit down. A few minutes later the rehearsal was over and Karajan disappeared but the message soon came back that he wanted a full apology from the orchestra, signed by each one of them and that Gibbs would not play at the evening concert.

Thus began a frantic afternoon of frayed tempers, telephone calls and mounting tension. Many of the Philharmonia principals flatly refused to sign or even to play the concert unless Gibbs *was* allowed to play, not so much because they condoned his ill-timed confrontation but because they agreed with the content of what he had said. They even pressed the point by asking for a signed apology from Karajan – but now was not the time to give it to him. Jane Withers told Shirley Baxter to type out something, as badly as she could, and give it to Mattoni, Karajan's personal assistant, thereby playing down the whole affair until at least the concert was over. This was done, and the document was never seen again. The concert went ahead, with Gibbs playing, with Karajan conducting – albeit a few anxious moments late – the audience blissfully unaware of anything untoward.

So ended the Philharmonia's 1955 USA tour. What had it achieved in real musical terms? It made nearly every major American orchestra look very closely at their own ranks and compare themselves with this ten-year-old fledgling that played in the world class. It was even rumoured that the New York Philharmonic held an inquest after the Philharmonia visit and sacked some of its players. A successful tour abroad was certainly good for orchestral morale, and following in the wake of the Berlin Philharmonic, they could be well pleased. Winthrop Sargeant in the *New Yorker* (5 November 1955) made a very perceptive analysis of the Philharmonia both corporately and individually. He ranked the Philharmonia as superior to both the Berlin Philharmonic and the Amsterdam Concertgebouw, who had been recent visitors to New York, and put its superiority down to 'a highly fastidious process of selection ... the players matched as deftly as a jeweller might match the diamonds in a tiara'. Sargeant saw in Karajan's performances a less fiery and impassioned approach than he showed with the Berlin Philharmonic, seeming more painstaking and objective. He also picked out individual players: 'The most arresting of the wind players,' he wrote, 'is unquestionably the first horn player, Mr Dennis Brain.' He singled out Gareth Morris as having 'a tone of unusual richness' and Sidney Sutcliffe as capable of producing 'some of the most spectacular pianissimos I have ever heard from this instrument. Mr Bernard Walton, the first clarinettist, is also a superb performer.'

The tour also gave Angel Records a very welcome boost for their record sales. Seeing the orchestra 'in the flesh' has always been a useful means of promoting records abroad and after three years of modest business, Angel and the Sorias were given a very welcome fillip.

Karajan's abrupt disappearance after the Boston episode gave some cause for concern. There followed a month of agonizing suspense about his future with the Philharmonia in general and January's Salzburg Mozart Festival concerts and tour in particular. EMI saw this as serious, as did Walter Legge. The Philharmonia was not a contracted orchestra. Karajan was now the principal conductor of the Berlin Philharmonic, whose players *were* contracted, and there was now a very real danger of losing him to Deutsche Grammophon.

All through December a sword of Damocles hung over the Philharmonia as no news came from Karajan over the Salzburg tour. At last, on Christmas Eve, word came that the 'maestro' would be there.

6. *A Chorus and a Cycle, 1956-9*

The early part of 1956 had a distinctly Russian flavour, with David Oistrakh making one of his rare visits for two concerts and some recording. Scriabin's *Poème de l'Extase* was recorded, compensating in his huge orchestration those players who had been left behind during the January tour. Legge had produced the Oistrakh sessions, and at the EMI February repertoire meeting he put forward the name of a promising Russian pianist who could record with the Philharmonia: Sviatoslav Richter. Legge had heard tapes of recitals and some American recordings, and now Oistrakh had added his personal endorsement of his abilities; he had grown up with Richter, and they were close friends. The principal obstacle was that shared by Oistrakh, namely that the Soviet Ministry of Culture made it virtually impossible for artists to get out of Russia only to record – they had to have guarantees of public appearances too. Legge's position with the Philharmonia Concert Society was an obvious lever, and so he wrote on 5 March, offering Richter eight concertos and some solo works to be recorded, and two concerts with the Philharmonia Orchestra, suggesting November 1956 and January 1957, or March and May 1957. Legge guaranteed his air fares as well as fees. Some scepticism was shown by EMI, but Richter had good business sense and had soon pushed up the recording fees originally offered and doubled the concert fees. Even so, a cable from Russia in August 1956 put an end to any hopes of a 1957 tour by Richter.

The concerts promoted by the Philharmonia Concert Society during this period tended to favour the standard repertoire. Legge's policy was to play the standard classics well. As he said: 'A great performance of a masterpiece has always been more important than the world première of a "novelty".' This made good box-office sense and kept the Concert Society's funds well in balance; the novelties could be indulged in the recording studios or by other concert promoters. A good example was a programme presented by van Wyck in May 1956 when Lipatti's widow, Madeleine, was invited to give the first performance of her husband's *Concertino in Classical Style* with the Philharmonia. The work had been recorded a year before by Felicia Blumenthal, also with the Philharmonia, but had not been issued. Now it formed part of a strikingly daring concert which, gratifyingly, attracted a large audience. Madame Lipatti proved an accomplished soloist, and her husband's symphonic suite *Tziganes* was also performed, together with Florent Schmitt's *La Tragédie de Salomé* for which the eighty-five-year-old composer had specially crossed the Channel. It was altogether an adventurous evening and well rewarded.

May 1956 proved interesting in the recording studio, too. Erich Leinsdorf recorded Cornelius's opera *The Barber of Bagdad*, a work which Legge adored but which no opera house would risk. Legge's musical assistant, Walter Jellinek, trained the chorus, and the result was very pleasing. The Philharmonia found Leinsdorf gentlemanly and charming to work with and quite exciting, but not quite in the top class. In many ways he resembled Sawallisch, who now recorded Carl Orff's *Die Kluge*. This, too, was an adventurous undertaking but, as usual, Legge chose his cast wisely and gave the recording the added refinement of being personally supervised by Orff himself, who also spoke the Introduction and the Epilogue. First violinist Hans Geiger translated Orff's German for the orchestra. *Die Kluge* was still only thirteen years old but had already won a place as one of Orff's most popular works, using as it did lyrical folk elements. The choice of Sawallisch to conduct was interesting: now in his third season at Aachen, he had little time for the modern repertoire. He was particularly good in the German Romantic tradition, and it was this quality he could draw from the performers in a later work.

Since his last recordings with the Philharmonia in August 1955, Cantelli had been developing his international career and acquiring a musical personality of his own that was modelled less and less on Toscanini and was also infinitely more relaxed and more mature. He had toured Europe with La Scala's orchestra and with the New York Philharmonic, taking the latter to the 1955 Edinburgh Festival. Then, for the opening of the Piccola Scala Theatre in Milan, Toscanini had planned to conduct *Falstaff* but on doctor's orders he had to withdraw and Cantelli was invited to conduct *Così fan tutte* to coincide with the Mozart bicentenary celebrations. When he came to London to record with the Philharmonia in May 1956, La Scala were already thinking seriously of appointing the young man to succeed Giulini. Already he was booked to take the *Così* production to Johannesburg in October and to the 1957 Edinburgh Festival. The Philharmonia found 'the boy' was now a mature conductor, and the sessions were more relaxed than ever before.

Cantelli returned to Britain for two performances of the Verdi *Requiem*, on 1 and 6 July, in the Festival Hall, with Elisabeth Schwarzkopf, Ebe Stignani, Ferruccio Tagliavini, Giuseppe Modesti and the Croydon Philharmonic Choir. The Verdi *Requiem* was a work that had not held much popularity since Toscanini had championed it in the 1930s: now Cantelli gave it performances that were very true to the composer and compelling for the audiences.

There had been more Verdi, in June 1956, with Karajan's recording of *Falstaff*. Ever since *Tristan und Isolde* in 1952, Legge had insisted on quality in the opera recordings, right down to the smallest principal, and scrupulous preparation. Soloists would be coached exhaustively at Legge's house in Oakhill Avenue for several days before a single note was recorded. Karajan would be there regularly to supervise the rehearsals, and the system allowed everyone to concentrate on the recording and not have to worry about the actual notes. For *Falstaff* nothing was left to chance: even the guitarist was the young Julian Bream, then just embarking on his prestigious career.

A change of orchestral managership came in July 1956, when Barrie Iliffe left to take up an appointment in Capetown. The following month John Nicholls was appointed in his place, in time for the Philharmonia's second visit to the Lucerne Festival. This time only three concerts were booked, one each with Karajan, Szell and Reiner. With Reiner on 1 September the Philharmonia played with the pianist Gieseking for the last time. A kindly giant of a man, Gieseking had recorded extensively with the Philharmonia, beginning with a magnificent set of four concertos with Karajan in June 1951 that were models of accompaniment as well as solo playing. He had also recorded the complete piano works of Mozart for Legge and was now in the middle of recording all the Beethoven sonatas. At Lucerne it was Beethoven that he played with the Philharmonia, the Fourth Concerto in G; two months later he was dead, the Beethoven cycle still incomplete.

4 September brought the Philharmonia's first encounter with Georg Szell. Legge had known him since the 1930s. A stern disciplinarian and perhaps disliked and feared by more musicians than any other, Szell brought a dose of authority that was undoubtedly good for the Philharmonia and which did make them sit a little nearer the edge of their seats than usual. As usual, autumn was a busy time in the recording studios. The latter half of September was taken up with the recording of four piano concertos with Solomon and Herbert Menges, and October saw the return of Giulini for an intensive fortnight, followed by a week with the young Australian-born conductor Charles Mackerras. Klemperer began recording the Brahms symphonies on 29 October, but then, on 1 November his wife died; leaving immediately for Zürich, he promised to return as soon as he could.

The composer Paul Hindemith came to London in the third week of November 1956 to record with the Philharmonia a collection of his own music. It was not very widely appreciated in Britain in the 1950s, and

Legge was taking a risk in trying a series of works. The risk, however, was well calculated since the orchestra was uniquely able to cope with the difficulties of the music, and Hindemith's own professionalism as a conductor made for a good working relationship.

On the last day of the Hindemith recordings, Saturday 24 November 1956, news reached London that Cantelli, just thirty-six years old, had been killed in an air-crash at Paris's Orly Airport. It had been apparent from the June sessions that he had outgrown his earlier self-torturing criticism. On both personal and musical levels he had mellowed and he had loved to work with the Philharmonia. Legge had encouraged the association. Cantelli was good for the Philharmonia, and as Karajan seemed gradually to be slipping away from the principal conductorship, the young Italian was a possible replacement. The news of his death was shattering. Even players whom he had crucified at rehearsals felt a personal sense of loss, and musically his death left a gap that would be very difficult to fill. Giulini was highly promising but his repertoire was far narrower than Cantelli's, and he still had to establish his own rapport with the players. Kletzki still worked regularly with the Philharmonia but could not get on with Legge. After Cantelli's death he was transferred to the HMV label, along with Beecham, to give the HMV catalogue more reputable conductors on their lists.

Karajan was still under contract to record with the Philharmonia, and in December 1956 they made a superb recording of Strauss's *Der Rosenkavalier*. No trouble was spared to cast the opera with singers of the highest calibre, and the 'regulars' were very much in evidence – Elisabeth Schwarzkopf, Otto Edelmann, Nicolai Gedda – and even minor roles were taken by some of the leading principals. A newcomer was Christa Ludwig, the young mezzo-soprano, and her engagement was an example of Legge's ear for potential talent. It even prevailed, in this case, over Karajan's nervousness about recording with an artist he did not already know. Christa Ludwig had already sung in *The Marriage of Figaro* with Elisabeth Schwarzkopf earlier that year, and Legge had promptly signed her up for Columbia in what was now her first major recording.

Legge's musical instincts seemed infallible: only his methods were unorthodox and sometimes disorganized, to say the least. He knew the right people and preferred to work by telephone as a rule; details such as fees were not discussed often until after the recordings were completed. He demanded the best, regardless of cost, a course which produced a glittering line of superb recordings but caused EMI's financial directors no little anxiety. There had been changes in staffing at EMI: David Bicknell had been appointed International Classical Manager in 1956 in succession to Bernard Mittel. This was a post long coveted by Legge whose own position had been made more secure in 1952 with the confirmation of his management of the Columbia label, replacing Leonard Smith. Legge's work as a recording producer with the Philharmonia had been since 1953 for the Columbia section only. The HMV label now passed from David Bicknell's control to two newcomers, Victor Olof and Peter Andry, who had left Decca and now had the task of rebuilding a rather depleted HMV classical catalogue. For the Philharmonia these changes meant a guarantee of continuing regular recording with a variety of outstanding record producers. For nearly two years now, experiments had gone on in the new stereophonic medium, and once EMI accepted it as a viable commodity it meant that much of the repertoire would need re-recording – this also was a guarantee of work for the Philharmonia.

Christmas 1956 was the mid-point of the Philharmonia's busiest-ever recording year: 309 sessions were logged between June 1956 and June 1957, and under the new Musicians' Union rates the Philharmonia players were the best paid in London. For some the money was not enough. Three sessions per day left no time for any real private or family life, and the sheer physical strain was often unbearable. The average number of concerts was still only about thirty per year but that represented nearly one a week, and the comparative informality of recording sessions, for which one did not have to dress up, did little to compensate for the constant drain on energy. For Max Salpeter, deputy leader since 1949, it had become too much, and at the end of December 1956 he left the Philharmonia. Very tired, he regretted leaving the orchestra but not the treadmill of three-session days.

About the same time, Manoug Parikian gave Legge warning that he intended to leave the Philharmonia before very long. For Legge this was a bombshell, particularly coming so soon after Max Salpeter's departure. His years in the Philharmonia had been both happy and rewarding but he still felt he lacked experience, most notably in the solo field. As a leader he had brought charm and dignity to his position and been the perfect liaison officer between orchestra and conductor. He had also ensured fair play between Legge and the orchestra. As Max Salpeter's replacement, and his own when he came to leave at the end of 1957, Parikian suggested Hugh Bean, whose meteoric career was like his own in so many ways. After a while filling in at the back of first and second violins, Bean was offered No. 6 in the second violins in time for the 1955 USA tour. Now his name was before Legge as the new No. 2 in the firsts, deputy leader in fact.

The turn of the year 1956–7 thus heralded a time of changes within the Philharmonia, some for better, some for worse.

On 21 February 1957 the Philharmonia Chorus was born, with its first rehearsal in the Gandhi Hall. For a long time Legge had wanted to form a chorus that would match the Philharmonia Orchestra and with which he could record such big choral works as Beethoven's *Choral* Symphony, the *Missa Solemnis* and the Brahms *Requiem.* One thing stood in his way, and that was his inability to find a suitable chorus-master. In the summer of 1956 he realized that he had been looking at the ideal man for some years. That man was Wilhelm Pitz, first conductor at Aachen Opera since 1947 and chorus-master at Bayreuth. Now Legge persuaded him to come weekly from Germany to rehearse his new chorus of amateur singers and train them into a performing body of professional standard. The following advertisement was placed in the papers in October 1956:

PHILHARMONIA CHORUS
(Artistic Director: Walter Legge)

Chorus Master: Wilhelm Pitz
Conductor of Bayreuth Festival Chorus

Applications are invited for membership of this newly-formed amateur chorus. No entrance fee or subscription. Works to be studied in first season include Beethoven's Ninth Symphony, Handel's *Messiah* for performances 1957–8 with Dr Klemperer. Send a postcard for application form to Philharmonia Ltd, 103 Cannon Street EC4.

About 220 applied initially, and auditions were held for over a week under the rigorous but kindly eye of Pitz and his wife. Just over 140 voices were selected, chosen not so much for their owners' ability to read music as for the quality of tone, and this was to prove to be the Philharmonia's trump card in its success as a major London chorus. More voices came gradually, and for a while the chorus was 'stiffened' by professionals from the John McCarthy Singers, particularly for recordings.

Joyce Reah, the secretary, had the parts for the '*Wach'auf*' chorus from *Die Meistersinger*, and Pitz worked on this for the first two rehearsals, ready for an early visit from Wolfgang Wagner. Then rehearsals began in earnest for Beethoven's *Choral* Symphony, which was planned for performance in the late autumn of 1957. Pitz rarely missed a rehearsal, flying in from his home at Aachen for the Wednesday and Thursday evening rehearsals and flying back to Aachen on Friday.

In March 1957 Klemperer returned for a series of concerts and to complete the Brahms symphonies which had been interrupted the previous November on the death of his wife. All were recorded and eventually issued in stereo, and plans were made to record the complete

Beethoven symphonies in the autumn of 1957 in conjunction with a Beethoven cycle of concerts at the Festival Hall. Klemperer's dry sense of humour endeared him to the Philharmonia players even though he could be bitterly cruel at an individual's expense. Klemperer stories abound in the folklore of British musical life but the best and the most genuine belong to his Philharmonia days. Like Karajan, he was considerate to his players but in a much more formal way. Unlike Karajan, if he wanted to correct a player, he would make straight for him, scattering stands and music as he went. As he became less mobile, he resorted to verbal attacks. The famous story of the violinist who, when Klemperer began to overrun the session, pointedly shook his watch and then his head in feigned disbelief, only to be asked with sarcastic concern by Klemperer 'It is still going?' is a mark of the authority he commanded to do things *his* way.

The players' relationships with their conductors varied, of course. There was, for example, Efrem Kurtz who, after a nearly two-year gap, began to record some Russian repertoire again. The Philharmonia found Kurtz very different from Klemperer. The latter's beat was small but his control was hypnotic, whereas Kurtz lacked a convincing command over the players and would stamp his foot to reinforce the rhythm. On a small tour of Ireland in May 1957, in a concert at the Cork Festival, Kurtz distinguished himself by giving an extra beat at the end of Beethoven's *Egmont* Overture which the orchestra promptly ignored. The audience went wild and applauded furiously, which pleased Kurtz so much that the next day, at the seating rehearsal for the concert in Limerick, each member of the orchestra found a present of an Irish linen handkerchief on their stand, whether for ignoring the extra beat or for the applause was never revealed.

It was now three years since the Philharmonia had appeared at the Edinburgh Festival and their first concert, on 29 August 1957, was with Klemperer. He chose not Beethoven or Brahms, which he had already conducted supremely well at Edinburgh with the Bavarian Radio Orchestra, but Mozart and Mahler. The former was represented by the 29th Symphony in A, which dazzled the critics with the immaculate articulation of the strings. Mahler's *Das Lied von der Erde* had Anton Dermota and Dietrich Fischer-Dieskau as soloists: Klemperer's conducting and the Philharmonia's playing were beyond criticism, but the work was too tied up with memories of Edinburgh performances by Kathleen Ferrier to move the audience on this occasion in quite the same way. It may also have had something to do with the fact that, to Klemperer's surprise and irritation, the Philharmonia had not played the work before.

The last of three concerts, on Saturday 31 August, was an all-Tchaikovsky programme conducted by Ormandy. The *Pathétique* Symphony was particularly moving, and made the Festival audiences wish the

Philharmonia were staying longer, but a heavy recording schedule lay ahead with Sawallisch, starting on Monday morning in Kingsway Hall with *Capriccio* by Richard Strauss. Some of the orchestra took the overnight sleeper home while others stayed in their hotel to make their way home by train or car during Sunday.

By breakfast the next morning most of the orchestra had learned the terrible news that Dennis Brain had been killed as he drove home overnight from Edinburgh. About six a.m., only a few miles from home, his sports car had skidded off the road, overturned and smashed into a tree.

The death of Dennis Brain stunned the Philharmonia almost more than anything it had suffered in its twelve years. It is no exaggeration to say that he was the best-loved player in the orchestra, admired not only for his phenomenal virtuosity and infallible musicality but also for his boyish sense of fun. That he had been the highest paid member of the Philharmonia for over four years had aroused not the slightest jealousy, and his fame as an international soloist had done nothing to spoil his shy modesty or his approachability. Dennis was only thirty-six when he died, but he had been a founder member of the Philharmonia, sitting as principal horn from the first day it was assembled to the last day of his life; his time with the Philharmonia had included such novelties as playing the organ in Karajan's recording of the Intermezzo from *Cavaleria Rusticana*.

When the Philharmonia assembled in Kingsway Hall on Monday morning, 2 September, the atmosphere was dreadful. Legge made a brief announcement, although by then just about everybody had heard the news. Alan Civil, who had been co-principal horn since the American tour in 1955, took over first horn and acquitted himself superbly well in what were very difficult circumstances. It was difficult, too, for Sawallisch, who was conducting, but as he said, quite sensibly, with a shrug of his shoulders: 'What can we do? We must go on.' This recording of *Capriccio* was in fact extraordinarily good. The orchestra seemed to find solace in busying themselves with Strauss's intricate score, and Sawallisch brought to bear all his steady professionalism as a first-rate conductor of opera.

Sawallisch had still not conducted the Philharmonia in public. He had made his London début earlier in 1957, accompanying Elisabeth Schwarzkopf in a Wolf *Lieder* recital of outstanding quality. When he made his conducting début, in November 1957, with the Philharmonia, it was something of the anticlimax that dogged many of his performances. His work at rehearsals and in recordings was very good indeed, but while his sincerity and integrity were manifestly apparent to his audiences, they did not find the electricity that came from the performances of his rivals.

The highlight of the autumn of 1957, anyway, was the first Klemperer Beethoven cycle of concerts at the Festival Hall. Eleven concerts were planned, from 11 October to 15 November, and would include all the symphonies and concertos (except the Triple Concerto), mostly twice over. Claudio Arrau played the piano concertos and proved an inspired choice as soloist for this gala group of concerts. Less fortunate was the choice of violinist Tossy Spivakovsky, who had made a promising London début a year before. In the Beethoven concerto he seemed to suffer from an excess of nervousness which had an unsettling effect on his intonation. Spivakovsky seemed unaware of the problem and tackled Klemperer with the idea of recording the work. 'It would be a great monument, Maestro,' he told Klemperer who promptly muttered to Legge: 'He means tombstone.'

The symphonies were being recorded in parallel with the concerts, usually about two weeks before each performance. The Third, Fifth and Seventh were not recorded at this group of sessions as they had been recorded already, admittedly only in mono, in 1955. The sessions, in Kingsway Hall, continued to forge the strong links between Klemperer and the Philharmonia. His approach to recording was a preference for long takes to ensure musical continuity and in general was preferred by the musicians to the patchwork technique favoured by many conductors. In fact, the possibilities of editing took a long time to impinge themselves on Klemperer's imagination, and it was with great reluctance that he was induced to re-record 'bits' to cover over mistakes.

The climax of the Beethoven 1957 cycle was the performance of the Ninth Symphony which also marked the public début of the Philharmonia Chorus. Wilhelm Pitz had worked on it for nearly nine months, flying over weekly from his home in Aachen to rehearse the young singers. Their enthusiasm was in part due to the chance offered of lessons with Schwarzkopf, Hotter and other notable singers, but mostly they enjoyed working with this short, stocky German who had practically no English but made up for it with a charming and relaxed friendliness. A few days before the concert, Klemperer took over and Pitz hovered beside him, anxious that all should go well. Even more anxiously he sat on the edge of his seat in the centre of the Festival Hall stalls on 12 November, until the audience rose in tribute to singing of a quality that few of them had heard before. As *The Times* put it: 'Miraculously, the finale exceeded in grandeur and brilliance all that the foregoing movements had implied, for the Philharmonia Chorus, which now made its début, can really sing the music of the finale, sing it accurately and with full, musicianly tone in every part ... the results were dazzling.'

Even before their début, the Philharmonia Chorus had offers of a contract with EMI which would pay £1,500 on signing and asked in return two major works and two double-sided LPs to be recorded.

After the complete Beethoven cycle had been recorded, Manoug Parikian left the Philharmonia, and Hugh Bean took his place.

A change of leadership undoubtedly brought with it some changes to the character of the Philharmonia, many for the better. What lay heavier on Legge's mind at this time was the changing state of the conductorship of the Philharmonia. In the whole of 1957 Karajan had recorded just two sessions with the Philharmonia. He had begun to record quite extensively with the Berlin Philharmonic, and it was evident that his career was moving away from an almost total dependence on the Philharmonia, a fact that Legge and the Philharmonia would have to accept and cope with. The Philharmonia could now sell itself on its own name alone. This was rare in a world where people bought records for the name of the conductor almost more than the composer, and Legge's early rule that the Philharmonia would have 'style, not *a* style' held true, even though Karajan had to all intents been a permanent conductor for over eight years. Now they would have to make a readjustment to conductors such as Klemperer, for example, with whom Legge was obviously building up a more permanent association.

There was no doubt that Karajan made the Philharmonia sound and play better than most, but equally he had used them to bring him the exposure he needed in Europe to lay claim to the great musical prizes that were at stake – Berlin, Vienna and Salzburg. However, he still felt unhappy about his image in America, where, although the Philharmonia and EMI had given him exposure, his reputation was still slight. Even the 1955 USA tour with the Philharmonia had done relatively little to enhance his record sales on EMI's Angel label. Now this outlet vanished (passed over to Capitol), and it seemed only a matter of time before Karajan would seek a company or a contract that would enhance his American reputation on a scale to match his European achievements. (The American market was good for the Philharmonia too, and it was frustrating that, just when stereo was taking hold and promising a renewed boost to the orchestra's recording work, EMI now had no major outlet in the USA.

In January 1958 Barrie Iliffe returned to work for the Philharmonia, this time as Concerts Manager. But now the Manager's job was split into two clearly separate halves. Barrie Iliffe was responsible for the organization of concerts, pencilling and confirming the booking of dates and sorting out the programmes, while John Nicholls, as Orchestral Manager, engaged the final personnel for each session or concert. Iliffe's return was welcomed, as he was not only firm and efficient but well liked, too. Over all reigned the imperturbable Jane Withers as Managing Director. Her title brought with it the doubtful privilege of acting as buffer between Legge and the orchestra, between whom there was not a great deal of personal contact. She had the task of passing on all the bad news to the players, as well as the good, and it is little wonder that her health occasionally suffered in the process.

The concerts for the early part of 1958 saw the return of such conductors as Silvestri and Sawallisch, and there was also the first appearance of the promising young American Thomas Schippers, who conducted them for a Leeds concert in March. This was Leeds' introduction to the Philharmonia and led to regular invitations to the Triennial Festivals. The Philharmonia rarely appeared outside London except for the Edinburgh Festival, the occasional concert in Leicester's de Montfort Hall, and at Brighton.

There had been talk of Klemperer taking the Philharmonia to Paris for two or three Beethoven concerts in late 1957, but the plans came to nothing. Instead, in April 1958, he conducted two concerts of music by Sibelius, Richard Strauss and Mozart.

In May 1958 David Oistrakh made two of his rare concert appearances in Britain. Sargent was conductor for both concerts, and for the second Oistrakh was joined by his colleagues Knushevitsky and Oborin in Beethoven's Triple Concerto, which they then recorded two days later. Oistrakh recorded Prokofiev's Second Concerto, with Galliera conducting, and began Mozart's D major Concerto. Galliera had to leave for other engagements before they had finished the Mozart, so Legge suggested that Oistrakh should direct the work himself. Oistrakh enjoyed the experience enormously. In his youth he had spent some time studying conducting and now was able to begin a new phase of his career.

For the 1958 Edinburgh Festival, the Philharmonia orchestral programmes had been conservative, and although the opening concert was made up of Beethoven symphonies, conducted by Klemperer, audiences looked forward with more relish to the prospect of Menuhin playing the Shostakovich Violin Concerto the following evening. The veteran Swiss conductor Ernest Ansermet made his first appearance with the Philharmonia on 25 August and seemed much more at ease with Tchaikovsky's Sixth Symphony, to which he brought a truly Russian flavour, than accompanying Menuhin in the Shostakovich concerto. The critics did at least find Menuhin's self-effacing restraint a welcome quality and the Philharmonia's playing sensitive and masterful.

The 1958 Lucerne Festival included the Philharmonia in just two concerts. William Steinberg conducted the first, on 8 September, in an enterprising programme that combined Mendelssohn's *Italian* Symphony with Stravinsky's *Rite of Spring* and sandwiched between them a performance of Stravinsky's Violin Concerto, with Arthur Grumiaux as soloist. Two days later, Klemperer conducted a more conventional programme of Beethoven – the *Egmont* Overture, the C minor Piano Concerto (with Rudolf Firkusny) and the Seventh Symphony. Then it was on to Vienna, for a Karajan recording of Beethoven's *Missa Solemnis* too smooth for those who prefer the almost apocalyptic drama of Toscanini or the majestic grandeur of Klemperer. There was some time left at the end of the sessions and so Karajan recorded the Mozart *Prague* Symphony.

Those who preferred Klemperer's Beethoven would have their opportunity in the October Leeds Triennial Festival. Three concerts were to be given, all conducted by Klemperer, with the *Missa Solemnis*, Stravinsky's *Symphony of Psalms*, Walton's *Belshazzar's Feast* and the first performance of Fricker's *The Vision of Judgement*. Klemperer fans were, alas, to be disappointed. Legge had reckoned without the quirks of Klemperer's almost manic-depressive nature and unpredictable health. Just before starting rehearsals for Leeds he developed bronchitis, badly enough to have to cancel Leeds but hopeful of being in London in late October for the beginning of a projected Beethoven cycle of concerts.

Luckily, Horenstein was available for 11 October to conduct the *Missa Solemnis*, and the Philharmonia knew it well from their recent recording in Vienna. John Pritchard was also available for the other concerts, and the success of the Philharmonia's appearances in Leeds promised well for future festivals.

With one crisis over, another attended the Beethoven cycle. Klemperer suffered severe burns as a result of smoking in bed in hospital, just when he was recovering from the bronchitis, and for a while his life hung in the balance. Some frantic replanning found Cluytens, and van Beinum as replacements. For the two performances of the Ninth, Klemperer had persuaded Legge, much against his better judgement, to engage Hindemith. Excellent though Hindemith was, with the Philharmonia in particular, the choice was not the most suitable. Audiences used to Klemperer's taut and measured interpretation found Hindemith's sagging and piecemeal despite his rushing about the rostrum.

Scarcely had the new year begun than yet another blow befell the Philharmonia. Karajan signed a contract with Decca towards the end of January 1959, thus ending his exclusive relationship with EMI which had lasted since 1946 and with the Philharmonia since 1951. Karajan's new contract was in fact with the Teldec combine, which offered him at a stroke an agreement with Decca, to record with the Vienna Philharmonic, RCA and the American orchestras, and the Berlin Philharmonic with a choice of companies, including Deutsche Grammophon. The loss was less to the Philharmonia than to EMI in general and to Legge in particular, for even in the mid-1950s the Philharmonia had been able to adjust from one conductor to another with ease, and during the past two years they had seen less and less of Karajan.

That spring a Mozart and Brahms series of concerts had been planned, and André Vandernoot and Rudolf Kempe conducted most of these for Klemperer. For a Mozart concert on 6 April the only available man was the young Colin Davis, fortunate in having as soloist the experienced and very distinguished Clara Haskil for the D minor Piano Concerto, though his own performance won him great credit for its imagination and stylish attention to detail.

On the recording side there was the complete *Lucia di Lammermoor* with Tullio Serafin and with Maria Callas in the title role. The number of recording sessions was showing a marked decline, and there was some unease in both camps as the Philharmonia's contract came up for renewal in June 1960. There had been 309 sessions in 1957 and 225 in 1958, but only 176 had been used in the year June 1958–June 1959, which was only a little over the minimum 150 laid down in the current contract. After the Berlin Philharmonic, the Philharmonia was the most expensive orchestra to employ for recording, costing about £525 per session, compared with £490 for the Royal Philharmonic whose contract only laid down a minimum of seventy-five sessions per annum, fifty of which were to be with Sir Thomas Beecham. In EMI's opinion, the Philharmonia were only better in their string sections; the woodwind, they felt, were slightly inferior to the Royal Philharmonic. Moreover, under the existing contract, record club sales in America were allowed only on Karajan's recordings, and he was now no longer exclusive to EMI or the Philharmonia. The present list of conductors regularly associated with the Philharmonia in the studio represented some seventy sessions per year, which left a large gap to be made up.

All this was largely EMI thinking out loud, but it shows the trends in the industry at the time. It was becoming apparent that the Philharmonia could no longer rely almost totally on its recording work for its income and would perhaps have to consider entering the open market and feel the wind of competition on its cheeks. It was a prospect that did not fill Legge with much joy at the time and which was to preoccupy him more and more in the coming years. His own position with EMI he found increasingly unsatisfactory as he was allowed less freedom to deal with artists and programmes in the way to which he was accustomed. Then in June 1959 David Bicknell recommended a five-year renewal of the Philharmonia's contract for 150 sessions per year and firmly declined a proposal that they should become non-exclusive. Legge could breathe again, for a while at least.

During the summer months of 1959, the orchestra could look forward to three trips abroad. The first was a short tour of Switzerland with Giulini, with concerts in Basle, Zürich, Geneva and Berne. The Philharmonia had then been invited by the Calouste Gulbenkian Foundation in Lisbon to take part in four concerts for the Third Gulbenkian Festival of Music, from 20 to 23 June.

The conductor for the first three concerts was the twenty-nine-year-old Lorin Maazel, and two days of intensive rehearsal preceded the orchestra's departure from London, as he faced the Philharmonia for the first time in Wembley Town Hall to rehearse Stravinsky's *Chant du Rossignol*. The general reaction was one of surprised admiration. The young man had a baton technique which was a little unusual, with its often subdivided beat, but utterly reliable. Few conductors can convey such complete mechanical confidence that the players can get straight on with the music, but Maazel did that. He further astonished the Philharmonia players with his photographic memory of the score when they rehearsed Bartók's *Concerto for Orchestra*: if there was any query, he could call out bar numbers and the player's notes without any reference to the score.

After the Portuguese concerts, Legge was so impressed by Maazel that he offered him a contract as second principal conductor of the Philharmonia, with the opportunity to succeed Klemperer when the time came. But when Maazel named the fees he would expect, Legge dropped the idea in horror. There was certainly not the money to pay that kind of price, even for the talent that Maazel could undoubtedly offer the Philharmonia. Besides, there were other young conductors available, and there were signs now that Klemperer was on the road to recovery.

On 5 September came the long-awaited return of Klemperer. At the rehearsal for the first of his two concerts (at the Lucerne Festival) Legge welcomed him back in front of the whole orchestra and as a gesture of gratitude and relief made him Conductor-for-Life of the Philharmonia. Klemperer was much moved and, although far from totally recovered, it did much to lift his spirits.

The last Lucerne concert, on 10 September 1959, was an historic one on several counts. A performance of Handel's *Messiah*, it marked the first foreign engagement for the Philharmonia Chorus. It was also the first collaboration with Sir Thomas Beecham since he had conducted the orchestra at its public début fourteen years previously. Beecham's own new performing edition of *Messiah* was being used, and it had already caused quite a stir. Even at the age of eighty, Beecham asserted his individuality over the performance. In one of the big choruses he suddenly stopped. 'Don't drag!' he hissed at the astonished chorus, in a whisper that could be heard all over the hall, and then started the number again. Pitz was furious; he took the incident as Beecham's way of insulting his Philharmonia Chorus and had to be dissuaded very firmly from giving a blistering interview to the Press during the interval.

On the return from Lucerne there were two big opera recordings planned, to be coupled with concert performances in the Festival Hall. Legge gave full credit for the latter idea to the Festival Hall's manager, T.E. Bean, who had suggested something similar after hearing Karajan's *Falstaff* recording. The programme for the first concert, Mozart's *Marriage of Figaro* conducted by Giulini, on 25 September, claimed that prior to the concert there had been 160 hours of intensive rehearsal and preparation, a figure that must have included every last minute from the first tentative bookings to the final editing but which nevertheless indicated the measure of care taken over the recordings in the true Legge style. On the night itself there were some who found the effect disappointing, with a lack of action and poor balance between singers and orchestra, but the public in general were highly delighted with the quality. The same procedure was planned for the first weeks of October, when *Don Giovanni* would be conducted by Klemperer, but again fate intervened when Klemperer ran a high temperature after just two days' recording. Legge had a crisis on his hands. Giulini was available to take over the recording, although he did not know the work very well, but he had to return to Italy immediately after and would not be able to conduct the two concert performances. In desperation, Legge telephoned Colin Davis to ask him if he would 'take it on'. As Colin Davis later recalled: 'Walter Legge used to take a gamble and it tickled him, I think, to put a little-known Englishman in front of an international cast and see what would happen'. As history tells, Davis made his name almost overnight with his authoritative conducting of the two performances and their rehearsals.

With the falling number of recording sessions for the Philharmonia, it was evident that the emphasis of its activity would now need to shift gradually away from almost total reliance on studio work and more towards the concert platform. With this in mind, it was decided to employ a General Manager, and on 1 December 1959 Stephen Gray was appointed to that post with the Philharmonia Orchestra and as General Manager and Secretary of the Philharmonia Concert Society. (The PCS was the Philharmonia's own concert-promoting body, and it made good sense to have a General Manager who could exercise control over both it and the orchestra itself.) Walter Legge and Jane Withers made it no secret that Gray's responsibility was to promote the concert side of the Philharmonia's activities, and for this he was well qualified.

The one common link between the Philharmonia Orchestra and the

Philharmonia Concert Society was Walter Legge himself, founder of one and artistic director of the other. The Concert Society was the major, but not sole, agent for the orchestra's concerts; it also regularly promoted chamber recitals of high quality. As a non-profit making company the Concert Society was eligible for financial aid which the orchestra itself was not; by maintaining the two organizations in parallel, the orchestra was in a position to finance the Concert Society which in turn employed the orchestra for concerts and could in its own right be subsidized. The Philharmonia began to increase its concert-giving at a time when there were moves afoot to tidy up the whole area of London orchestral activity. It could no longer hide behind the security of a lucrative recording contract to ensure its survival.

7. *Klemperer – and Crisis, 1960-4*

Throughout 1959 EMI had continued to 'think aloud' on the subject of the Philharmonia's contract, due for renewal in June 1960. After the original proposal to renew for five years, at 150 sessions per annum, both EMI and the Philharmonia had second thoughts, and by September 1959 a three-year contract of 150 sessions per annum was agreed. A second factor now entered the negotiations, with the records of *Don Giovanni* and the *Marriage of Figaro*. Both Mozart operas used only a small orchestra, and it was becoming difficult to retain some of the superfluous players. The Philharmonia suggested that the 150 sessions of the contract should apply only to orchestras of more than fifty players. EMI could not consider this, as the number of sessions was falling with the gradual completion of the re-recording of the catalogue in stereo. The number of future 'pencilled' dates was down, so they countered with a proposal that the contract be for 150 sessions and that for those occasion when less than fifty players were employed the rest would be retained at standard Musicians' Union rank-and-file rate. The fine print would be sorted out during the winter.

The retention of the Philharmonia was still important to EMI's business, as it earned considerable foreign currency and worked with most of their leading conductors, who had themselves now become a critical factor in the negotiations, significantly with the recent move by Karajan and with the impending expiry of contracts of many conductors who had worked regularly with the Philharmonia – those of Galliera, Klemperer, Kurtz, Matačić, Sargent, Markevich and Silvestri were all due to expire in 1960 and that of Kletzki in 1961. The sum total of Philharmonia sessions represented by these was just over seventy, less than half the contract minimum. Karajan had in the mid-1950s done as many as sixty sessions in a year, and now he was down to just a handful. So far, Klemperer's work had been sporadic, and any real hopes that he could fill the gap left by Karajan must now have seemed very slim indeed.

The retention of players in the Philharmonia encompassed two extremes: there were those who found themselves under-used, as in the

Mozart opera recordings, and might be tempted away, but there were also the principals who were often attracted by outside offers and whom the Philharmonia were particularly keen to keep. About twelve players were held on contract or Service Agreement as it was known, but for many a verbal agreement sufficed. Hugh Bean, as leader, for example, had no writen contract at any time, but it would have been unnecessary in his case, as for many others. The strong point about the lack of a universal contract had always been that it gave the Philharmonia a flexibility that ensured the engagement of the best players, who would be totally loyal anyway. Walter Legge put it more succinctly: 'I must retain the inalienable right to hire and fire: security breeds contempt.' In fact, in twenty years Legge fired only three players – a rank-and-file violinist, a bassoonist and a horn-player. Other 'departures' were undoubtedly engineered, but the personnel was highly consistent during the 1950s and early 1960s.

When the new recording contract with EMI was at last signed, the terms were quite favourable after the long discussions during the winter. It was for three years with a minimum of 150 sessions per annum: significantly, for all sessions full fees would be paid to fifty players, to include Flutes 1 and 2, Oboes 1 and 2, Clarinets 1 and 2, Bassoons 1 and 2, Horns 1 to 4, Trombones 1 to 3, Tuba, Trumpets 1 and 2, Percussion and Harp, with rank-and-file payments to the remaining players not used.

The number of players applying to join the Philharmonia was growing, and auditions became more frequent. They were tough, but fair. Once a shortlist had been drawn up, the candidates would be invited to play to a panel (hidden behind a curtain) usually consisting of Hugh Bean, Walter Legge and the principals of the section concerned. The format was the traditional one, a piece, some sight-reading and a chat afterwards. For the players, auditions were invariably a frightening ordeal; sometimes they could be re-auditioning for their own job. The Philharmonia long had the reputation of being a 'cloak and dagger' orchestra, for Legge was very quick to pick up comments from conductors whose judgement he respected. He once re-auditioned the whole trombone section after a chance remark by a conductor.

One very eminent lady violinist remembers her audition well. She was given a Mozart minuet to play at sight and was so nervous that she persistently played it four beats to a bar, until Hugh Bean went over to her and, unseen by Legge, beat time for her, for which she has been thankful ever since. She needed the job badly and got it, deservedly in the light of her subsequent career.

Two aspects of Legge's genius came through at auditions. First, he had a remarkable ear for potential talent and an interest in the job, perhaps from those who had stumbled through an audition but could offer something. Secondly, he could be disconcertingly fair and sympathetic, particularly to young players. Often he would keep two or three of them back, explaining gently that everyone had been very impressed but they were still very young; he would suggest they played for a while in one of the big provincial orchestras to learn the repertoire and then, please, come again and play for a place in the Philharmonia. This sort of approach gave great confidence to a young player and was a side of Legge's nature that is often understated.

After all the uncertainty about Klemperer's fulfilling his sessions with the Philharmonia, the first three months of 1960 were spent almost entirely on sessions with him. The repertoire was largely Wagner and Richard Strauss, composers admirably suited to his temperament and abilities, but the early days were spent on some Haydn and the complete Mendelssohn *Midsummer Night's Dream* music.

Klemperer was in fine form for the recording sessions and was able to complement them with a Brahms cycle of concerts in February and then a Mozart series in early May. After the Mozart concerts he went with the Philharmonia to Vienna for the 1960 Wiener Festwochen. The framework of the Philharmonia visit was a Beethoven cycle. Five concerts covered all the symphonies and the Violin Concerto with Szeryng. Klemperer was in splendid form: in Vienna he always had big successes and was popular, and the 1960 Festival won him, and the Philharmonia, great acclaim. His performances of Beethoven were a welcome relief from some of the more 'freaky' interpretations that Vienna had seen in recent months. Grand, straight-up-and-down performances were just what the Viennese wanted.

The Philharmonia were quickly adjusting to Klemperer's style and grew to love him for it. Some hint of the old days with Karajan was given when he returned in late March 1960 to record with them some Rossini overtures and Sibelius' Second Symphony. He had not recorded the Sibelius before, and with the old rapport still evidently at work this was a highly successful version. Indeed, he did not record it again until 1981, with the Berlin Philharmonic. On 1 April 1960 Karajan followed the recordings with a concert in the Festival Hall. He directed Bach's B minor Suite from the harpsichord and then conducted a performance of Strauss's *Tod und Verklärung* with shattering intensity, a quality which, one critic noted, 'one had begun to think the Philharmonia had forgotten'.

In Vienna three concerts gave the Philharmonia a break from Klemperer and his capricious high spirits, as Heinz Wallberg and Giulini took the baton.

The summer break was followed by the Philharmonia's sixth visit to Edinburgh for the 1960 Festival, and on 21 August, in the Usher Hall, they opened the Festival with Verdi's *Requiem*: Giulini conducted, and the Philharmonia Chorus made their Edinburgh début. It set a standard not just for the whole 1960 Festival but for the Philharmonia's own performances to live up to. Soloists, chorus and orchestra all came in for praise for a performance that was 'as near perfection as I ever hope to experience', as one critic remarked.

For Giulini's second concert in the Festival there had been some anxiety, as Claudio Arrau had been ill, but a tremendous reception greeted him as he came on to the Usher Hall to play Beethoven's First Piano Concerto. His playing betrayed nothing of his illness, and the audience saw in Giulini all the sensitivity of Cantelli in the shaping of phrases with his expressive hands and well-judged tempi. The following evening's concert fell into the trap which always lay wide open for the Philharmonia and even for distinguished conductors – the trap of routine excellence. The critics' comment on Beethoven's Seventh Symphony, which ended the concert and the Philharmonia's contribution to the 1960 Edinburgh Festival, is particularly telling: 'It rode powerfully down the runway without ever becoming airborne ... for all its technical brilliance this performance became machine-made and not, as they say in American, "custom-built".'

One week later, the Philharmonia were in Lucerne for four concerts, two with Klemperer and one each with Giulini and Szell. Klemperer's first concert, on 1 September, opened with Bach's Brandenburg No. 1 and then featured Christa Ludwig and Ernst Haefliger in Mahler's *Das Lied von der Erde*. The concert was being broadcast, and at the rehearsal Hugh Bean found Klemperer's beat, which was always economical, even smaller and vaguer than usual and realized he would have to direct most of the work himself. It was vital that he saw as much as he could of those elusive hands, but a very real obstacle presented itself with the placing of the soloists directly in his line of vision, threatening to obscure Klemperer completely if they moved from their positions marked out by the radio technicians. During the break Hugh Bean had a word with them and made them promise not to move – on peril of their lives. Came the evening of the concert and Klemperer seemed completely lost. As one paper neatly put it: 'At this point an English fog descended on the performance, but it was not the fault of the orchestra.' In fact, 'Jock' Sutcliffe picked up a vital oboe cue and turned up the volume and everyone was able to hang on. Next morning the Philharmonia had their first rehearsal with Szell, who had sat through the Mahler concert in the front row, arms resting on his umbrella and his face carved from granite. On his way out after the concert Hugh Bean came face to face with Szell.

All teeth and glasses, Szell fixed him with a glare: 'Get a good night's sleep. You have a hard day tomorrow!'

After Lucerne it was back to recording in London. The Capitol label was now well established for the classical repertoire, and Erich Leinsdorf was a regular contributor with the Philharmonia. A very pleasant, gentlemanly conductor, he brought both insight and excitement to the pieces he conducted. These September 1960 sessions were items by Richard Strauss, and he was particularly good in the Intermezzo from *Die Frau ohne Schatten*, negotiating his way through the difficult piece ably and musically.

Then, for the third week in September 1960, Karajan came for what was to be his last group of sessions with the Philharmonia. He began with a second version of Sibelius' Fifth Symphony which seemed rather soft-centred by comparison with his 1952 version, and then spent four days on light orchestral classics and ballet music from the operas. The whole week seemed like a holiday for Karajan, so easily did he take things, a far cry from the busy, heady days of the 1950s. Time after time he would set a piece going and then run the session from the control room backstage in Kingsway Hall; pieces such as Chabrier's *España* were recorded over and over again. It was a rather tame ending to a partnership that had been so productive to both sides.

EMI looked at the Philharmonia's position again and saw that by the end of January 1961 only seventy-eight sessions would be used out of the contractual 150, leaving seventy-two to be completed in only four months. Some attempts were made to catch up: sessions were brought forward that were not due until the next contractual year and some effort was made to get four sessions' work into three. The first did something to alleviate the deficit on the current year's sessions but only postpone the problem for one season; the second just did not work. Some works in fact took longer, very often the result of the late confirmation of bookings which meant that certain key players were missing from vital sessions. *Le Coq d'Or* for example, with Kurtz in April 1961, needed extra sessions as neither principal flute nor principal viola was available for the very time they had important solos.

There had been some talk within EMI over the idea of buying the Philharmonia outright. There would be a number of advantages, the most significant for the players being that the Philharmonia would then become the permanent 'house' orchestra – the players would welcome a guaranteed salary. However, Jane Withers pointed out that the Philharmonia, in any deal, would have to insist that 1) the continuation of the orchestra would be assured along with its contractual agreements, 2) there would be a guarantee of employment for the administrative staff, and 3) there would be a capital sum payable for the consequent loss of royalties, name and goodwill.

Now that the Philharmonia was giving more concerts, it became involved in moves towards a more coherent concert-giving policy for all the big London orchestras, initiated by T.E. Bean, Manager of the Royal Festival Hall. At a meeting on 4 December 1960 attended by all the big established orchestras (London Philharmonic, London Symphony, Philharmonia Concert Society, Thomas Beecham Concert Society, BBC), Bean outlined the problem facing the Festival Hall management. Very simply, the orchestras were asking for more dates in the 1960–1 season than could be given them under the present method of allocation. So far approximately 170 dates had been given for orchestral concerts, with a hundred dates for promotion directly by the established orchestras or societies, seventy to the freelance or *ad hoc* promoters; this latter group would of course include concerts that involved the established orchestras but under different promoters and were often a vehicle of promotion for promising conductors or soloists who could not secure engagements with the orchestras directly. Programme-planning had been left to individual orchestras and was both haphazard and repetitive.

Bean pointed out that if the orchestras wanted more dates for themselves, it would have to be at the expense of the freelance promoters. He was willing to change the balance this way but could not do so arbitrarily, giving out more dates at other people's expense so that the orchestras could become, as it were, a closed shop. He could, as General Manager, recommend more dates to be granted by the London County Council, but it would have to be on certain conditions. The planning and dovetailing of programmes would have to be much more closely co-ordinated; there would have to be agreement, for example, on who was going to present the next Beethoven cycle. Some way would have to be found of sharing out the promotion of works which were not good box-office attractions but which deserved to be played, and more opportunities should be given to promising young talent through the orchestras directly, especially as they were proposing to reduce the outlets available through the freelance promoters. All this, Bean pointed out, could be achieved without loss of any individual identity or competition for supremacy: competition would be free to continue but within the framework of much closer co-operation and consultation in programme planning.

This was patent common sense. A close look at the programmes for the Philharmonia's last two seasons revealed a lack of variety and novelty that could not be refuted. For much of the Philharmonia's life under Legge's management he had been able to indulge himself in the luxury of fewer concerts of generally 'conservative' music and leave the novelties to the other orchestras. The recording studio could then be used to risk works which did not have to sell concert tickets. The inescapable fact now, however, was that the Philharmonia's income from recordings would soon begin to dwindle, and that the orchestra would have to accept the open concert market on the sort of terms T.E. Bean was proposing. It would certainly be the only way the Philharmonia Concert Society could hope to attract public funds, which it would now need to replace the comfortable support of gramophone royalties.

The Philharmonia's contractual recording year ended on 5 June 1961, just thirteen sessions short of the 150, but eleven of these were taken up by Klemperer sessions planned for the next year and used early. It meant a £2,300 deficit had to be paid to the Philharmonia for the lost sessions, something which EMI did not want to repeat. The number of sessions would be carefully monitored over the coming year. The biggest gap now seemed to be through July and August, months when Karajan had formerly been available to take the Philharmonia through a large batch of recording dates.

Much would now depend on Klemperer, who was going from strength to strength since his recovery from the last bout of illness. The recording engineers got used to his complete ignorance of editing and his preference for long, unbroken takes – the complete antithesis of Karajan. Even when he grasped the idea that a short passage could be re-recorded to cover bad entries or wrong notes, the 'old man', as the recording staff affectionately dubbed him, would return to the studio after being asked to remake a few bars and murmur quietly to the Philharmonia: 'The whole movement from the beginning – with repeats.'

The plans for the 1961 Edinburgh Festival reflected a change of artistic directorship. Robert Ponsonby had relinquished the post to the Earl of Harewood, who for his first Festival announced the idea of a linking thread. The 150th anniversary of the birth of Liszt and the tenth anniversary of the death of Schoenberg formed the 'thread' for the 1961 Festival, but neither composer featured in the Philharmonia's four concerts. Nevertheless, Lord Harewood had the foresight to present Klemperer in music other than Beethoven and Brahms with which he had in the public eye become almost exclusively linked. The catholicity of his taste was to be found in the opening concert on 5 September when he conducted a programme of Mendelssohn, Bartók and Schumann. His performance of Mahler's Second Symphony on 8 September drew superlative singing from the Edinburgh Royal Choral Union and made the concert one of the leading events of the Festival. Giulini had already conducted a shattering Russian evening with the Philharmonia on 7 September, with the Philharmonia responding magnificently to 'those magic hands which seemed to mould the very phrases out of the empty air and give them tangible form and substance'. It was Giulini who had the task of closing the official Festival on the Saturday night. The first half was all-Mozart and then, in the presence of the composer, Britten's *Serenade* and *Young Person's Guide to the Orchestra* closed the second half. Such was the effect of the latter on the audience as well as the appearance of Britten himself on the platform that the Fugue had to be repeated. Taken just about as fast as it could go, it brought the house down.

With the Edinburgh and Leeds Festivals out of the way, it was back to the routine and to recordings and concerts with Klemperer. Another Beethoven cycle was scheduled to begin with the *Missa Solemnis* on 29 October. Behind Klemperer's fragmentary gestures and despite some blemishes of ensemble, it was a performance 'worthy of Beethoven' in the words of one critic, and a grand opening to the cycle of concerts.

The violinist for the 1961 cycle was Nathan Milstein, the only soloist ever to get the better of Klemperer, and in a public concert. At the last rehearsal of the Violin Concerto the orchestra stopped before the final cadenza. Klemperer always liked to hear the cadenzas right through in rehearsal but Milstein demurred. After Klemperer had insisted, Milstein shrugged his shoulders and played a dozen bars of textbook cadenza, finished with a trill, and Klemperer brought in the orchestra with a self-satisfied smile. At the concert, Klemperer halted the orchestra at the same point and waited for the short cadenza. After ten bars the great hand rose slowly in anticipation of the final trill, but there it stayed, frozen in powerless immobility for nearly ten minutes. Milstein simply took off, enjoying himself in an enormously long and intricate display, and Klemperer was absolutely powerless to do anything about it.

All through the autumn of 1961 there was more anxiety on both sides of the EMI-Philharmonia recording contract. Looking at the present three-year contract, the first year had been short on sessions and the second promised to be about thirty-five sessions short. The third year would also be over thirty sessions short, provided Klemperer and Callas could fulfil their bookings; if they did not, there would be a shortfall of nearly eighty sessions. It was becoming increasingly clear to both sides that by remaining exclusive to EMI the Philharmonia was losing recording work. Nevertheless, EMI felt sure enough of the Philharmonia's dependence on them to suggest a new contract from December 1961 to December 1966 for a total of 460 sessions on a sliding scale. It included eliminating the 'fifty players minimum' guarantee but in return offered $3\frac{1}{2}$ extra years contracted work over and above the present terms. No further moves were made, and the existing contract, due to expire in June 1963, continued to operate, with an anticipation of a busy start to 1962.

If recording work was causing the Philharmonia anxiety, the concerts maintained a high standard with a growing public. 1961 had been the year of festivals, in Edinburgh and Leeds: for 1962 plans were well in hand for a visit to the Vienna Festival and a short European tour in May and June. Josef Krips was eventually engaged for a Brahms cycle of concerts for the Vienna visit, but in December 1961 an unexpected tribute came from Willi Boskowsky after he had conducted a Viennese evening in the Festival Hall with the Philharmonia on the 16th. Leader of the Vienna Philharmonic Orchestra, he was developing a career as a conductor both in the concert hall and in the recording studio. His Philharmonia concert had been an all-Strauss programme, and his immediate reaction to working with them was widely reported: 'This London orchestra is so good that I want to try to arrange to take it to Vienna some time this year – to show Viennese orchestras how Viennese music ought to be played.'

The completion of a *St Matthew Passion* recording with Klemperer at the end of November 1961 meant that, true to custom, the Philharmonia were now due to give a public performance of it, and this they did on 25 February 1962. Klemperer had spent the first two weeks of February recording *Fidelio* with the Philharmonia. With a cast that was of Legge's choosing rather than that which he had used for his 1961 Covent Garden success, the omens had not been good, but Legge's instinct paid off with uncanny accuracy. *Fidelio* seemed to summarize all that was best in the Philharmonia's activities at the time. The Bach had been spread over two years, but *Fidelio* was concentrated into a fortnight's intensive recording. Admittedly, in concession to Klemperer's advancing age, 'intensive' now meant one three-hour session per day instead of the usual two, but there was continuity, and the Philharmonia responded with consistently high playing born out of respect for a man who was a supreme Beethoven conductor in a work which he loved almost best of all. It turned a recording session into an occasion.

Much credit for this must go to Legge and his engineers. Legge's conception of stereo differed in many respects from that of his Decca colleagues, who often used it to create effects impossible in live performance. Legge used stereo to capture a theatre atmosphere, and in *Fidelio* he did this to perfection, the singers moving perceptibly from point to point yet subtly and without any hint of gimmickry. In the wake of such a masterpiece of recording as *Fidelio* and, just a month later, a superb Mahler Second Symphony, Legge put Klemperer in front of the Philharmonia to record Stravinsky's *Symphony in Three Movements*. True, in his heyday, Klemperer had been one of the great champions and interpreters of contemporary music, but this was 1962 and Klemperer was really past coping with the intricacies of such a work, even in the studio. Legge would have to accept that Klemperer should be confined to the composers he could conduct best: the recent *Fidelio* and *St Matthew Passion* were ample testimony to that. It was in the interests of the Philharmonia Orchestra itself and the concert-giving public; it was also, very importantly, in the interests of harmonious relations between Legge and Klemperer, which were coming under some strain at this time.

Maria Callas had been associated with the Philharmonia since September 1954 and with Walter Legge since 1952. Now she appeared with the Philharmonia in February 1962 in a concert recital of solo arias. Since her 1952 début at Covent Garden, Callas had returned several times to the Royal Opera House and had recorded regularly at La Scala with Tullio Serafin and under Legge's supervision. Her first effort at a concert recital had been in September 1959 with the London Symphony Orchestra and Nicola Rescigno. The top register of her voice was beginning to show some roughness but the biggest disappointment of that evening had been the orchestral playing, which was untidy in the orchestral items and poor when accompanying her.

For Callas herself, and for her reputation, the concert on 27 February was a mixed blessing. The top notes were even less secure than in 1959, but most of the programme lay in the middle register, as had her most recent LP recital with Prêtre and the Paris Orchestra. One critic asked in a headline next morning: 'Will Mme Maria Callas become a mezzo?' and with some justification.

In the hall, everything had been done to create an atmosphere of glamour and theatricality. The auditorium was blacked out and a roving spotlight followed Callas's shuffling, geisha-like progress across the platform in a tight dress that could not have created greater excitement had she changed it for every aria. All this, together with her frivolous 'throw-away' manner, had the effect of distracting attention from her singing. This was a pity, for herein lay her strength. She was not just a visual stage performer: she used her voice to project her ideas and could command gripped attention by vocal inflexion alone, but on this occasion she was not allowed to do so. A huge ovation followed each item, however.

Already, in June 1960 and November 1961, Callas had recorded two selections of arias with Antonino Tonini and the Philharmonia, but these and some further sessions following the Festival Hall concert in the first few days of March 1962 were beset with problems. A complete *Traviata* had been set up with the Philharmonia, with Callas in the title role. The project was cancelled at the last minute, and a recital disc was planned to use up the sessions. The July 1960 sessions, at Watford

Town Hall, found Callas tired, having rested her voice for nearly eight months. The March 1962 sessions were cancelled and two days re-scheduled for 9 and 13 April. By now Callas had a cold and a grim determination to finish the items for the recital disc but after two sessions it was clear that nothing was going to be fit for issue.

In 1962 Vienna Festival opened with a concert, on the morning of 27 May, given by Karajan and the Vienna Philharmonic. That evening Krips and the Philharmonia gave the first of a series of Brahms concerts which was to include the piano concertos, with Wilhelm Backhaus, the violin concerto, with David Oistrakh, and the double concerto, with Oistrakh and Rostropovich. As with Klemperer's Beethoven two years previously, the concerts were highly acclaimed by the Viennese. The morning after each concert, Krips would grin at the orchestra and in his high-pitched voice squeak: 'Another British victory!' Oistrakh also joined Giulini for a Beethoven concert on 30 May, and then on Sunday morning 3 June Willi Boskowsky gave his promised Johann Strauss concert to 'show the Viennese how Viennese music should be played'.

It was highly successful with the Viennese audience, and the encores came thick and fast. The Philharmonia's achievements in their visit were rewarded in the City of Vienna's presentation to the orchestra of an Augarten porcelain statuette of Johann Strauss.

After Munich on 4 June there was Augsburg, and then Zürich on 7 June. The rehearsal in the Tonhalle started at 10 a.m., and the orchestra wearily sat down to face three hours of Klemperer and Beethoven. At ten past ten Klemperer stopped and said: 'We haff konzert this evening. Good morning, gentlemen!' and everyone raced out into the sunshine before he could change his mind, to go sailing, sunbathing or wandering round the shops. The concert went all the better for the time off.

The following night, in Milan, Giulini was far from happy, as well he might be. The audience talked almost incessantly through Mussorgsky's *Pictures*, with two well-to-do ladies in a box directly behind Giulini's right shoulder discussing, with opulent gestures, their gala hair-dos. The next evening the programme was to be repeated, and the Orchestral Manager, Michael Maxwell, tried to get the orchestra together for an afternoon rehearsal, but in vain. The schedule said 'free afternoon', and the players reacted with a loud 'No!' The concert was a total success. The audience was mainly made up of young people and there was a tremendous response from the hall – from 'real people' as one Philharmonia player described them.

On their return from Europe the Philharmonia spent two days completing the Stravinsky *Symphony* recording with Klemperer. Then, for the next six months they recorded no more with him nor performed any concerts. Legge had told EMI that Klemperer's diary up to May

1963 yielded only twenty-two days, one session per day, and of these the Philharmonia and Kingsway Hall were available for only twelve days. Giulini was available and Legge continued to widen his repertoire with Debussy, Tchaikovsky and Britten, as well as the Brahms symphonies. This latter was a courageous move in view of Klemperer's long-established claim on their interpretation. Legge also encouraged Maazel, whom he still coveted on a more permanent basis for the Philharmonia.

In 1958 Sir John Barbirolli had resigned as permanent conductor of the Hallé Orchestra in order to have the chance to conduct more of the international orchestras both in concert and in the recording studio. Pye had not served him well in recent years since he had been recording for them, and now, in 1962, he returned to HMV much to his, and the Philharmonia's, delight. His first recording for HMV with the Philharmonia was in May 1962 and was of Vaughan Williams' Fifth Symphony together with Elgar's *Enigma Variations*. In August there followed recordings of Elgar's First Symphony and *Cockaigne* Overture, all first-class performances of good English music under the baton of a man who cared for them deeply and conducted them supremely well. Indeed, the summer of 1962 was dominated by natives, for all three conductors for their first Promenade Concerts were all British – John Pritchard, Sir Malcolm Sargent and Sir Adrian Boult.

With the Proms it seemed that work was picking up again for the Philharmonia. With the exception of two weeks' holiday, the months of June and July saw only five days without engagements of any kind, and a significant proportion of those had been recordings. The sessions with Maazel had been spent on large-scale works and therefore used more players; there had also been a substantial opera recording with Matačić of the *Merry Widow*, a milestone in the year's recordings, for Matačić had all the advantage of stereo, the Philharmonia Chorus (under Reinhold Schmid) and Elisabeth Schwarzkopf leading a new term of brilliant soloists, all launched on the new Angel label which now formed part of the British EMI series.

The centrepiece of the 1962 Edinburgh Festival was the music of Shostakovich, who was present throughout as guest of honour. Several leading Soviet performers were there to add their support to this theme, and the Philharmonia were to take a leading part, too. Their first concert, in the Usher Hall on 4 September, crowded 108 players onto the platform for the first performance in the west of Shostakovich's Twelfth Symphony, completed only the previous year. That the Philharmonia played it outstandingly well was due in no small measure to the conducting of Gennady Rozhdestvensky, with whom they had had no fewer than five rehearsals before leaving London, in addition to the rehearsal on the day of the concert.

On 7 September the Philharmonia gave their final tribute to Shostakovich. Just two works gave the public and the composer himself a memorable evening. David Oistrakh had given the Violin Concerto its first performance in Leningrad in 1955 and then its London première just four months later with the Philharmonia and Nicolai Malko on 23 February 1956. Now Oistrakh gave it another inspired performance, a work of great variety and creativity played by the supreme artist for whom it had been composed, and the Philharmonia provided flawless support. They gave equal dedication to the mysterious Fourth Symphony, which was being heard for the first time in the West more than twenty-five years after its completion. Shostakovich had withdrawn it just before its planned première in Leningrad in 1936 and, quite aside from the artistic criticism that had been levelled at him at the time, he admitted himself it was 'too long' and 'suffered from megalomania'. The Usher Hall audience had some sympathy for these comments as it listened to an hour-long work that involved nine horns, two tubas, five trumpets and triple woodwind – an advance of five players on the Tuesday night orchestra. It made an astonishing contrast with the sight of its composer, a timid little man who had to return repeatedly to the platform and be pushed on to acknowledge the ovation.

The summer had seen some heart-searching by all concerned with the Arts on the subject of the small amount spent by the Government and the salaries received by orchestral players in London and the provinces. A strike threatened by the London orchestras from 10 October in support of their provincial colleagues was happily averted, but some bitterness remained about the country's attitude to music as seen in the amount it chose to spend on it. One example quoted at the time was a May Gala Concert at the Royal Albert Hall in which the Philharmonia had taken part: the artists' fees alone totalled £60,000 – admittedly money privately owned and privately spent – but a sum that alone could have saved the Carl Rosa Opera Company, for example, or the Yorkshire Symphony Orchestra.

In June 1962 Jane Withers had pressed EMI for a long-term commitment on recording or the Philharmonia would be forced to turn elsewhere – that is, to become non-exclusive and thus be open to direct competition for work with the other leading orchestras. In September 1962 EMI made their position quite clear. They had put their support, in both influence and finance, behind the Philharmonia since 1946 as it was the only EMI-backed orchestra of any promise. Their support had meant fees to the players above Union rates and royalty payments to the Philharmonia company owned by Legge averaging about £30,000 per annum, making the Philharmonia unique in living off its recordings. Since the late 1950s there had been a decline, through EMI's completion of the mono and stereo catalogue and with the demise or loss of many distinguished soloists and conductors. With increasing costs there was a drop expected in the company's requirements, and the suggestion was now made that the Philharmonia look for some form of subsidy, whether from EMI themselves or from outside, or to agree to a non-exclusive contract.

When one recalls Sir Thomas Beecham's remark to Walter Legge in October 1945 about the name 'Philharmonia', it is ironic that EMI added the suggestion now that even the name of the orchestra was not ideal for the commercial market. This applied particularly in the United States where 'Philharmonia Orchestra of London' was liable to be confused with the London Philharmonic or even Royal Philharmonic Orchestras. On the constructive side, however, EMI suggested the inclusion of more major works to help boost the number of sessions: *Die Meistersinger, Wozzeck* and *Elijah* alone would take up forty-two sessions, but with the same breath they were making cuts in the proposed spending for recording the Verdi *Requiem* by reducing the size of the chorus and pegging the fees at the same rate as they had been paid for the Brahms *Requiem* and Beethoven's Ninth Symphony.

Klemperer was available for more recording in the first months of 1963, and the Philharmonia suggested a new contract with EMI of seventy-five sessions with him for one year. EMI considered this too high a number in the time, especially taking into account Klemperer's age and variable health. Matters seemed to be reaching something of a crisis: for nearly three years the contract discussions had simmered without any real solution to what was the Philharmonia's lifeline. By March 1963 the only real proposal acceptable to both sides seemed to be a joint contract with EMI and Deutsche Grammophon, and this existed in draft form. The role of the Philharmonia had certainly changed. It was no longer primarily a recording orchestra but a concert-giving body in open competition with the other big London orchestras. Thought needed to be given to retain the players' loyalty, for the competition, particularly from the London Symphony and BBC Symphony orchestras, was growing stronger.

Following T.E. Bean's proposals in 1960, three of the major London orchestras, the London Symphony, the London Philharmonic and the Philharmonia, were taking part in a scheme of co-ordinated concert-planning for the 1963–4 season. The bait took the form of increased grants from the LCC and the Arts Council – £36,000 from each Council – in return for which they would plan their season as a whole in conjunction with the Arts Council and the Festival Hall management. The scheme was long overdue but the money was insufficient to guarantee a level of rehearsal beyond the minimum. For seven months during 1964 all the orchestras were going to have to find alternative accommodation while the Festival Hall was closed for renovation and completion. The coming winter would tell if such a scheme was viable and pave the way for more rigid planning for the future.

At all this Walter Legge pulled a long face. The thought of his programmes being 'rationalized' filled him with horror, but the Philharmonia would be wise to co-operate now its finances depended more heavily on its concert-giving. To be absolutely accurate, it was the Philharmonia Concert Society that received the grants, not the Philharmonia Orchestra itself: the Society was a company not having a share capital and therefore in the position to be able to receive financial assistance from public funds which it could then use to employ the Orchestra. Legge hated bureaucracy in any form, and the idea was thus doomed from the start.

Legge was finding the spectre of bureaucracy rising before him in nearly every aspect of his working life. On the board of Covent Garden he found himself powerless to influence any major decision and was growing increasingly disenchanted with his position in a sphere for which he cared passionately. He claimed that his work at EMI was becoming 'committee-ridden': whether this was more imagined than real is open to conjecture, but there is no doubt that the management of EMI was having to rethink its classical recording programme and could no longer lash out the lavish sums needed to sustain the kind of luxurious freedom hitherto enjoyed by Legge. The repertoire committees, which met regularly to approve or defer recording projects, were not aimed specifically at Legge but they sought to keep a tighter control on the planning and financing of the larger-scale recordings particularly. For some while now, Legge had been producing only for Giulini and Klemperer, and his relations with the latter were far from easy. On 27 June 1963 Legge wrote to EMI giving them a year's notice.

The committee 'bogey' was only one of a number of factors that influenced Legge in deciding to leave EMI. Another was the continuing problems with the Philharmonia's recording contract. This had been extended to October 1963 while the proposed joint contract with EMI and Deutsche Grammophon was discussed. EMI were willing to put to DGG a proposal for three years, but Jane Withers said the Philharmonia would only be interested in one year with an option on a further two years, thus giving time to look further afield. After a delay for the summer holidays the reply came from Deutsche Grammophon. They could not agree to a one-year contract and certainly could not consider paying an orchestra a royalty of three per cent, even on reduced session numbers. The Berlin Philharmonic received only one per cent. The question now seemed to hinge more and more on the royalty payment, and EMI themselves had also decided that they could not continue a five per cent royalty for the Philharmonia on an indefinite basis. The situation was fast approaching a stalemate, and it was clear that before many more months a radical answer would have to be found.

The new element of insecurity made some players reconsider their positions in the Philharmonia more carefully. Even in the 1950s, few except the top principal players had been able to rely entirely on the Philharmonia for their income. With the decline in recording work the principal players were attracted by the extension of the BBC's co-principal scheme to include wind players. After three years' rejuvenation of the Proms and the BBC regional orchestras, Glock was revitalizing the BBC Symphony Orchestra with his co-principal scheme which offered to the best players the ideal combination of a regular salary with enough free time to pursue other solo work. Several string players had already been enticed from the London Symphony Orchestra and the Philharmonia. One of the first wind player's to go was Sidney ('Jock') Sutcliffe, the Philharmonia's principal oboist for fourteen years: for him the schedules, even now, were too full for him to enjoy a rewarding family life. This had been brought home to him one night when, returning from a session, he met his eldest daughter on the stairs, and both realized it was the first time they had bumped into each other for nearly two months.

The first six months of 1963 had included an interesting variety of music-making. June was by far the busiest month in the recording studios, with a heavy schedule that ranged from the *Holberg Suite* to Stravinsky's *Firebird*. In the middle of the busiest period came one of Giulini's regular Verdi *Requiem* performances, on 23 June. Any suspicion that audiences might be tiring of the work or its conductor and performers was dispelled by a packed Festival Hall. A week later the Philharmonia helped launch an enterprising venture with the Greek harpsichordist Lina Lalandi: the first Bach Festival in Oxford. The orchestra's participation seemed to set a high standard for the whole Festival and make its future look secure.

July brought the Proms, with the Philharmonia booked for five concerts, and September the Lucerne Festival, but the focal point of the whole summer was a tour of South America, with Barbirolli conducting nine concerts in Brazil, Uruguay and Argentina.

On Sunday 18 August the Philharmonia began two days intensive rehearsal in Battersea Town Hall in preparation for the tour. The excitement was undeniable: it would be the first Latin American tour by any British orchestra. The choice of Barbirolli as principal conductor for the tour might have seemed a little surprising at first sight, but his reputation as a leading *British* conductor coupled with a world-wide renown that included the Americas made him a first-class candidate to take Britain's leading orchestra abroad. He was now thoroughly used to working with the Philharmonia, to their mutual enjoyment, and neither Klemperer nor Giulini would have been any real match for his versatility or his own inimitably *English* style.

The programmes had as their basis the standard symphonies such as Brahms' Second, Sibelius's Second and Dvořák's Eighth, but there was also Vaughan Williams's Fifth, and nearly every programme included one other British work. The climax of the tour was to be a concert of Stravinsky's music in Rio de Janeiro, conducted by the composer himself.

The Teatro Sodre was the venue for the two concerts in Montevideo, and the first of these made an outstanding impression. Appropriately, it was the date of Debussy's birth – 22 August – and the Philharmonia played *La Mer* to a capacity audience who demanded an encore and got one the overture to *Die Meistersinger*. The second concert's British offering was Barbirolli's own *Elizabethan Suite*, an arrangement of early pieces that he had written during the War. *El Pais*, Montevideo, commented: 'After listening to American orchestras with exceptional sound qualities (Cleveland and Philadelphia especially) the London ensemble has a sonority that shatters all memories.' 'The splendour, the varying quality of sounds, the purity of tones, the harmony, showed the stupendous perfection of the orchestra.' Many of the Philharmonia's principals came in for special mention by the Press, *La Nacion* wrote: 'A hundred instrumentalists of superior rank, with real artistic conscience, technically perfect, brought together to create an exemplary instrument.' *El Mundo* added: 'The orchestra is, in itself, a work of art. The variety of its colours is infinite: its dynamics are immense. Absolute order reigns in its ranks. The result is sincerely awe-inspiring.'

Then it was on to São Paulo for two routine programmes, and next Rio de Janeiro for the three concerts forming part of the International Music Festival, the climax of the tour.

One Rio paper said: 'The Philharmonia is, as we heard it on Saturday, one of the leading symphony organisations of our time, not only for the intrinsic quality of each instrumentalist and each group of instruments and for the professional qualifications which distinguish its musicians, but also for the superb vitality which inflames it and gives it extraordinary rhythmic force, compelling the prompt and sensitive response of all the instruments to the dictatorship of the conductor.'

The final concert in Rio was on 3 September and consisted of three works by Stravinsky – *Fireworks* and the *Symphony in Three Movements* which Robert Craft would conduct, and the Suite *Baiser de* la Fée to be conducted by Stravinsky himself. The Philharmonia did not take to Craft very well but they were perhaps anxious to meet the great man himself. They were not disappointed: the tiny figure of the eighty-one-year-old composer impressed them tremendously, chiefly in the way he simply took charge of the rehearsal with no noise, no fuss, but a complete command of the musical demands. The response by the orchestra gave rise to the following by *O Globo*: 'The Philharmonia Teaches the Experts: the Philharmonia's subtleties, its rounded and brilliant sonority, will for long to come be the object of commentaries in our musical circles.'

The orchestra left Brazil the next day, flying immediately to Italy, where they played one concert, with Giulini, in Stresa (fortunately of well-tried classics). Then a long coach journey brought them to Lucerne, where Maazel launched them into Brahms' Third Symphony. Maazel still tended to play the clever young American at rehearsals, keeping his best qualities for the concerts, which were usually superb. Now the Philharmonia were tired, and he found them sluggish and even, eventually, rebellious. Gradually, however, the Lucerne pace slackened, and there was Giulini again on Tuesday, with Milstein as soloist in the Tchaikovsky Violin Concerto, a Viennese evening with Boskowsky and then Karl Böhm and Geza Anda on the last Saturday, 14 September.

The Philharmonia left Lucerne by train immediately after the Böhm concert that Saturday night, arriving in London on Sunday afternoon. Since they had left home on 20 August, there had been only three official free days in the gruelling 3½ week schedule. Nevertheless, work started on Monday morning, 16 September, with the long-awaited recording of Verdi's *Requiem*. It is a tribute to their stamina that the recording came up to the very high expectations aroused by recent performances. Even a full fortnight of recording was some respite from jet and coach and train, irregular hours and the strain of repeated public concerts on tour.

The British Council, which had sponsored the South American Tour, was also underwriting a second visit abroad that autumn which was the result of the invitation to the Philharmonia Orchestra and Chorus, together with Giulini, to open the Verdi 150th anniversary celebrations in Parma with performances of the *Requiem* and the *Four Sacred Pieces*. The *Requiem*, in particular, was fresh in everyone's mind from recent recording. There had been some local resentment at the fact that the Philharmonia had been given the major share of the singing rather than an Italian chorus, and it was with some trepidation that they faced an audience notorious for the harsh receptions it gave to singers who failed to come up to standard. The *Four Pieces* were given a polite, even a mildly surprised amount of respect, and so there were good augurs for the *Requiem* the following night.

Sunday was a gala occasion. Every note had been rehearsed to perfection, the crowd were excitedly expectant in a theatre decorated overall with flowers and with trumpeters positioned in the high boxes. The performance was brilliant, and the audience would not let Giulini continue until he had repeated the Sanctus. At the end there was tumultuous applause, and carnations in their thousands were showered down from the decorated boxes. It was a high spot in a very busy autumn and great tribute to orchestra, chorus and conductor. Next day the Teatro chorus crowded round the buses taking the chorus to the airport and escorted them through the street of Parma, singing happily.

The chorus flew home from Parma while the orchestra went on by coach to Florence for a concert with Giulini in the Teatro Communale. It was nearly midnight before orchestra and instruments were taken to Pisa Airport for a 3 a.m. take-off for London.

It is not surprising to find that the Philharmonia players were tired on their return from Italy early on Tuesday morning and not full of enthusiasm for the beginning of the 1963 Klemperer Beethoven cycle on Thursday evening. The concert revealed signs of strain, with some ragged playing, and Klemperer not in such tight control as usual. The Festival Hall was not full, and only when at the end of the *Eroica* Symphony Klemperer dragged his massive frame to its feet did the strings regain their accustomed polish. The soloists for the concerto concerts, Arrau and Milstein, seemed to do something to lift the performances by their unobtrusive but guiding presence. And yet, taken as a whole, the Philharmonia's ten Festival Hall concerts in the last quarter of 1963 – seven Beethoven Klemperer programmes, two other Klemperer concerts and one by Giulini – attracted an average paid attendance of 98.9 per cent, and this at prices higher than those charged by the other orchestras on average. In a period when Festival Hall attendances had dropped markedly for the others, it put still more pressure on the idea of tighter control over programmes.

Already, in return for the promise of increased grants from the London County Council and the Arts Council, the London Symphony Orchestra, London Philharmonic Orchestra and the Philharmonia Concert Society had agreed to plan the season for 1963–4 as a whole in collaboration with the Arts Council and the Festival Hall management. In practice there was still a marked imbalance, particularly in the presentation of modern repertoire. The Philharmonia still relied on its privileged position of a reliance upon recordings, albeit a diminishing role, and concerts of accepted masterpieces by the great interpreters of the time, such as the recent Klemperer Beethoven cycle. The 'modern stuff' was left to the LSO and the LPO, and they wanted to spread the load more widely and more fairly.

October 1963 saw significant developments in the negotiations between EMI and the Philharmonia over the recording contract, which had been in a kind of nervous limbo since the collapse of the Deutsche Grammophon deal in August. EMI had even suspected that Legge had tried to bring off his own private deal with Deutsche Grammophon for the Philharmonia, as well as for Schwarzkopf and even for Klemperer. The latter was certainly restive over his own contract and exasperated with the Philharmonia's delay in sorting out its own affairs. The strain of all this began to tell on Walter Legge. Now in his mid-fifties, he regularly worked a twenty-hour day; his health had suffered already, and now pressure made him obstinate in the pursuit of his own way and with a manner that made his colleagues edgy and exasperated.

EMI agreed to extend the contract from October 1963 to May 1964, for a total of fifty sessions, but it was only a stop-gap measure. Klemperer's own future was becoming bound up with that of the Philharmonia. The idea had been mooted that of those fifty sessions, twenty-five should be conducted by Klemperer, but this could be accepted by the Philharmonia. Klemperer was tired and after a few sessions in October 1963 he cancelled everything except his planned recordings of *Messiah* and *Magic Flute*. His own contract was also extended to May 1964, after which he indicated that he would be still willing to work with EMI after Legge's departure, but with a non-exclusive contract to give him more freedom of repertoire. He had also been told that 'EMI would not have at its disposal the Philharmonia Orchestra' after that date.

At this critical stage it was important that problems of management and business should not become common knowledge among the players. It was not part of Philharmonia policy that they should take more than a very mild interest anyway. The system was autocratic, but most liked it that way and surfaced only when there was flagrant injustice, which was rare indeed. The November 1963 schedule promised a full year's work ahead, with a healthy number of recordings, the Proms again and even a prolonged tour to the Spoleto Festival in the summer of 1964. In retrospect it is clear that many of the dates – notably the Spoleto Festival – were meant to sustain a sense of security and continuity.

At the end of January 1964 EMI began to press the Philharmonia for a decision. EMI were favourable to the idea of retaining the Philharmonia and were concerned about their future well-being, but since January 1962 they had made several constructive offers to guarantee that well-being, none of which had been taken up. EMI's final offer came on 26 February. Three types of contract were offered to give the Philharmonia the freedom to spread its options if it so desired. They were: 1) An exclusive contract with EMI of fifty sessions per annum, paying 3½ per cent royalty with a guaranteed income of £50,000 over the next two years; 2) A joint contract with EMI and one other recording company with two per cent royalty and an income of £40,000 but for thirty-five sessions per annum; 3) A non-exclusive contract, no royalty, for thirty sessions per annum and an income of £30,000.

The Philharmonia's management was urged to make a decision soon, and EMI soon had their reply, but not in the way they anticipated. Legge had been thinking hard. With his own departure from EMI imminent in June 1964, and now both Klemperer's and the Philharmonia's contracts expiring in May 1964, he felt he could hold out until then at least. Under the latest pressure, however, together with a growing feeling in London that the whole orchestral structure needed a radical review in terms of both organization and policy, Legge felt that action was needed, and needed soon. He was genuinely scared at the step he knew he had to take, but after much heart-searching and little sleep he acted.

On Sunday evening 8 March he invited Hugh Bean, Gareth Morris, Bernard Walton and Jane Withers to dinner. Legge came straight to the point.

'We cannot go on,' he told them frankly. 'I intend to suspend the Philharmonia. I will make a full statement to the Press on Tuesday evening, and the players will be informed at the same time.'

PHILHARMONIA ORCHESTRA

55 Heath Street,
London, N.W.3.

10th March 1964

Dear

Wednesday's papers will publish an announcement which may or may not correspond to the statement which is enclosed so that you may know exactly what has been said.

It is impossible for me to express my regret that this is necessary: I feel as if I am cutting out my own heart from my living body; but better that than that the name Philharmonia, which has been representative of a new and higher standard of performance than Britain has ever had, should deteriorate.

Yours sincerely,

WALTER LEGGE

PHILHARMONIA ORCHESTRA

55 Heath Street,
London, N.W.3.

10th March 1964

Mr. Walter Legge, Founder and Artistic Director of the Philharmonia Orchestra, announces on behalf of Philharmonia Ltd.:-

It is with the deepest regret that I have been forced to the conclusion that it is no longer possible, in present circumstances, to maintain the standards which have been the hallmark of the Philharmonia Orchestra since I founded it. I have therefore decided that after the fulfilment of its present commitments the activities of the Philharmonia Orchestra will be suspended for an indefinite period.

Several factors have contributed to this decision:

1 In my considered view there are not in Britain enough players of the quality to make two orchestras equal to the present standards, for example, of the Cleveland Orchestra and the Berlin Philharmonic Orchestra.
2 Not even New York has more than one full-time symphony orchestra of international quality.
3 The Berlin Philharmonic Orchestra has approximately four times the subvention the Arts Council and the London County Council together are able to divide between the three leading London orchestras.
4 The general contraction in the amount of recording of classical music by the major companies has made it impossible to command the undivided loyalties of the players essential to maintain Philharmonia standards.
5 The intense competition for the services of key players by broadcasting and television organizations.
6 The lack of public support for concerts given by any but the most famous conductors and soloists.

The Philharmonia Orchestra will fulfil its engagements at all concerts to which it is contractually committed (these include the Philharmonia Concert Society, the Leeds Festival, the Promenade Concerts and the City of London Festival) and will complete its current recording programme.

I am convinced that an orchestra of the type and quality I have built and developed as the Philharmonia cannot properly fulfil its purpose unless the country's musical life as a whole is radically reorganized from the earliest stages of education.

8. *Suspension and Rebirth, 1964-5*

On Tuesday 10 March Legge released his statement to the Press, and letters had been posted to every member of the orchestra to arrive on Wednesday morning. This plan misfired slightly in that many of the players heard the news on the radio or read their morning papers before the post arrived. None the less, over one hundred members of an internationally famous recording orchestra were suddenly disbanded, made redundant.

The statement made front-page news in most of the national daily newspapers on 11 March, becoming a major news item even in many non-musical circles. The next day the BBC reported pressure by a small group of MPs in an effort to force the Government to secure the future of the Philharmonia. Walter Legge announced on the same day four conditions under which he was willing for the orchestra to continue in existence: 1) that means were guaranteed to enable the orchestra to give permanent employment for five years to about one hundred instrumentalists; 2) that funds were made available for at least one 'extended tour' each year – Legge to choose both programmes and conductors; 3) that membership of the reconstituted orchestra should be selected by a committee consisting of the orchestra's principal conductor. Legge and such persons as were decided suitable to serve on such a jury; 4) that Legge was not prepared to spend public money unless he was satisfied that the public would get its 'full money's worth, and the quality to which it is entitled'.

Taken at a glance, there is little to dispute in the statement issued to players and public. Legge's contention that 'the country's musical life as a whole' should be 'radically reorganized from the earliest stages of education' is as true today as it was in 1964. Reading between the lines, however, and in the light of subsequent writing by Legge himself, one is driven to the conclusion that the essential reason for disbanding the Philharmonia lay in the man himself. The factors mentioned in the Press statement were only contributory elements.

The opening remarks, about the impossibility of maintaining the Philharmonia's standards, implied (and in a later article he categorically stated) that those standards had declined dramatically. There had in fact been no noticeable recession in the Philharmonia's standards of playing, and the only threat to its position of superiority had come from welcome improvements elsewhere, chiefly in the London Symphony Orchestra. The overall slur on London's orchestral players was hardly justified by the evidence.

The point about the number of London orchestras was an old issue. Since 1945 Legge had maintained that London did not need the number of full symphony orchestras it had and for nearly twenty years he had fought to keep the best players in the Philharmonia, with notable success. It had been dubbed by many 'the cloak-and-dagger' orchestra, which implied that positions were regarded cheaply by the management and that jobs could disappear overnight. The facts are that only two or three players were actually sacked, in the true sense of the word, and although there was some sense of insecurity and many players had left after some significant degree of 'pressure', during the busiest years (from about 1950 to 1963) the personnel was astonishingly stable – much more so than that of many of the orchestra's rivals. Indeed, the very insecurity of the Philharmonia players was one of its chief strengths in maintaining its standards. The good players had little need to fear it and found a sense of some excitement in it; the second-rate players were the ones most likely to suffer from it and probably should not have been there anyway. This makes Legge's phrase 'undivided loyalty of the players' difficult to understand, for the loyalty of the players was never in question. It was the very stuff of which the Philharmonia was made. Outside engagements had always been part-and-parcel of any arrangements and in most cases formed a healthy complement to the work of a freelance body of outstanding instrumentalists. It is more than likely that Legge was attacking the BBC's new joint-principal scheme, but the Philharmonia had not suffered unduly and reports were that the system was not proving as attractive as it seemed from the outside. The loss of players through this and through death or retirement (Dennis Brain and Harold Jackson, for example) was regrettable, but time and again Legge had proved his ability to attract the best players. The Philharmonia of 1964 *was* different from the Philharmonia of 1954 – different, not inferior.

Legge's complaint about public subsidies, or lack of them, was one shared by the other three big orchestras. Their answer had been to take on far more outside engagements and programmes of dubious quality than were compatible with maintaining the highest artistic standards. Being self-employed, they had no alternative, and it at least offered them a breathing space until they could raise standards over a longer period in the future. The Philharmonia's costs were rising, and Legge was not prepared to compromise with sub-standard performances, however attractive financially, and as the employer of the Philharmonia Orchestra he was not prepared to finance it on conditions imposed from without.

Legge did much to foster the impression that the Philharmonia Orchestra received no public finance whatever, even boasting that the Philharmonia neither needed nor received any public subvention. In practice the Philharmonia Concert Society, a non profit-sharing company, did receive money from the Philharmonia Orchestra, the Arts Council and the LCC; the PCS then engaged the Philharmonia Orchestra for twenty-odd concerts each season. What was now relevant in this context was that, with the growing importance of concerts in the life of the Philharmonia, Legge would need to co-operate much more with the bodies from whom he needed more money, namely the LCC and the Arts Council. The Philharmonia Orchestra itself would gradually be able to contribute less cash as its income from recordings began to decline.

The statement that there had been 'a general contraction in the amount of recording of classical music by the major companies' was hotly denied by Decca almost as soon as it was uttered, but it was undoubtedly true of the Philharmonia's relations with EMI. It also glossed over the rather inflexible negotiations on recording contracts of the past few years which had brought matters to crisis point and which stemmed largely from Legge's refusal to accept a changing role for the Philharmonia. The phrase 'in present circumstances' clearly meant 'in the way I [Walter Legge] want': the Philharmonia Orchestra, if it was to survive, had to be one of the big four orchestras, and Legge was never 'one of' anything.

This last point brings us back to the true reasons for the suspension of the Philharmonia, which lay in Walter Legge himself. The character of the orchestra was changing and the natural corollary was that Legge felt it slipping away from him. He no longer held the total power he had exerted over its every activity, and he could not bring himself to loosen the reins even more, the one price that would ensure its continued survival. There was no hiding the fact that he was disappointed, even disillusioned. The three passions in his life – the Philharmonia, recording and opera – seemed slowly to be slipping from his fingers. He had fully expected to succeed Bernard Mittel as head of EMI's International Classical Division in 1956 and made no secret of the disappointment he felt when David Bicknell was appointed to the post. When the International Classical Repertoire Committee was set up to keep a close watch on the business side of recording, he no longer felt free to run things his own way: he no longer was free to do so, for his unorthodox ways of working did not endear him to many of his superiors at EMI. His resignation from EMI in June 1963 was followed five months later by his resignation from the board of Covent Garden, where since 1958 he had tried to get his finger back on the pulse of British operatic life, with frustratingly little success.

Walter Legge had a bureaucracy-phobia; he sensed bureaucracy boring its way into the recording industry, opera, and now into his own Philharmonia. It meant the end of his 'benevolent dictatorship', and that was too much; the Philharmonia would have to go, too.

If Legge thought that by suspending the Philharmonia Orchestra he was killing it, he had reckoned without the players. On Wednesday 11 March the Philharmonia were in the middle of recording *Messiah* with Klemperer. Only about forty string players were involved. Many of the other orchestral players, however, made their way to Kingsway Hall that day to discuss what was to be done. It was immediately clear that no one was prepared to give way without a struggle. Klemperer himself was right behind the players. He was furious that he had first learned of the proposed suspension almost by accident on Monday, at a recording session. Legge claimed later that he had asked for Klemperer's comments on the draft Press statement before the Sunday dinner meeting and that he had received no reply; both Klemperer and his daughter denied any previous hint of Legge's intentions.

A meeting of all the orchestra was called for the following Tuesday, 17 March; sixty-five out of the seventy players turned up, thus confirming the optimism they felt. At this stage optimism was about all they could count on. Some recording engagements were still outstanding, together with some concerts, to take them up to the autumn, but next season's concerts had never really reached the drawing-board. By this time in the year conductors, soloists, halls and programmes would normally be well in hand. The first constructive step they could take was to re-form as a self-governing orchestra and set up a company to administer it. They needed a name for the orchestra, a name that would enable them to retain their identity without conflicting with any other commercial interests. That Tuesday night the most popular name was Philharmonia Symphony Orchestra, but approval needed to be sought from the Board of Trade. Legge would not part with anything willingly, but the President of the Board of Trade was Edward Heath, a noted supporter of the Arts and a musician himself. Certainly some continuity of identity was vital since continuity of personnel was almost total. One player had already planned to leave to teach next season, and one or two players were considering transfers to other orchestras.

A governing body was elected – Bernard Walton (Chairman), Hugh Bean, Gareth Morris, Alan Civil and William Monro – but the matter of the name was deferred. One player, however, was quick to point out that they should register *a* name anyway, to protect their interests and enable them to set about finding money to sustain the new orchestra and work to develop it. 'Musical Harmony Limited' was accepted by the Board of Trade as an interim working title, and with the help of Robert Wright and Arnold Goodman negotiations went ahead to secure a permanent name. Robert Wright was a barrister and a friend of Bernard Walton. He had not been one of the original subscribers but had been co-opted onto the Council, under Rule 40, to advise them on legal matters. He was soon elected Secretary of the Council.

The orchestra also needed a new manager. Stephen Gray had already applied for a similar post in Liverpool in February and had been placed on the short-list when Legge suspended the Philharmonia. Gray tendered his resignation the same day and asked for it to be accepted from 30 April; he was appointed General Manager of the Royal Liverpool Philharmonic Society on 31 March and took up his new appointment in June. Bernard Walton thought of Barrie Iliffe and telephoned him to ask if he was interested in coming back to the Philharmonia if they could get things going again. Iliffe agreed and started as General Manager on 1 May.

Support for the new organization came from many quarters: Hugh Bean had already been telephoned by Barbirolli and by Boult, both highly indignant at the news. At the very next Philharmonia concert, on 23 March, Boult made his feelings known publicly. There was a sense of occasion in the air anyway, and when he came on to conduct, he made a short speech, urging the audience to back the orchestra in their intentions not to allow 'this glorious body of players to be snuffed out like a candle'.

Further support came from the chorus: 'To Hugh Bean, Esq. (leader). We, of the Philharmonia Chorus, wish to record our deep dismay at the threatened extinction of "our orchestra" with whom we have made great music for seven years. We offer the Orchestra our fullest support in their gallant struggle for survival.' It was signed by every chorus member.

The first of the surviving Festival engagements was Leeds from 18 to 21 April, with three concerts conducted by Giulini. He had also made his support known to the orchestra in a short but moving speech in Abbey Road, in which he made the point that it was the survival of their music that was at stake as much as a livelihood. On their return from Leeds the players again met, on 22 April, to discuss plans for the future. The best news was that the Board of Trade had finally accepted the name 'New Philharmonia Orchestra Limited' which nicely combined identity with continuity.

April had also seen the recording of the *Magic Flute* with Klemperer, who was a man who liked to work *his* way and resented, more than a little, Legge's way of managing every aspect of their work from the first casting to the final editing. Certain things, he felt, were his prerogative, and one was the first piano rehearsals with the soloists which were invariably held in his suite at the Hyde Park Hotel. Klemperer therefore telephoned Legge and asked him frankly and cordially that he should not come to the rehearsals for the *Magic Flute*. Legge's reaction was sudden and uncompromising: he *would* be at the rehearsals. The adamant nature of his reaction disturbed Klemperer because Legge's interference with matters of interpretation had already played on his nerves, and this only added to the tension. Klemperer wired EMI to ask if he was contractually obliged to hold piano-rehearsals with the producer present. When he was told he was not, he insisted that Legge should not attend. Legge replied by withdrawing from the recording (Peter Andry took most of the sessions) and bitterly wired Klemperer that he would never set foot in the same building again.

More relaxed were some sessions to complete the Verdi *Requiem* with Giulini. Once these were over, Legge completed the process by suspending the Philharmonia Chorus, on 2 May. Like its parent orchestra, it did not remain suspended long. Wilhelm Pitz flew to London from Germany specially for a full meeting of the chorus on 5 May. In a crowded Memorial Hall in Farringdon Street, 230 out of the 240 members voted to keep the chorus going and that they should adopt the name 'New Philharmonia Chorus'. Pitz agreed to remain chorus-master and artistic director, and Charles Spencer, the newly elected Chairman of the new self-governing body, undertook to start negotiations with the New Philharmonia Orchestra to plan future seasons. It was an emotional evening: Pitz was evidently much moved, and as he left the meeting he smiled: 'God bless you and your singing!'

The cry from the singers was no less enthusiastic. 'The Philharmonia Chorus is dead. Long live the New Philharmonia Chorus!'

Wilhelm Pitz, smiled happily at the dedication of his singers. 'Those wonderful amateur singers!' Pitz said later. 'Everyone turns up on a Sunday – it's marvellous! That is the English. It never happens in Europe: there they turn up for money.'

The new management soon found new offices, rather dingy and cramped, in Carey Street on the opposite side of the road from the famous bankruptcy court. The address became the butt of many humorous quips, but at this stage the humour was a little heavy and rather too near the mark, as finance was still the biggest problem. Recording contracts with EMI and Decca were being sought, with assurances to EMI that the orchestra was identical with the old Philharmonia and that the New Philharmonia's council of management were happy with a non-exclusive contract. One was soon hammered out and signed: one year's work of twenty-five sessions (minimum) for a guaranteed minimum of fifty players at Musicians' Union plus twenty per cent rates, no royalties. It was not the ultimate, but it was a start. Decca's terms, eventually agreed later in the summer, were less formal but at least added to the overall number of sessions. The BBC Transcription Service were in fact the very first to offer recording work, Fricker's First Symphony, which was recorded with Charles Mackerras on 4 July.

Good will from the profession and the public existed in abundance, and financial support was promised from a number of sources. Most reassuring was that the grants already earmarked for the Philharmonia Concert Society by the Arts Council and the LCC would be made available to the new orchestra. This allowed the New Philharmonia to plan twenty-one concerts for the 1964–5 season, six in the Royal Albert Hall, eleven in the Royal Festival Hall when it re-opened, and four at the Fairfield Hall, Croydon, with help from Croydon Corporation. A foreign tour to South America in August 1965 was already under discussion before the suspension and would be useful to follow up if financial backing were available.

Within this framework, however, the orchestra still needed to be able to promote up to thirty or forty concerts at its own risk, each of which could incur a loss of nearly £1,000 if any kind of progressive artistic policy was to be pursued. The orchestra and chorus had no funds to meet such losses or to cover overhead costs and provide a fund to lay down a reserve for security of employment. The decision was therefore taken to form a trust fund, administered by a board of distinguished trustees, with the aim of raising upwards of £30,000 per year. The Musicians' Union gave £2,000 towards initial overhead expenses, and on 28 April the Trust was set up. People could make donations or bequests, or they could enter a seven-year covenant and thus avoid paying tax on the amount assigned. They could even undertake to sponsor particular concerts.

For a while the players continued to work under 'double management', fulfilling outstanding engagements as the Philharmonia and starting to obtain bookings as the New Philharmonia. The Welsh Council sponsored a Philharmonia tour of South Wales in the first few days of May. Back in London, the Royal Festival Hall had closed on 31 May for six months repairs and alterations, and so the Royal Albert Hall became the major London venue, with Croydon's Fairfield Hall a very useful second. Boult had made his point about the old Philharmonia: he showed his loyalty by conducting the first public concert under the new name on 4 June in the Albert Hall.

The 1964 City of London Festival was one engagement booked under the old management, but as Klemperer was conducting he insisted that the 'New' should be added. By either name the Mozart programme suffered under his heavy hand. One critic described the *Serenata Notturna* as 'moving like a steam-roller on its irresistible way, the opening Marcia clumping through the hall in heavy boots, the Minuet in a strait-jacket and the finale without a trace of a smile'. Klemperer's grim determination to stand by the Philharmonia in its hour of need would have to be swallowed with such dry performances as these, but compensation could still be found in his Beethoven and Brahms. The players had sufficient respect and affection to offer him the post of Honorary President, an honour he graciously accepted on 21 July; the chorus were to pay him the same compliment in October.

A useful bridge over the summer was offered by the 1964 Promenade Concerts, of which the Philharmonia were booked to play five, from 30 July to 7 September. Giulini, Mackerras, Groves and Del Mar were the conductors. The most adventurous in a very traditional series of programmes was, appropriately, the last, when Del Mar conducted excerpts from Richard Strauss's operas – Elektra's Monologue, the *Dance of the Seven Veils* and the closing scene from *Salome*. Closing scene indeed: Monday 7 September 1964 was the last public concert given by the 'old' Philharmonia Orchestra.

The players had survived but there were many loose ends to tie up. Walter Legge now had no further interest in the orchestra and planned to retire abroad as soon as he had completed his commitments to EMI. These included the final sessions on the Verdi *Requiem* and a few other items but mainly involved clearing his office desk and cupboards ready for his successor, Christopher Bishop.

Walter Legge owned the Philharmonia company personally, ninety-seven per cent of the shares in fact. He was ready to sell both his shareholding and the Philharmonia's various assets, which included the music library, valued at around £300, the library van, the fine set of four Wagner tubas and an assortment of percussion instruments.

Clem Relf was now librarian for the New Philharmonia, and he made Legge an offer for the music, but Legge refused, out of spite, and eventually sold it to the Bournemouth Symphony Orchestra. Relf's task of rebuilding the music library had the sympathetic help of the BBC library and the Goodwin & Tabb lending library; he was able to start with single string parts that he could mark up with bowings to use as 'masters' until he could obtain full materials. A shortage of cash meant

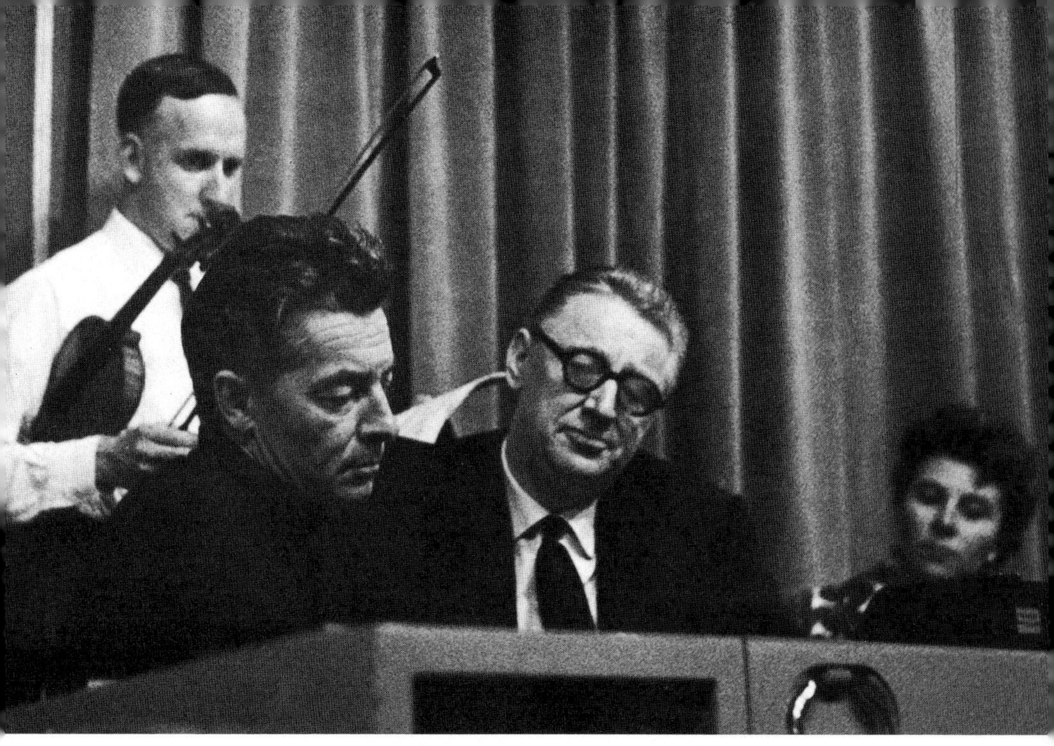

September 1958; the Philharmonia record Beethoven's *Missa Solemnis* in Vienna with Karajan. Karajan, Legge and Christa Ludwig (seated) listen to a playback with leader Hugh Bean standing behind.

In the hall of the Musikverein, Hugh Bean stands in front of Christa Ludwig for his violin solo while Karajan discusses the balance of the voices.

Beecham's second concert with the Philharmonia, conducting his own version of *Messiah* at the Lucerne Festival on 10 September 1959. The soloists are (from left to right) Nicolai Gedda, Elisabeth Schwarzkopf, Monica Sinclair and Donald Bell.

Colin Davis conducts Luigi Alva at a rehearsal in the Festival Hall on 18 October 1959 for a concert performance of *Don Giovanni.* The concert should have been conducted by Otto Klemperer but he was ill and Davis made his reputation overnight.

The Philharmonia Chorus at work with their first Chorus-master, Wilhelm Pitz, in the Gandhi Hall.

With Giulini in a Verdi *Requiem* rehearsal.

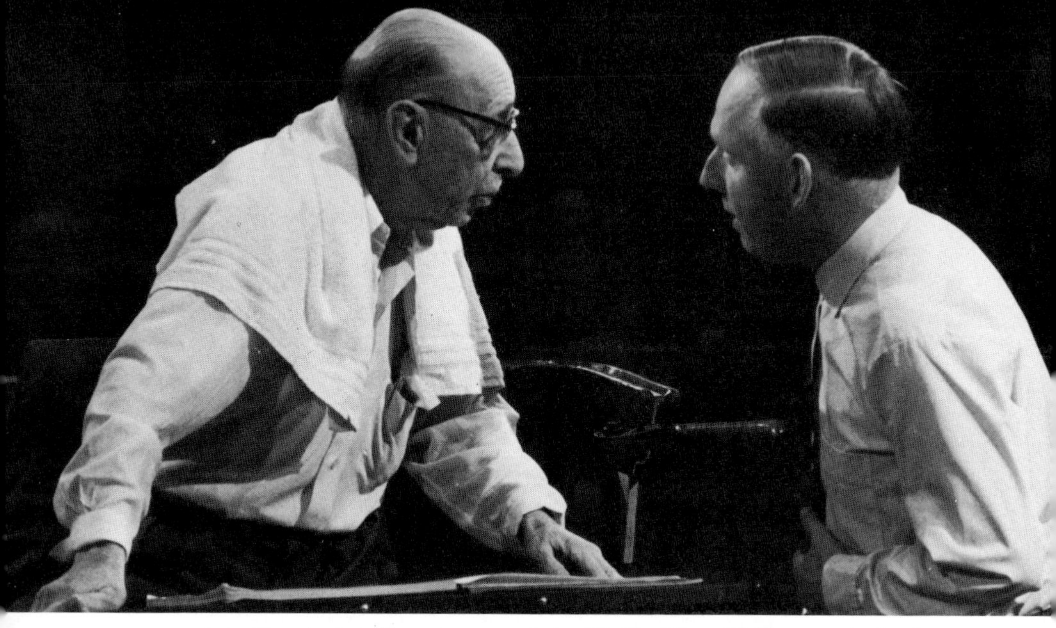

Igor Stravinsky discusses a point with the New Philharmonia leader Hugh Bean at a rehearsal for his concert in September 1965.

The Gala Concert in the Royal Albert Hall on 27 October 1964 when Klemperer conducted the New Philharmonia Orchestra and Chorus in a performance of Beethoven's Ninth Symphony to launch the orchestra's Trust Appeal.

Thirteen of the Philharmonia principal players give the third ever performance of Wagner's *Siegfried Idyll* at the house at Triebschen where it was first played to Cosima Wagner in 1870. This was a private concert at the 1963 Lucerne Festival.

The annual concert of the Grand Gala du Disque in 1965 when the New Philharmonia Orchestra became the first British orchestra to be invited to play for the event and when Giulini received an Edison award for his recording of the Verdi *Requiem* with the Orchestra. Giulini receives the award from the Dutch Minister of Culture, Mr Vrolijk.

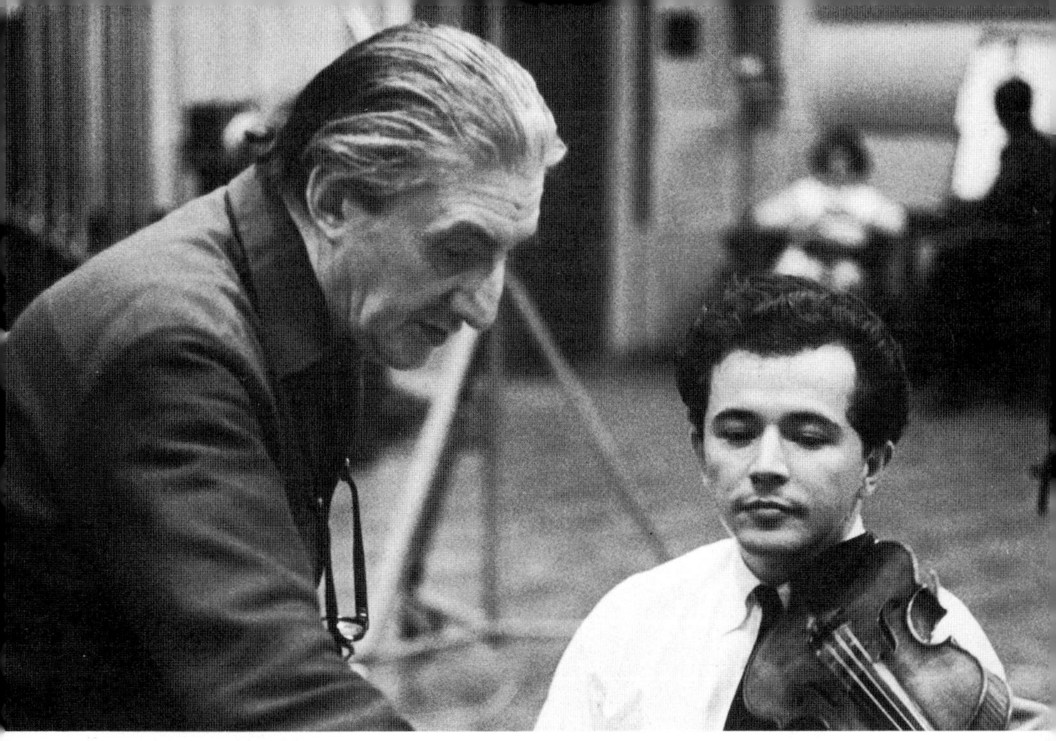

Barbirolli rehearses with the New Philharmonia for their tour of Japan in 1970. Only hours later, Barbirolli was dead. Here he talks with the leader of the New Philharmonia, Carlos Villa.

Tour of Japan 1970: John Pritchard took over many of the concerts due to be conducted by Barbirolli. Here he conducts Janet Baker in Mahler.

Otto Klemperer's 85th birthday in the Festival Hall 14 May 1970. After a performance of Mahler's *Das Lied von der Erde*, Gareth Morris (left) presents him with a silver salver from the Orchestra.

Lorin Maazel has had two appointments with the New Philharmonia Orchestra. In November 1970 he was made Associate Principal Conductor under Klemperer. The day before this appointment was announced he appeared as soloist and conductor in Mozart's A Major Violin Concerto with the Orchestra in the Festival Hall.

that a lot of second-hand material had to be used, and when, later, a photocopying machine became available, Clem was able to reproduce non-copyrights which were out of print.

The Wagner tubas and the percussion instruments were sold to the New Philharmonia along with the old library van to tide them over until a better vehicle could be afforded. By 30 September 1964 all the sums had been done, and after tax, dividends on shares, sundry debts and estimated outstanding costs, the balance sheet showed a figure in excess of £111,000. Jane Withers, as the sole remaining director, started the process of winding up the company. At a meeting in Brown's Hotel, Dover Street, W1 on 14 November 1964, Philharmonia Limited was declared to be solvent and the intention stated that the company would be wound up voluntarily.

The Philharmonia Concert Society was a separate concern. It had to abandon its claims on grants from the Arts Council and the LCC as well as its responsibility for promoting the Philharmonia Orchestra concerts but it survived into the 1980s with the sponsorship of one or two recitals a year.

Any intending purchaser of Philharmonia Limited would acquire with the shares just one valuable asset, the royalties that would continue to be paid on recordings made by the Philharmonia up to 1964 and still issued commercially. EMI were naturally very keen on buying the shares themselves but delayed showing an interest until they had investigated very thoroughly the possibility of taking legal action against Legge. He had been both owner of the orchestra (and thus entitled to all the money earned by it) and an employee of the company who provided the majority of that money.

Whatever else he may have been, Legge was no fool on this issue. As early as May 1946 EMI found that he had been given written permission to promote concerts and musical activities provided this activity did not encroach on the time given to EMI. For years, too, he had had no official contract with EMI so that was a rather difficult issue to pursue in any case. When he did finally enter into an elaborate Service Agreement, on 29 November 1957, Legge had asked specifically if it would mean giving up his interest in the Philharmonia and was quite clearly told by EMI that it would not. On the Philharmonia Company's records his shareholding was always shown as held by 'Barclays Bank nominees', a common business ploy to disguise one's financial interests, but in all Philharmonia publicity and correspondence he was described as Founder and Artistic Director, so his interest was always quite clear to EMI and the world in general. The legal department could find no grounds for any action on Legge, and so the idea was dropped.

EMI now put in a bid for the Philharmonia shares, and after much discussion they were finally purchased in February 1968 for £53,800. Legge was living in Switzerland and so avoided a heavy tax burden on the deal. EMI now became entitled to the royalties, and when in 1977 the New Philharmonia reverted to the original name, the liquidator's control was handed over to EMI's legal department.

The position of the New Philharmonia in September 1964 was reasonably strong and very optimistic for the future. The first priority was to demonstrate to the world that there was continuity not only of personnel but of high artistic standards, backed by the security of a sound financial basis. Recording with EMI had already started by virtue of some overlap with old Philharmonia work, particularly with Klemperer, and some still needed to be completed, notably the re-recording of the contralto arias from *Messiah* with Grace Hoffman and sections of Mahler's *Das Lied von der Erde* with Fritz Wunderlich. A start was made with Decca on 11 September with a selection of operatic arias by Renata Tebaldi, conducted by Oliviero de Fabritiis. Some casualness at these latter sessions was soon jumped on by Bernard Walton, who, in a letter to the players, pointed out every individual's responsibility for the security of the New Philharmonia. He also reminded them how much hung on the work of the Trust.

A brochure on the Trust had been produced and circulated. Money was coming in steadily, and a welcome boost was given by a press conference held at the Waldorf Hotel on 17 September, at which Barrie Iliffe outlined the orchestra's new contracts with EMI and Decca, remarking that EMI had in fact donated £500 to the Trust. He also outlined the plans for the coming season and made a particular point of the intention to have as many rehearsals for each concert as had been the practice in the past. The first of the New Philharmonia's self-promoted concerts would be on 27 October 1964 in the Albert Hall. It would be a gala concert to launch the Trust and be conducted by the orchestra's Honorary President, Otto Klemperer, who was making special arrangements to get to London in time to fit the concert and rehearsals in with the EMI recording schedule. Everyone concerned with the concert, Klemperer, Wilhelm Pitz, the New Philharmonia Orchestra and Chorus, intended donating their fees to the Trust.

On the night of 27 October the Albert Hall was full to overflowing, and the excitement was intense. The concert was late starting as principal bassoonist Gwydion Brooke was held up in heavy traffic. Eventually, Hugh Bean, plump, genial and keyed up, came on to great applause, and then the tall, angular, granite figure of Klemperer, leaning on his stick and making his slow progress to the podium, brought audience, orchestra and chorus to their feet for a tremendous ovation.

Klemperer eased himself into his chair. Musically, the evening had its share of patchiness, but the total effect was a shattering success and brought the audience to their feet again, this time shouting their appreciation. Over £4,000 was raised for the Trust and, with enquiry desks at three strategic points in the hall during the interval and after the concert, the list of subscribers grew significantly. Between 4 and 24 November alone, over one hundred new subscribers were added to the list.

Antal Dorati was the first guest conductor of the new season, on 13 November. As well as Bartók's *Concerto for Orchestra* and Stravinsky's *Petrushka*, he wanted to conduct the Kodály *Peacock Variations* rather than the *Dances of Galanta*, as planned. One wag in the orchestra observed that Dorati was in danger of using up his entire repertoire in the one concert. Dorati relented over the *Galanta Dances* but demanded an extra rehearsal in return, an expensive luxury in view of the rather sparse audience that turned out but well rewarded in terms of exhilarating performances.

The third and last NPO-promoted Albert Hall concert of 1964 was with Giulini. This performance of the Verdi *Requiem*, as well as a *Messiah* to be conducted by Pitz in April 1965, was part of an overall plan to emphasize continuity, a point made again at a Dorchester Hotel lunch given for Giulini by the New Philharmonia on 26 November when he repeated his support for the orchestra's efforts. The Verdi *Requiem* of 6 December was one of the best in the long line that Giulini had now given with that orchestra and chorus. The Albert Hall was full again, and every aspect of the evening's performance emphasized that continuity was indeed there, in full measure.

The growth in work for the New Philharmonia made it easier to hold players but a lot still depended on their loyalty. Principal Horn Alan Civil was offered a post with the Berlin Philharmonic by Karajan when the Philharmonia was suspended; this was a great honour since the Berlin orchestra had never before engaged musicians from outside Germany, and naturally Alan Civil was interested, but when the New Philharmonia was formed he immediately cancelled his Berlin plans and in fact became one of the first members of the orchestra's governing council. The offers continued to come from Berlin, and in January 1965 he joined the Berlin Philharmonic for an American tour of twelve concerts, their latest attempt to woo him away. His remaining loyal to the New Philharmonia but accepting the occasional Berlin engagements brought considerable credit to the New Philharmonia.

After nearly half a season in the Albert Hall the New Philharmonia found a welcome relief in the re-opening of the Festival Hall on 1 February 1965, with its new coats of paint and the completion of much structural work begun nearly fifteen years before. The LCC presented them in the third of the concerts to mark the opening of the hall, with Klemperer conducting a Brahms programme on 3 February. Inside, the Festival Hall looked much the same, but it now had 'assisted reverberation' to help cope with the previously rather dry acoustics. A series of hidden microphones, tuned chromatically from the lowest likely note up to middle C, meant that the life of any of these notes was now longer than the structural properties (unaided) of the hall would allow.

The new acoustics of the Festival Hall were put to good effect on 25 March when Colin Davis conducted Part I of Berlioz's *The Trojans*. The singing of Josephine Veasey and Colin Davis's conducting made a strong case for the complete opera's revival at Covent Garden. Concert performances of operas sometimes fall flat but the superb playing of the New Philharmonia, assisted by two bands played in the Terrace Stall foyers, made the whole evening a real occasion. The performance also highlighted the contrasts in work now undertaken by the orchestra, for in the same week they were making their first recordings for Philips of light music; it was a compromise but it was work, and a year later they were engaged to record regularly for Philips.

On 29 June 1964 Sawallisch closed the New Philharmonia's first season with the Berlioz *Symphonie Fantastique*. The New Philharmonia had given eleven concerts under its own auspices as well as twenty-five promoted by others, made thirty-seven recording sessions and nineteen radio and television performances. Considering that bookings would have normally been made two years ahead and that the number of their own promotions was thus restricted by the availability of dates, this had been no mean achievement. Players had supplemented their income with private engagements, and the psychological factor of being their own employers had given them the incentive to maintain standards of quality. In a progress report, the New Philharmonia's Chairman, Bernard Walton, wrote: 'We feel that this, our first full season of concerts, is already showing the pattern on which the orchestra's claims for survival were based last year. We are alive again, a great orchestra, a great chorus, with great conductors.' Walton then went on to remind his readers of the financial burden of running the orchestra, particularly in the light of the newly published Goodman Report.

The New Philharmonia Orchestra's new financial predicament, coupled with the Royal Philharmonic Orchestra's own recent near-collapse, had made the appointment of an inquiry into the financing of the London orchestras even more necessary. On 21 December 1964 the Goodman Committee on the London Orchestras was set up by the Arts Council, in consultation with the LCC (the Greater

London Council from 1 April 1965). Its brief was: 1) to consider the four major London orchestras (London Symphony, London Philharmonic, New Philharmonia and Royal Philharmonic) and consider whether the number should be reduced, increased or maintained, what form any regroupings should take and how conditions for orchestral musicians should be improved, and 2) to examine how concert-giving could be on a more organized and co-ordinated basis with a maintenance of high artistic standards and employment.

All four orchestras under consideration were now self-administered, and with increased competition for audiences, rising costs and falling revenue from recording, they all faced financial difficulties without substantial public funds. Self-promoted concerts at the Festival Hall, even with full houses, made a loss, a pattern made worse by the introduction of the Festival Hall's own cheap voucher ticket scheme.

The Committee found the self-government of the four orchestras generally very efficient but felt it could benefit from a lessening of the burden of responsibility for concert promotion. Players needed more security in their jobs without the necessity for overwork; concerts should be a service to the public and not just a source of employment for the musicians, and this meant a co-ordinated programme policy. In the long term, at least one of the four orchestras would need to find its own home for concert-giving to allow the other three enough available concert dates. Some promise of this was seen in the plans for the new Barbican complex. Looking at the present pattern of work, the Committee concluded that there was about enough for 3½ orchestras. One solution would be to disband one of the present four and increase the playing strength of the other three; all the orchestras would certainly welcome an increase in numbers, and it would eliminate the need to engage extra players. The Committee, however, was against cannabilizing one of the four orchestras since it realized that the present position was a state of transition, with the New Philharmonia and the Royal Philharmonic needing time to settle down, the effects of close programme-planning to be felt and the re-opening of the Festival Hall making more dates available. It was therefore recommended that the playing strength of at least one of the four orchestras should be increased and the position reviewed at a later stage.

The recommendations of the Committee in its Report (submitted to the Arts Council on 28 April 1965) were broadly twofold: the setting up of the London Orchestral Concerts Boards (under the wings of the GLC and the Arts Council) to co-ordinate concert dates, subsidies and budgets of each of the orchestras, and the allocation of £40,000 per annum per orchestra subject to conditions laid down by the London Orchestral Concerts Board. It further recommended that conditions of employment should be regularized, including sick pay and holiday conditions.

The Goodman Report had implications for the New Philharmonia at a time when it could benefit most from them. Any delay in response by the government could be crucial, as dates for the 1966–7 Festival Hall season soon needed to be fixed, and those orchestras which planned to increase their permanent playing strength could not yet do so. There *was* a delay until late in the autumn of 1965 before the government guardedly indicated its 'acceptance in principle' of the Goodman Report, and the London Orchestral Concerts Board was to be set up on 1 April 1966 to look at the money needed for the 1966–7 season. That meant no money at all for the 1965–6 season, then under review: the New Philharmonia had survived its first season in the residue of goodwill and cash it had inherited and clung to through the period of suspension and reformation. The next few months would be critical both financially and artistically.

9. *The Pangs of Rebirth, 1965-6*

A tour of South America had been planned for the summer of 1965 before the suspension of the Philharmonia and soon after reorganization the idea was taken up in more detail. The British Council offered £25,000, doubtless encouraged by the success of the first South American tour in August 1963. On the strength of this offer, Kletzki, Barbirolli and Stanley Pope were invited to conduct a total of twenty-seven concerts over a period of five weeks, from 9 July to 14 August, visiting ten countries. It would be by far the biggest venture under the new management and a real challenge in organization.

The playing strength of the orchestra was raised for the tour from seventy-eight to ninety-eight, a costly but essential luxury: such a gruelling tour needed some players 'in reserve', for the programmes included such larger-scale works as Stravinsky's *Firebird* and Britten's *Young Person's Guide*. The total cost of the tour was in the region of £96,000, and so it was a shattering blow when the British Council withdrew its offer of financial support only six weeks before departure. Barrie Iliffe wasted no time: he went straight to the Controller of the Council's Arts Division and persuaded them to reconsider, but the sum now offered was reduced to £15,000. The New Philharmonia themselves managed to find another £3,000 from other sources, but it still looked as if some £5,000 would need to be made up.

The long, testing tour had more than its fair share of hazards and trials. In Mexico City, at four thousand feet altitude, many of the wind players had difficulty playing in the rarefied air; their problem worsened as they climbed to seven thousand feet at Puebla, and over eight thousand at Bogota. The only answer was to rephrase the music, overlapping the sound to allow members of a section to breathe in relays. Also at Puebla, their agent's credit card was blacklisted, and everyone's luggage was impounded until Iliffe found the money to pay their hotel bill. At Rosario, a cello fell to pieces as it was taken out of its case – the result of rough handling by porters. At Buenos Aires one of the orchestra's planes developed an oil leak and had to return to the airport, necessitating the cancellation of the first of the concerts in São Paulo, Brazil, their next stop.

It all seemed like a test of the orchestra's stamina. Only the enthusiastic welcomes and their audiences' appreciation made up for the trail of agonies they had left behind them.

On arrival back in Britain, they had just a few hours rest before they were off to Edinburgh to play a major part in the 1965 Festival. They were booked for fifteen performances in all.

On their return, Stokowski was in London to record with them, and within a week there was a concert with Stravinsky. There was no denying the excitement created by the approach of the Festival Hall concert on 14 September, which was to prove to be the last the eighty-three-year-old composer would conduct in London. The Press had been staggered at the alert ease with which the small, bent figure, half-hidden behind dark glasses, dealt with the reporters' questions. When he met the New Philharmonia later in Kingsway Hall to rehearse, the players were equally surprised at the way he coped with the cut-and-thrust of a rehearsal. They all stood up respectfully to welcome him, then, in shirt-sleeves, baggy trousers and slippers, he launched into the *Firebird* Suite. The version of *Firebird* being used was Stravinsky's own 1945 rescoring, and problems kept cropping up over the numerous pencilled corrections made to the original 1919 version which was being used. Stravinsky finally became so impatient that he snapped: 'I do not compose in pencil!' and that was the end of the matter.

Stravinsky had the ability to transmit his intentions with the smallest of gestures and with the added advantage of a very clearly defined beat. The New Philharmonia's reaction was a mixture of affection and admiration. He seemed to judge the speeds so exactly right and gave the music great flexibility and warmth. The audience responded, too, and could only be persuaded to go when the composer appeared on the platform in his overcoat.

This first concert of the orchestra's 1965–6 season brought some new financial assistance in the form of sponsorship by the Rank Organization, which also put up the money for two further October concerts with Giulini.

And so the autumn passed, no less busily than the summer, with appearances in Amsterdam, at the Grand Gala du Disque Classique, and in November a three-week tour of Austria, Italy, Switzerland and Germany.

The tour had been planned immediately after the 1964 reformation of the orchestra and aimed to reaffirm the orchestra's artistic prosperity and identity in the principal cultural centres of Europe. It was intended that Klemperer would conduct the tour but he was now too frail to cope with such a gruelling schedule, though in Zürich on 24 November his conducting drew from the Press the accolade of 'perfection which far surpassed mere technical perfection'. Munch and Markevich shared the conducting on the tour, which began in Vienna on 9 November and ended in March on the 30th.

In the Musikvereinsaal in Vienna, all two thousand seats were taken and people were standing six deep at the back of the hall. Some of the climaxes in *Daphneis and Chloë* sounded as if a hurricane had been let loose in the hall and Brahms's First Symphony, a bold choice for a Viennese audience, was driven hard, but at the end Munch and the New Philharmonia were given a fifteen-minute standing ovation. At Milan's La Scala, two days later, Markevich's very cool and rational approach made Prokofiev's *Classical* Symphony sound a little dull and mechanical, but the 'society' audiences responded with wild cheers and again a standing ovation, refusing to let the orchestra go until they had played two encores. After meeting up with Klemperer for the Zürich concerts there were appearances in Berne, Lausanne, Geneva and St Gallen, and then Frühbeck joined them for the final concert in Munich. When the New Philharmonia arrived back at London's Heathrow Airport on 1 December, it was with a collection of Press reviews that said over and over again that the tour's objective had been achieved, the reaffirmation of the orchestra's European reputation. *Die Presse* of Vienna summed it up by simply stating: 'The Orchestra now has a new name, yet the old qualities.'

The orchestra returned with an armful of glowing notices but a financial headache in the form of a loss on the tour of over £5,000. No government help had been available to help finance the tour, and this loss now had to be added to debts of over £7,000 on home concerts. Bernard Walton was quick to make public his dissatisfaction. 'It is very degrading,' he told the Press. 'We have a world-class orchestra which travels under conditions no foreign orchestra would tolerate.'

It was a depressing note on which to finish such a successful tour, but Walton was stating the hard facts that faced the New Philharmonia – and still do today. He was also warming to the task of running the affairs of the orchestra, a hard one to combine with his position as principal clarinettist. He had worked tirelessly throughout the eighteen months since reorganization, with the support of the Council and particularly of Robert Wright. There were signs, however, that some in the orchestra saw in this combination too powerful a force at work; ever since the days of Walter Legge there had been an almost neurotic fear of any form of dictatorship and a suspicion of anything that resembled its reappearance in any way. Gradually there was a split of loyalties between those who saw the hard work done by Walton and Wright and chose to ignore the attendant dangers, and those who were content to leave the work of running the orchestra to its General Manager and get on themselves with the business of making music.

This division had driven something of a wedge between Walton and Barrie Iliffe. Walton was ambitious and Iliffe had difficulty in defending his position. When the British Council offered him a post in their Music Department, he accepted. The turn of the year saw his departure and a new arrival. Lord Harewood joined the orchestra as Artistic Adviser, having been involved with the New Philharmonia Trust since the summer of 1965 and having known the orchestra from his many years at both the Leeds and Edinburgh Festivals.

As winter ended, the main excitement was the plan for a Verdi *Requiem* to be conducted by Karajan on 13 March. It obviously promised to be a huge box-office success, although Karajan insisted, naturally, on a star team of soloists – Gwyneth Jones, Christa Ludwig, Luciano Pavarotti and Nicolai Ghiaurov; together with his own fees, the total costs threatened to bankrupt the orchestra. It would be a real scoop to have Karajan back in front of the orchestra after over five years. In the event it turned out to be about the most accident-prone performance in Festival Hall history and yet still a musical triumph.

First, Pavarotti could not be released by La Scala and then Karajan himself withdrew, claiming the pressure of television commitments. Next Ghiaurov cancelled, and then *his* replacement, Giovanni Foiani, became ill. Days before the concert Christa Ludwig withdrew because of a cold; only Gwyneth Jones remained of the original team, and fingers were crossed that she and the replacements – Marga Höffgen, Carlo Cossutta and Nicola Zaccuria – would not succumb to some sudden flu virus. They did not, and despite ticket prices up to 3 guineas, the Festival Hall was full on the night. For the replacement conductor, Frühbeck, it was a night to show what he was made of, and, without a score, his enthusiastic and commanding control established a performance that was stunning. With all the last-minute changes it was inevitable there would be some problems of ensemble, but as one critic said: 'If this is what accidents produce, I feel we should have more of them.' The New Philharmonia Chorus were the stars of the evening, and Andrew Porter, writing in the *Financial Times*, went so far as to say: 'Sometimes one feels that the condition of being engaged for soloist in a New Philharmonia Requiem should be that the singer joins the chorus for a season.'

At the end of March 1966 there came to the surface a great storm of suspicion and discontent within the administration of the orchestra. On the last day of the month Bernard Walton and Robert Wright resigned from the orchestra, and the players were left without a Chairman and a legal adviser; they had also lost their principal clarinettist.

Bernard Walton had worked tirelessly since 1964 to put the New Philharmonia on its feet and that had meant sacrifices. As early as the summer of 1965 Walton had taken the first step towards the protection of his position as Chairman. At a recording session in Wembley Town Hall he called the Council together for a quick, informal meeting. They were asked to look at a document which guaranteed Walton a minimum sum per year so that he would not lose financially because he was Chairman *and* principal clarinettist. No amount was specified on the document but there appeared later in the minutes of a meeting on 22 October the ratification of an amount of £4,800 per year, a considerable sum in those days. At the orchestra's Annual General Meeting, on 26 October, the players were asked to vote on a change to the Constitution that would allow any Council member to be compensated for loss of earnings while on orchestral business. Many of them sympathized with Walton's difficulty, but they felt that such a change could be open to abuse, and the proposal was rejected by a show of hands.

When Barrie Iliffe left in January 1966, Bernard Walton seemed in no hurry to appoint a new General Manager. In fact, in February he told the Council that frankly he was not happy with the idea of a General Manager in principle, but he was prepared to work alongside one until the post was no longer necessary. He clearly had ambitions for the position himself, and at a Council meeting on 10 February he declared his hand by proposing that from 1 April 1966 he should concentrate on administrative work only and give up playing the clarinet. This was a radical proposal and one which the rest of the Council said would have to be put before the whole orchestra, for it was not covered in the Constitution. The Chairman of the orchestra was elected annually from the members of the Council who, with the sole exception of Robert Wright, were playing members of the orchestra. Walton's proposal was for a non-playing member to be paid full-time for the position and to be able to retain it indefinitely.

Matters came to a head at an Extraordinary General Meeting of the orchestra on 31 March. This had been called at the request of seventeen members of the orchestra who wanted more frequent consultation with the Council on orchestral business and were also impatient at the delay over the appointment of a General Manager. Feelings already ran high among the players, many of whom did not appreciate the full facts of the situation but in general terms were or were not supportive of Walton's position. Gareth Morris was a clear leader of the opposition, and he had been busy investigating the facts as thoroughly as he could, taking legal advice and discussing the case with colleagues in the orchestra. In the Festival Hall's Recital Room on 31 March the vote would clearly resolve the divided loyalties of the players.

That afternoon there was first the issue of who should chair the meeting. Bernard Walton felt too personally involved and suggested

Robert Wright. It was then pointed out that Wright was only a member of Council as an ordinary member and under Rule 40 should have relinquished his position at the October Annual General Meeting. After some heated argument, Wright left the platform and Walton took the chair. Everything hinged on the question of Walton's position as a player *and* administrator, and a ballot was held of the sixty-eight members present. There were in fact forty-four in favour but a three-quarters majority was necessary to pass the motion and so it was declared lost. Bernard Walton resigned immediately but Robert Wright was not so easily convinced; he saw in the vote a personal defeat as well. His name had been on the original agreement and his own ambitions were closely linked with those of Walton. The meeting finally broke up in disarray.

Next morning it was decided to send Walton a letter asking him to return as a player only, and despite Morris's opposition this became a significant issue over the next few weeks. Walton claimed that he had only resigned as Chairman and demanded to be reinstated as principal clarinettist; Robert Wright was also threatening legal proceedings, and rather than let matters get out of hand two courses of action were taken. First, since the orchestra now had no legal adviser, it appointed Sir Charles Russell, on the advice of Lord Harewood, and asked Robert Wright to return all documents relating to the orchestra's legal affairs to Sir Charles. Secondly, in view of Walton's own attitude and an apparent ignorance of all the facts of the case by Klemperer, a letter was drafted to Walton asking him to clarify the reason why he had left the orchestra.

Gareth Morris was duly elected Chairman of the orchestra and he felt that a full meeting of the members of the orchestra should be held to 'clear the air' on the attitude to Walton's return. This was held at the Festival Hall on 5 May. Morris felt too involved to chair the meeting and felt it important to have the meeting minuted, at least informally, by someone of experience. Basil ('Nick') Tschaikov reluctantly agreed to do it: he played only occasionally for the orchestra but was very experienced in union matters and known as a tough but fair negotiator. At the meeting Gareth Morris spoke on the case as he saw it, that there had been manipulation of the affairs of the orchestra of such a nature that far outweighed any argument that Walton should return as a player. A case was then made for Walton's return: not only was he irreplaceable, in many people's view, but his loss would jeopardize the orchestra's credibility with certain important conductors. Much else was said, particularly with reference to Robert Wright's behaviour throughout the affair and the implications of allowing Walton to return to playing. The meeting concluded by adopting the advice of the orchestra's solicitor, that the draft letter should be sent to Walton asking him for a full explanation: if none came, the orchestra should hold a referendum on whether he should return.

No reply came and the ballot was held: it overwhelmingly said 'No' to Walton's return to the New Philharmonia, but there was worse to come. Nick Tschaikov's notes on the 5 May meeting were shown to the Council members for their approval. All agreed on them except one player who was in a hurry and asked to keep them overnight to have a better look at them. He obviously did more than that, for the day following the rejection of Walton's application to return to the orchestra writs for libel were served on Gareth Morris and Nick Tschaikov. It was obvious that the notes had been copied and had passed into the hands of Walton and Wright.

Bernard Walton made one more attempt to return to the New Philharmonia by getting a 'round robin' letter circulated amongst the players but to no effect. The break was made and all he could now pursue was compensation for loss of earnings which he did for some time afterwards. John McCaw was soon appointed principal clarinettist from the London Philharmonic Orchestra, and Bernard Walton took his place there. One wound was thus healed. What took longer was the wound caused by the legal action on Gareth Morris and Nick Tschaikov. Tschaikov had only been involved on the periphery of the affair and it is to his eternal credit that he did not back out at any point when the going began to get rough, least of all when it came to legal action. Morris was also steadfast in defence of his case: when repeated pleas were made to him to back down and let the matter drop 'for the sake of the orchestra', he replied that he stood by what he believed to be the truth 'for the sake of the orchestra'. It took a heavy toll on his nerves and his private life but he felt that he was defending more than his own personal integrity. In the end it was Wright who backed down; he would have lost the case if he had pursued it.

The events of March and April 1966 have been discussed fully since they are a part of the history of the orchestra over which a veil has settled that has distorted the facts. Of more long-term significance is the effect they had on the subsequent years of the orchestra's development. It became more inward-looking, playing for safety and thus losing some of the gloss that had made it pre-eminent in London's orchestral life. Losses on foreign tours and the lack of public subsidy meant that the orchestra would have to concentrate more on more concerts, broadcasts and recording. Gareth Morris, as the new Chairman, clearly indicated that his interest was to get on with playing but reserving the Council's right to criticize the results. This would work well with an able and firm General Manager, and so the Council turned their attentions to this in early April. As an interim measure Rosemarie Schnutz, who had resigned as Assistant General Manager in December 1965, was reappointed as Concerts Manager. A number of applications for the post of General Manager were on file, and these were now looked at with the hope of an early appointment.

Substantial progress was made with the appointment of a new General Manager, George Stringer, a Cambridge solicitor with many Arts connections, who arrived in the first week of July. The immediate prospect must have daunted him. Although the London Orchestral Concerts Board had at last been set up with effect from 1 April 1966, as a result of the Goodman Report, there was little prospect of immediate help for the orchestra. It looked hopeful on paper, but in hard cash terms even the amounts recommended in the Goodman Report would still fall short of the subsidy which would enable the New Philharmonia to live and make music in a civilized way.

One of Stringer's first tasks was to find a replacement for leader Hugh Bean, who had given notice that he intended leaving the orchestra the following year, in order to build up more solo work and to develop his Music Group of London. He would be difficult to replace; even more than his predecessor, Manoug Parikian, he had spent almost his entire time leading and had now spent nearly ten years in the leader's chair. His utter loyalty and reliability had carried the orchestra through a difficult time, and his integrity and total inability to say anything unkind about anyone had endeared him to orchestra and audience alike.

In August, even that problem had to be shelved, for Klemperer fell and broke his hip while on holiday in Switzerland. He had been booked to open the New Philharmonia's Beethoven cycle on 27 September, and at first the prospect of finding his replacement must have seemed daunting, but in fact a number of conductors were able to help out: Pierre Boulez, Carl Melles, Wilhelm Schüchter and Sir Adrian Boult.

Boulez had not worked with the New Philharmonia before; he claimed he had not heard Beethoven's Fifth Symphony for nearly twenty years. He did have a formidable reputation as a champion of twentieth-century music and had won the support and encouragement of Klemperer. On the rostrum Boulez was very efficient, cold as ice and with a very clear beat, but also very gentle-mannered. His conducting of Beethoven was also very efficient but to the point of being mechanical. He succeeded in giving the opening of the Ninth a mysterious, veiled quality that made it seem a new work, and the Chorus loved him. Boulez now began to work with them on a regular basis, recording some Debussy with them later in the year. His readings of *La Mer, Jeux* and *Préludes* were regarded by many as definitive, the only reservation being the use of a British orchestra whose instrumental tone colours did not seem quite to suit French music.

On 26 February 1967 Klemperer returned to the rostrum for the first time to conduct the New Philharmonia since his accident. There were two performances of Mahler's Ninth Symphony, the culmination of two weeks hard work recording it for EMI. A large number of sessions were used, and it seemed that Klemperer's hearing was impaired as he demanded more and more trumpeters. It was almost eight months since Klemperer and the New Philharmonia had last worked together, and when he began to conduct the first session in Kingsway Hall a smile crossed his face as if meeting an old friend again after a long absence. He was using a baton again for the first time in nearly thirty years, and Edward Greenfield found the Festival Hall performance 'one of the most intense experiences I can ever remember in the concert hall'. The audiences gave Klemperer and the New Philharmonia a standing ovation for a performance that in Klemperer's own words had 'no more irony, sarcasm, resentment whatever ... only the majesty of death'. Greenfield also found the 'majesty of death' prevalent in the recording, which was steadier and less emotional than Barbirolli's famous 1963 Berlin account which had prevented Klemperer from recording it in Walter Legge's time.

In March the proposal was made, through an anonymous donor who was already helping the orchestra on a regular basis, to set up a music scholarship fund to support exceptional musical talent that stood on the threshold of a professional career. A sum of £10,000 was offered initially, with a request that the New Philharmonia should administer it through its own office facilities and musical expertise. This the orchestra was very honoured to do. The beauty of the Martin Musical Scholarship Fund, as it came to be known, was its simplicity. No fixed amounts or specific prizes were defined and the rules for eligibility were few. Applicants received preliminary auditions in the autumn and about half went on to the final auditions the following spring, performing at the Wigmore Hall before a panel that included members of the orchestra and invited judges – a distinguished conductor or pianist, a critic, someone from the BBC, and so on. The results could range from £50 for help with extra lessons to £1,500 to purchase a good instrument.

One of the first Martin Scholarship winners was the conductor Lionel Friend, and since 1968 a steady stream of young musicians have been awarded grants from the Fund: Anthony Goldstone, Roger Vignoles, Trevor Pinnock, Nigel Kennedy, Julian Lloyd-Webber, Jill Gomez and the entire Fitzwilliam Quartet are but a few of the holders over the eighteen years since the Fund's foundation. The Menuhin, Purcell and Chethams schools have always been well represented, the only age stipulation being an *upper* one of twenty-five years; a scholar can also be eligible for two awards. Since 1968 there have been few changes. The annual grant has grown to three times its original size and the scope widened to include composers, a student recording scheme and an instrument-maker. Administrators have come and gone, the present organizer being Vivienne Dimant. The Fund was directed at the music world at large but the New Philharmonia benefited directly itself over the years in fruitful work with conductors, soloists and new members who have all been scholarship holders.

Klemperer was now in Britain for some weeks, and two matters needed his advice and approval. The most urgent problem was that of finding a new leader to replace Hugh Bean. George Stringer thought it was the Council's job to make the selection, but they did not seem to be making much progress and there were signs of restlessness among the younger players. There were some auditions for back-desk players in February 1967 and among the applicants had been a young Columbian, Carlos Villa. Twenty-seven years old, he had studied with Galamian in Philadelphia and with Menuhin in Zürich and since then had pursued a solo career. He was currently employed as a peripatetic string teacher in Hertfordshire; his application for a back-desk post in the New Philharmonia had arrived too late for consideration, but Stringer was impressed by his credentials, on paper at least, and pressed the Council to consider him for leader.

Villa had recently recorded the *Kreutzer* Sonata of Beethoven for *Classics for Pleasure*. It had not yet been issued but Stringer obtained pressings. He was convinced, and so was Klemperer, so much so that he rang Stringer at 3 a.m. to tell him, 'Ve haf your leeter!' An audition was arranged for 27 March, and after a very impressive performance of the solo from *Ein Heldenleben* Villa was appointed to the leadership from 13 August. Unusually, he was to be a contracted employee responsible to the Council, not a *member* of the orchestra in the ordinary way. Time would tell whether this inexperience in leadership and orchestral playing generally would be a serious handicap or whether he would be able to follow the example of Manoug Parikian.

The second item for Klemperer's consideration was the possible appointment of a younger conductor to work beside him. Gareth Morris had explained to him that the orchestra needed a young conductor whose name would be regularly associated with that of the orchestra and who would be able to undertake foreign tours and Festival engagements. The conductor concerned would also undertake more of the concerts in the Festival Hall than had previously been allotted to any conductor, and it was intended that a contract should be signed. Both Morris and Stringer had Claudio Abbado very much in mind. He had much impressed the orchestra at Edinburgh in the 1966 Festival with his handling of Berg's *Three Orchestral Pieces*, and when they had bombarded Stringer with their appreciation of his technique, and of his rapport with them, Stringer had filed the orchestra's report in his memory. But Klemperer's approval of any move was essential and would be given only after careful deliberation: he would not be rushed.

Unfortunately, Stringer *was* prepared to be rushed, despite firm warning from the Council that any contacts with Abbado were to be exploratory only and no offer was to be made. Stringer had the enthusiastic support of Lord Harewood, the orchestra's Artistic Adviser, and when he heard that Abbado was being made firm offers in Italy and there was a real possibility of a closer association with another London orchestra, they decided to act. On 8 February they flew to see Abbado in Milan and after long discussions returned with an assurance from him that he would be delighted to consider a long-term post with the New Philharmonia but he was worried at the thought of Klemperer's attitude. The Council had already suggested that Abbado and Klemperer should meet in Paris, if possible, when the orchestra was due to give a concert there on 23 April.

In Paris, Klemperer and Abbado talked long and earnestly about music and the Mahler symphony being performed there, but little was said on the matter of the conductorship. Klemperer was clearly not unaware of the approaches that had already been made to Abbado, and he was furious. It was not that he objected to Abbado in particular but rather the idea of an associate principal conductor. He resented the fact that the talks had gone so far towards the discussion of a contract, and the reaction was swift. There was to be no second permanent conductor, Abbado or anyone else, and Stringer was quite out of order in approaching him.

Stringer resigned over the Abbado affair, at the end of April 1967, but agreed to remain for the tours of Florence, Parma and Portugal which he had set up. The orchestra had been invited to play the Toscanini Centenary Commemoration concert and, in view of the Florentine flood damage of November 1966, were giving their services free. Giulini was the ideal choice for conductor, and he had already spent the latter part of April with the orchestra with performances of some of the Leeds Festival items and the Verdi *Four Sacred Pieces* at the Festival Hall concerts. With the New Philharmonia Chorus he gave a stunning performance of Beethoven's *Missa Solemnis* on 13 May in Florence's Teatro Communale, and the reception from the audience matched that at the Verdi concerts in 1963, carnations, commemorative medals and all.

Just two weeks later, the orchestra went to Portugal with Lorin Maazel. He was supercritical of their playing, of intonation in particular, which put many players' backs up and yet was what the orchestra needed. Maazel was a good trainer but too much of a disciplinarian for the New Philharmonia. He also found it very difficult to see the human side of concert-giving. The first concert, in Oporto, opened with Britten's *Young Person's Guide to the Orchestra*, thus ensuring the presence of every player in the orchestra on the platform at the start of the concert. For the next night, at Coimbra, Maazel wanted to put it second on the programme, after Mozart's *Sinfonia Concertante*, and refused to see Stringer's point that it would give remaining players a good half an hour extra in the bar. The result, sure enough, was quite one of the worst performances of the Britten that they had ever given. Lisbon was rather better: in the huge Coliseu they followed a circus, and the smell of animals was almost overpowering, but the two concerts were well performed, the second with Ricci in the Tchaikovsky Violin Concerto and Maazel giving a very impressive reading of Bartók's *Miraculous Mandarin* Suite. By now Maazel was winning the respect of the more experienced players, and the Bartók contributed to that in no small measure.

The Festival Hall concert on 13 June 1967 was Hugh Bean's last as leader of the New Philharmonia. It was conducted by Sawallisch and came in the middle of a batch of recordings that completed Sawallisch's cycle of the Mendelssohn symphonies. Of all the symphonies the Second proved to be the most novel. The 13 June performance marked its first performance in Britain for at least a generation in its complete form. The choral finale, *Hymn of Praise*, was familiar to countless choral societies as a separate entity, and Sawallisch gave it a committed reading, with orchestra and New Philharmonia Chorus in fine form, and made it a convincing experiment.

That summer the Mendelssohn symphonies were recorded for Philips, with whom the orchestra now regularly worked, but EMI were still the major employer of the New Philharmonia in the recording studio, and the renewal of their contract in the summer of 1967 offered seventy-five players (as opposed to fifty in 1964) a minimum of sixty sessions per annum. The one reservation over this apparent advance in prospects was that the sessions were subject to Klemperer's availability, a reduction to forty-five sessions on his death or illness. This was a little worrying in the light of his recent absence after his car accident and in view of the fact that he came to London only twice a year on average, in January–March and September–October, with occasionally an extra visit in May. He was also fast approaching the end of his recordable repertoire, and the need for an associate conductor, at least, who had a major recording contract, was becoming more than just a luxury; it would soon be a necessity.

When the New Philharmonia had been without a General Manager for over six months, at last, from nearly 150 applicants, Harvey Mitchell was appointed as from 1 February 1968. The Council found him friendly and intelligent, and he seemed competent enough for the job. He joined the orchestra at the beginning of a busy spell of concerts, recordings and foreign tours, a period of work that would put him to the test, but he had the added help of George Wansborough, who had joined the orchestra as its business manager, and of Lord Harewood, now Chairman of the New Philharmonia Trust.

Just at a time when there was a feeling that Klemperer was too old and infirm to record a Wagner opera, he began to record *The Flying Dutchman* on 17 February 1968. Moreover, he succeeded in injecting into the recorded performance something of the spirit of Wagner's intentions which modern productions so often neglected. The New Philharmonia were able to contribute a precision and colour that supported the strong cast. Klemperer used the BBC Chorus again, and he was superbly supported by the EMI engineers in their discreet use of effects to create the various spatial illusions. As usual, the climax of the recording was a Festival Hall concert performance on 19 March, where no such spatial effects could be used but which one critic described as 'the concert of the season'. There were times when the orchestra was not together, and Klemperer's control was not infallible, but the live performance scored over the recording in the way it would flow, carefully and skilfully paced by Klemperer's guidance.

After a year at home, the prospect of a foreign tour during the second half of May 1968 was exciting. The British Council was sponsoring visits to Germany, Hungary and Czechoslovakia. In Germany there were six concerts in six days, conducted by Solti. The concert venues were a wide range of halls from the traditional splendour of Hamburg's Grosse Musikhalle to the advanced modern design of Berlin's Philharmonie Halle. The original plan had been to fly out on the day of the first concert, 16 May, but many complaints about the lack of a full rehearsal on the first day led to the date of departure being brought forward one day. The programme for all the German concerts was Wagner's *Tannhäuser* Overture, Brahms' Symphony No. 2 and the *Frank Bridge Variations* by Britten.

Britten was also represented in the two concerts given under Giulini in Budapest, this time *Les Illuminations*, with Jennifer Vyvyan as soloist. She made an unmistakable impression on the Hungarian audiences – one concert-goer said she 'sang like God'. The other soloist, in both Hungary and Czechoslovakia, was Clifford Curzon, an ambassador of long standing for British musicianship. The New Philharmonia took the bold step of playing Dvořák's Seventh Symphony in Bratislava and Prague – a British orchestra under an Italian conductor playing Czech music in the very heart of Dvořák's homeland. The audience at the Prague Spring Festival had every reason to be dispassionately critical, and the orchestra every right to feel nervous, but the results exceeded all expectations. A leading Slovak composer described the performance as 'monumental', 'a revelation', and the two Prague concerts were hailed as 'the artistic event of the Festival'. The Prague concerts, as well as those in Berlin and Budapest, were also relayed by radio, and so the audiences numbered millions rather than the thousands in the halls; this helped to serve the two purposes of the tour: to consolidate the international reputation of the orchestra and to foster cultural relations between the countries. Three months later, the players were shaken to hear of the news of Russia's invasion of Czechoslovakia.

On 30 June Frühbeck used the Chorus to give a memorable performance of Mendelssohn's *Elijah* in a New Philharmonia Festival Hall concert. *Elijah* is one of those works beloved of amateur choruses because it is not too difficult to sing, and it therefore often receives ham-fisted performances. Frühbeck's reading of it, with the orchestra and a distinguished team of soloists, was stunning; at the end of Part One the audience went wild. The control and balance that he achieved, coupled with a firm build-up of tension and drama, were carried over into the recording which he began, with the same forces, next day in Kingsway Hall. The recording is still in EMI's catalogue and has become a classic of the gramophone. Alec Robertson summed it up thus: 'It is patent how much he [Frühbeck] loves Mendelssohn's *Elijah*, and to be able to give expression to that love with all his heart and mind through the medium of such superb forces and recording must have constituted one of the happiest and most rewarding experiences of his life.'

Later that summer Philharmonia plunged into the 1968 Proms and an EMI recording of Verdi's *Otello*, with Barbirolli. The two batches of work could not have represented greater contrasts for the orchestra. With Barbirolli, in the spacious acoustic of Walthamstow Town Hall, they played warmly for the man whose father and grandfather had played it in the very first performance of *Otello* and for a team of soloists that had Gwyneth Jones, Dietrich Fischer-Dieskau and James McCracken. At the Proms, on 19 August, they found themselves playing Sessions' Fourth Symphony (dating from 1964) and Ives' *Fourth of July*. Conductor Frederick Prausnitz and the orchestra gave a cautious reading of the Sessions, which also suffered by being followed by a boisterous and extravagant performance of the Ives movement.

1968's composers represented at the Edinburgh Festival were Schubert and Britten, with the latter's *War Requiem* presented on 1 September. The work made an indelible impression, the three soloists for whom it was written – one Russian, one British, one German – making an eloquent plea for world peace. It was Giulini's first acquaintance with the work, but with Britten himself directing the chamber ensemble it was an 'authentic' performance and a very moving one. Abbado conducted Schubert at Edinburgh with the New Philharmonia, the vivacious little Second Symphony, as did Giulini with a serious view of the *Tragic* Fourth Symphony and a performance of the Eb Mass No. 6 which brought some astounding singing from the Festival Chorus. It made an interesting sequel to the previous evening's concert when Klemperer gave a deeply moving and leisurely paced account of Mahler's Ninth Symphony.

Both Abbado and Klemperer conducted the New Philharmonia at the 1968 Lucerne Festival, the first time the orchestra had appeared there since 1963. Abbado had Barenboim as soloist in the Brahms D minor Piano Concerto; he closed the concert with Wagner's Prelude and *Liebestod* from *Tristan*, with the same glittering success as in Edinburgh, and with it ended his association with the orchestra. He now chose to work principally with the London Symphony Orchestra, the first orchestra to give him a chance in London and with whom he worked very amicably. His experience over the Associate Conductorship with Klemperer with the previous year had not given him the promise of a close association with the New Philharmonia. At Edinburgh, a rather shaky performance of Bartók's First Piano Concerto had not given either side much confidence in the other, and after Lucerne they parted, but on the best of terms.

Klemperer opened the New Philharmonia's autumn season on 15 September with the Bach B minor Mass. The criticism that it was unenterprising to repeat a performance from the previous season was in part answered by the full Festival Hall that greeted it. After Klemperer's long wait to achieve his ideal interpretation, it was also right that he should be given another chance to air it before time set a limit on his conducting powers. The quality of the performance was well worth the risk, even with changes in the solo team. Two weeks later, Klemperer had less success with Mahler's Seventh Symphony. The occasion was an historic one, for almost sixty years earlier, to the day (19 September 1908), Mahler himself had conducted the first performance with the Vienna Philharmonic Orchestra in Prague, and at the rehearsals had been the young Klemperer, then assistant to the German Opera in Prague. In the course of numerous revisions before the 1908 première, Mahler had received help from Klemperer, as well as Berg and many others.

The success of Klemperer's first Paris visit with the New Philharmonia in 1967 encouraged Pathé-Marconi to subsidize a second trip in October 1968. It is seldom possible for a major symphony orchestra to go abroad for only one concert unless it is a for a major musical event, but the concert in Paris on 18 October was just such an occasion. A capacity audience in the Salle Pleyel heard Klemperer's own *Gavotte* and *Variations on a Theme of Rameau*, Mozart's *Prague* Symphony and Beethoven's Seventh, virtually a repeat of a Festival Hall concert on 10 October. The visit, spread over three days, undoubtedly gave the orchestra a great 'lift' and certainly made Klemperer very happy as he had a recording of the concert to keep as a memento of the occasion, made for him by the EMI engineers.

A further boost to the orchestra's morale came with a second invitation abroad, this time in mid-November 1968. It was for a special gala concert organized by the German recording industry in Berlin on 16 November and to be conducted by Erich Leinsdorf. Three international soloists had been engaged – Maurice André for Haydn's Trumpet Concerto, Arthur Grumiaux for Mozart's Violin Concerto K216 and Martha Argerich for Liszt's First Piano Concerto. The concert was tele-recorded for subsequent relay to a number of European countries, and there were also radio transmissions. The excitement caused by Maurice André arriving for the rehearsal minus his trumpet was soon forgotten in the glamour of the evening's concert and the tumultuous reception given to Leinsdorf and the New Philharmonia.

On the 18th the orchestra assembled in Kingsway Hall for a Decca recording of Stravinsky's *Firebird* with the veteran Swiss conductor Ernest Ansermet. It was his first major recording with a London orchestra for many years and, sadly, it was also to be his last: three months later he was dead. Fortunately, Decca recorded not only the complete *Firebird* but also two sides of rehearsal sequences which captured the old master at his best, now in his mid-eighties.

Ansermet had in fact given the first performance of Stravinsky's *Rite of Spring* in Paris in 1913, and now, on 1 December, the young Boulez gave his first performance of the work with the New Philharmonia, a performance that was probably one of the most dazzling that he had given of any work in Britain and which suggested that the New Philharmonia was still Britain's finest orchestra. It certainly reminded the orchestra that it was in need of a young, dynamic conductor of this calibre with whom it could develop a long-term relationship. The orchestra could have no further designs on Boulez for that position, however, as he had already accepted Glock's invitation to become Conductor-in-Chief of the BBC Symphony Orchestra from 1971. For the time being he could still offer them occasional concerts and recordings.

Older conductors such as Szell could still draw superb playing from the orchestra, and his concerts in November 1968 displayed this to the full. Yet, despite the high spots created by men such as Szell and Boulez, morale in the New Philharmonia was low. There had been some quite significant changes in personnel since 1964, and not always for the better. Klemperer's effect on the orchestra was becoming increasingly stifling as he aged. An example was his Festival Hall concert of 22 January 1969, when the general standard of playing in a Mendelssohn programme was far below the orchestra's standards, with indistinct playing and even, in the *Midsummer Night's Dream* Overture for example, gaps appearing at some places. The same concert brought the critics' fury down on Klemperer for replacing the last ninety-four bars of Mendelssohn's *Scottish* Symphony with an extension of the movement's second subject on the horns which slowly died away into what many felt was rather a damp squib. Klemperer insisted that 'every single note' was by Mendelssohn, but the audience felt cheated. The only recording that Klemperer undertook during the winter months was Schumann's Third Symphony, and this also provoked the comment that it sounded lifeless, when it had the potential to be so exciting a work, but he recorded three of his own works with the New Philharmonia at EMI's Abbey Road studios in March, paying for the sessions himself. This occurred in the middle of his season of Beethoven's *Fidelio* at Covent Garden. The shortness of *Fidelio* suited his diminishing stamina and was the idea vehicle for his far-seeing, rightness of pace and musical staging. The performances were also spread over three weeks.

One of the works that Klemperer recorded in March was his String Quartet. It was issued in 1970 on disc under the title 'Philharmonia Quartet', a nice revival of the name which had been the seed of the original orchestra. Leader of the quartet for the recording was Emanuel Hurwitz, who in April 1969, after a period as Guest Leader, joined the New Philharmonia as co-Leader with Carlos Villa. Villa took on a large number of solo engagements and was on a continental agent's lists as well, so he found it increasingly difficult to maintain the regular leadership in the way that his predecessors had done. Hurwitz's appointment helped with this, and he also brought a wealth of experience to the front desk of the first violins, coming as he did from the leadership of the English Chamber Orchestra.

After just a year as General Manager of the orchestra, in May 1969 Harvey Mitchell left the New Philharmonia. He had been competent enough but seemed unable to impose any kind of leadership on the orchestra's management team that could lift them out of the rather sleepy rut into which they had settled (The Council did not give good managers the freedom they needed to be effective and expected more from poor managers than they could produce.) It was not an auspicious time for the New Philharmonia to lose yet another manager, as on 18 June the first meeting was held in London of an independent committee of enquiry set up by the Arts Council to investigate Britain's orchestral resources and the funding of music outside London, by subsidies from national and local funds and contributions from industry and commerce.

On the more positive side, Giulini conducted varied and exciting programmes with the New Philharmonia in late May and then took them to the Bath and Aldeburgh Festivals in June. The latter was overshadowed by the tragic fire that had destroyed the lovely Maltings concert hall but only one festival concert was lost and the New Philharmonia's concert was transferred to Ely Cathedral. Giulini also took them into the EMI studios twice, to record a couple of overtures; nothing more substantial was planned at present although his EMI contract had another two years to run. Frankly, Giulini was becoming disheartened by the falling standards in the New Philharmonia since reorganization in 1964. He had been an ardent champion of its revival but could see no development of his relationship with them while they were so closely bound up with the career of Klemperer. Giulini would honour the engagements he was contracted to do and continue to conduct the occasional concert as guest conductor but he now felt that he wanted to withdraw from the special relationship he had built up with them.

Barbirolli brought the season to a happier close with the Mahler he conducted so well. After his award of Companion of Honour in the 1969 Queen's Birthday Honours, he followed the triumph with hard work on Mahler's Fifth Symphony with the Genoa orchestra, hard work but a good preparation for a recording of it with the New Philharmonia in mid-July. He also recorded Verdi's *Requiem* with them that summer, perhaps sensing that this recording would be his first and last; it made him doubly anxious that the results should be of the highest quality. The recording contained a great deal of human warmth with no hectic attacks purely for dramatic effect and a gentleness that comes from a great inner strength.

After London rehearsals the orchestra travelled overnight to Edinburgh for five concerts in the 1969 Festival. This year had an Italian flavour, representing significant periods of Italian musical history with a strong emphasis on the twentieth-century. The New Philharmonia's first concert, on 7 September, had little that was Italian, but Giulini came to the rescue on 9 September with Bonporti's *Concerto Grosso*, a *Magnificat* by Petrassi and Rossini's *Stabat Mater*.

One of the first projects on return to London was a complete recording of the Bach Orchestral Suites with Klemperer. The effort of conducting the recording sessions left him too frail to conduct the Festival Hall concert of the suites on 23 September. (It was the opening concert of the New Philharmonia's season, and leader Emanuel Hurwitz had to direct the whole evening with violin and bow.) He recovered to conduct the following Tuesday's concert, which included his own Second Symphony. His towering frame tottered and his gestures were more restricted than ever but his very presence gave an undeniable lift to Beethoven's Overture, Adagio and Finale from *Prometheus*, and a virile seriousness to Mozart's early G minor Symphony No. 25. His own symphony, a largely tonal work lasting just under half an hour, was something of an anticlimax, its lack of coherence and thinness of texture emphasizing the strange sound of the occasional atonal intrusions.

The New Philharmonia's new recording contract with EMI had been signed on 9 September, with effect from 1 July. A total of a hundred sessions, spread over three years, was guaranteed, but there was already some anxiety on both sides over dates. Giulini was losing interest in the orchestra, and there was the stranglehold of Klemperer's own exclusivity of repertoire. Some hope seemed to be offered in a planned complete *Die Walküre* which Klemperer was to begin in October. Plans were to complete Act I by 28 October, Act II between 28 October and 4 November and Act III soon after 8 November. It looked an optimistic schedule and proved to be. As soon as sessions began on 21 October, it was apparent that EMI would be lucky to complete Act I. The sessions went on and on: conductors such as Goodall, Lloyd Jones and Mackerras took the first half hour or so and then Klemperer would record for the remaining two hours. Instead of 28 October it was the 31st before Act I was completed, and Klemperer was in no state to finish another act that side of Christmas.

10. *Poverty and Despair 1970-2*

There were high hopes of a more settled administration for the New Philharmonia with the appointment of Gerald McDonald as General Manager at the end of 1969. McDonald was a musician with a great deal of experience as a musical administrator, formerly regional director for the Arts Council in Liverpool and for eight years manager of the Royal Liverpool Philharmonic Orchestra; he had also run the pioneering Musica Viva concerts under John Pritchard and initiated the international competitions which discovered Achucarro, Ogdon, Mehta and Atzmon. He came to the New Philharmonia from the BBC, where he had been Head of Music for their North Region, where he was closely associated with various schemes to assist young musicians.

McDonald's avowed aims for the New Philharmonia were that it should be the most enjoyable orchestra to listen to and the most interesting to play for. Certainly the plans for the future looked exciting enough: Klemperer's eighty-fifth birthday concert in May 1970 was to be followed by a televised Beethoven cycle in May and June. A two-week tour of Japan with Barbirolli and Edward Downes in August would be followed by concerts with Klemperer in Bonn to celebrate the Beethoven bicentenary. A tour of the United States in the autumn of 1971, with Lorin Maazel, was also being planned.

What McDonald did *not* say was anything of the daunting challenges that faced him. He knew he was taking charge of an orchestra whose standards were not what they had been and which was to some extent freewheeling on the strength of its gramophone recordings. Now they faced a situation where Decca were unwilling to re-engage the orchestra and EMI had the ageing Klemperer on their hands and little repertoire left to record. (Klemperer now realized that he would never complete *Die Walküre*, for example.) By comparison with other London orchestras the New Philharmonia were on about half sessions. McDonald saw his role as that of a salesman, and at his first meeting with the orchestra he pleaded with them: 'You must give me something to sell!'

The only reason that the orchestra was not already bankrupt was the accumulated reserves which had sustained it since 1964 and the continuing support of its anonymous benefactor, but the reserves could not last for ever in the face of diminishing work, and the signs were that the 1969–70 season would show a significant loss. Before very long the orchestra could face bankruptcy and extinction. McDonald had the unenviable task of halting the process. Three things were needed: a new, young principal conductor, financial backing and the injection of dynamic new talent into the ranks of the orchestra itself.

A new conductor would give the orchestra a real sense of purpose and direction. At present only two names stood out in the minds of those who gave the matter any thought. Giulini was an older man with limited concert and recording repertoire, who rightly saw a need for greater discipline and commitment within the ranks of the players; he was becoming increasingly disillusioned by the lack of either and would not guarantee his allegiance much longer. Barenboim was the right age but he wanted a high degree of command over the choice of personnel and programmes which the Council were not prepared to give him; he also had his sights on Berlin, where he was gaining little foothold with Karajan blocking his way. His major strength in this situation lay in his good relations with EMI, for whom he was financially a very good property. There was a third possibility in Lorin Maazel, who was nearing the end of his contract with the Deutsche Oper and who appeared from time to time with the New Philharmonia. Although audiences did not readily take to him, and his recordings did not sell very well, the possibility was very real that he was on the brink of that essential popularity.

The two record companies which still used the Philharmonia on anything like a regular basis were EMI and Philips, and January 1970 was divided almost equally between them. For Philips there was the completion of all Mozart's music for violin and orchestra with Szeryng and Gibson. Produced by Erik Smith, who also wrote the cadenzas for some of the concertos, they represented almost a definitive set of recordings of these works. Less definitive Mozart came in Klemperer's recording of *The Marriage of Figaro* for EMI. Over three weeks were spent on the work, although in fairness to Klemperer he was always ahead on the session schedule. The now customary slow tempi allowed one to hear detail that was usually lost but they produced a ponderous quality that was not easy to shake off. The recording was followed by a concert performance on 3 February in the Festival Hall which not only was disappointingly attended – about two thirds of the hall was full – but gave rise to a blistering review in *The Times*. William Mann wrote that he had to admit to leaving the performance half way through the last act 'for fear that my mounting indignation at Klemperer's didactic, humourless, tortoise-like manner would bring on a fatal coronary thrombosis'.

When Barenboim came back to conduct two concerts in March 1970, McDonald took the opportunity to discuss future policy with him. Both men felt that the orchestra had suffered over the last eighteen months or so because of the Klemperer method. Some players were not good enough, and too many paid such scant attention at rehearsals that the same musical point had to be made to each section in turn. Barenboim was nevertheless very interested in the New Philharmonia: he had now recorded nearly all the solo piano and chamber orchestra repertoire he wished to undertake and would be interested in starting to record the larger symphonic repertoire, even as early as 1971 or 1972. For this he was confident of a large-scale commitment by EMI and Decca (perhaps fifty and twenty-five per cent respectively), together with a second conductor such as Mehta to take the Decca slice. He would want to be Musical Director with considerable overall power, and in return the Council would have to respect his opinion and judgement and give the scheme time to show its merits.

At this stage this was too much for the Council to give one man. Barenboim's concerts with the orchestra showed undeniable technique but did not always 'sell' the works he undertook. For example, the March Festival Hall concerts included the difficult Bruckner Seventh Symphony whose structure is not easy to communicate anyway, and in Schoenberg's *Verklärte Nacht* he drew exquisite playing but failed to achieve the balance required for the work's contrapuntal interest to come through. This may have been due in some measure to the Festival Hall's dry acoustics and his placing of his string forces. Small points, maybe, but factors that had to be considered in looking for a man to be responsible for 'selling' the orchestra to the public again.

The end of the financial year brought the expected loss: at nearly £8,300 it was a considerable blow to morale as well as the bank balance.

14 May 1970 was Klemperer's eighty-fifth birthday, and his own musical celebration was to be to conduct his own New Philharmonia Orchestra and Chorus in Mahler's *Das Lied von der Erde*, with Janet Baker and Nicolai Gedda. His daughter, Lotte, had planned a practical present for him on 19 May by booking St John's, Smith Square, and the Bartók Quartet to give the first public performance of his Quartet No 7. The Philharmonia Quartet had already recorded it for EMI, and the score and parts had been sent out to Sydney where the Bartók Quartet were in the middle of a five-month tour. EMI's contribution to the celebrations was the issue of Klemperer's recording of his own Second Symphony and Quartet, as well as re-issuing the complete set of Beethoven symphonies made in 1957. Fate, which had given Klemperer many blows throughout his long life, saved some excitement for his birthday concert. On the day itself, at 7 a.m., Gedda rang to say he had a

bad cold and would not be able to sing. McDonald rang Richard Lewis in Rome: he desperately needed someone who knew the Mahler and who had previously worked with Klemperer, and Lewis had done both. Unfortunately, Lewis had to say no, but within minutes he was on the telephone again to McDonald to say that there was a Musicians' Union strike in Rome and that his prior engagement was now cancelled.

At the concert Klemperer was helped to the rostrum to a standing ovation from orchestra and audience. All they got was a curt nod and, when silence finally ensued, an unemotional and objective reading of his '*Spiritus rector*' Gustav Mahler's great masterpiece. The New Philharmonia, miraculously divining every intention from the imprecise beat, played their hearts out, and soloists and chorus matched the intensity of the occasion. Afterwards there were speeches and gifts: a Georgian silver salver from the orchestra, inscribed 'With affection from the members of the New Philharmonia Orchestra', which was presented by Gareth Morris with an affectionate and eloquent speech in which he congratulated Klemperer on behalf of the orchestra, the public and the 'whole world of music'. When he finished, a huge hand shot out and grabbed the salver, and a gruff '*Danke*!' came from the old man. There was also an ashtray from the New Philharmonia Chorus, and then after a couple of curtain calls Klemperer vanished, leaving the soloists to take their applause. Perhaps Klemperer, like at least one critic, resented the presence of a proportion of the audience who were there for non-musical reasons and whose coughing and fidgeting were obtrusive at times. Only the moving '*Abschied*' had silenced them.

It was not the last of Klemperer by any means. 1970 was the Beethoven bicentenary year, and from 26 May to 2 July he was to conduct a complete cycle of the symphonies. If there had been any doubts about his ability still to convince the public of his interpretative powers, that cycle dispelled them. They were rare occasions, indeed. The opening concert on 26 May was complete with television cameramen in evening dress as if they were part of the performance, which in a sense they were. The First Symphony was played, appropriately, with reduced forces, but made rather an uncertain start, while the *Eroica* was colossal in its architecture and its conviction. As the concerts progressed, it became evident that even in his eighty-sixth year Klemperer could still keep an open mind on the Beethoven symphonies. In the very familiar Fifth he kept his audience in suspense until the last section of the Finale, with no first movement repeat, an Andante that darkened as it progressed and a menacing Scherzo which only resolved in a blaze of light in the C major Finale.

The Ninth Symphony brought a full Festival Hall and long queues outside hoping for returned tickets. In the *Guardian* Edward Greenfield described the performance as an 'honest reading': this covered everything from the dry opening, a Scherzo that was far from the marked '*Molto vivace*' and which with all the repeats lasted longer than the first or third movements, a richly played Adagio, and a Finale in which Gwydion Brooke shone in the bassoon counterpoint to the long opening melody. The soloists – Teresa Zylis-Gara, Janet Baker, George Shirley and Theo Adam – and the New Philharmonia Chorus joined in a reading that won all concerned a standing ovation. The whole cycle had been tele-recorded for transmission a few days later in the month. For Wilhelm Pitz, the Ninth was the climax to a season that had brought him an OBE for services to British music, an honour of which he was very proud and which he richly deserved.

And it was a timely honour: while the chorus were in Sweden the following July, they heard that Pitz had had a stroke during the Festival at Bayreuth. There had already been some doubt as to his ability to continue with the New Philharmonia; now his illness made his resignation inevitable. It was the end of a magnificent era.

The last week of July 1970 saw the final preparations and rehearsals for the orchestra's first visit to Japan. They had been invited to represent British orchestral music in Expo 70 in Osaka and also to give concerts in Tokyo. Soloists John Ogdon and Janet Baker were to accompany them, and the principal conductor for the tour was to be Barbirolli, assisted by Edward Downes. Barbirolli's health was at this time in a grave state, but on Monday 27 July he rehearsed the Mahler First Symphony and the two song cycles with Janet Baker. He then spent the 28th on Britten's *Sinfonia da Requiem* and Beethoven's *Eroica* Symphony, which left just the Sibelius Second Symphony to do the next day. There was a short pre-tour press conference and photographs and then he went home. In the early hours of the next morning he was dead.

The loss felt by the Western music world was shared by the Japanese, who had looked forward keenly to seeing Barbirolli in the flesh for the first time in Japan. John Pritchard now faced not only the nightmare of replacing 'Glorious John' but a nightmare of a schedule. He had been to Japan before, with the London Philharmonic in 1969, but at a considerably more leisurely pace. He now took on the programmes exactly as they were planned, with a diary that read thus: 3 August, LSO Prom, London; 4 August, fly to Japan, arrive 5th in time for afternoon rehearsal; 6/7/8 August, concerts in Osaka; 9 August, fly back to London; 11 August, Glyndebourne Opera Prom, London; 12 August, fly to Japan, arrive 13th in time for rehearsal and concert, Tokyo; 14 August, concert, Tokyo; 15 August, fly via Hong Kong to Athens for Festival ... None of this would have worked without the generosity of

Edward Downes, who took on a performance of Mahler's First Symphony – his first performance – with the minimum of personal rehearsal; he had the task anyway of conducting in Osaka and Tokyo the performances of the *Symphony in One Movement*, commissioned from Alexander Goehr for Expo 70.

John Pritchard seemed to thrive on the exacting schedule, and the sight of him and John Ogdon receiving bouquets from the enchanting little kimono-clad Japanese girls, all bowing to each other, was one to be treasured. John Barbirolli had not been forgotten: in the hall in Osaka was an enlarged photograph surrounded with white chrysanthemums, and later, in Tokyo, a complete exhibition had been mounted. The playing was a tribute to the memory of Barbirolli, having to stand comparison with Berlin and Cleveland. The Press described the Philharmonia as having a uniquely beautiful sound and a virtuosity to compare with any orchestra in the world.

A week after arrival back from Japan the orchestra was in Edinburgh to open the 1970 Festival. Those who went by plane only just made it through the fog. It was again a case of 'dead men's shoes': Colin Davis stood in for Barbirolli, who should have conducted Beethoven's Ninth Symphony with the Edinburgh Festival Chorus. It was a daunting task even for a conductor of Davis's stature, but his performance was sturdy, often strangely extrovert. Barbirolli's memory, and that of Georg Szell who had died just a day after him, was respected with a three-minute silent tribute by audience and performers. Downes followed with the Goehr Symphony and Dvořák's Eighth Symphony fresh from the Japanese tour, and then on 27 August Giulini conducted the Beethoven *Missa Solemnis*.

McDonald took the opportunity to talk to Giulini about his relations with the London Symphony Orchestra and his future with the New Philharmonia. Giulini was most encouraging and expressed his confidence in the new management of the New Philharmonia to the extent that he would be willing to consider a position in which he could be one of a triumvirate, with Klemperer and Maazel as the leading lights. Certainly this was a promising step forward, as Giulini's participation in the New Philharmonia's concert calendar was a significant factor for both orchestra and chorus. His recordings were less marketable, and for the present McDonald intended to pursue the association with Maazel.

A major event in the September concert calendar was the orchestra's invitation to Bonn to take part in the Beethoven bicentenary celebrations there. Klemperer was to conduct Beethoven's First and Third Symphonies in two concerts, on 25 and 26 September. The Bonn concerts had been planned originally for 1969 but had been rescheduled in three cycles in May, September and December 1970; the New

Maazel conducts the New Philharmonia in Strauss' *Till Eulenspiegel* in Philadelphia on the November 1971 tour of the USA.

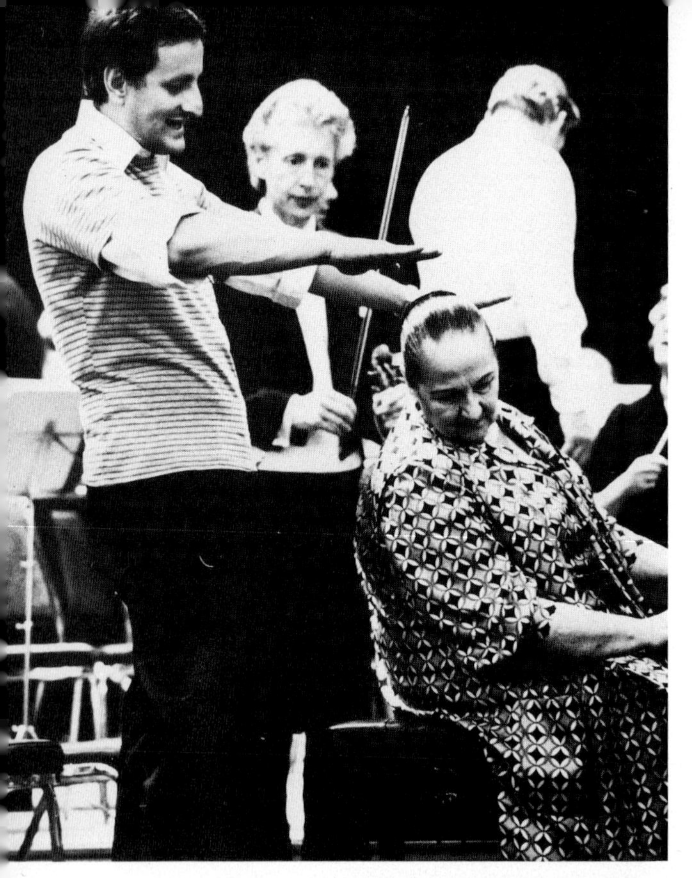

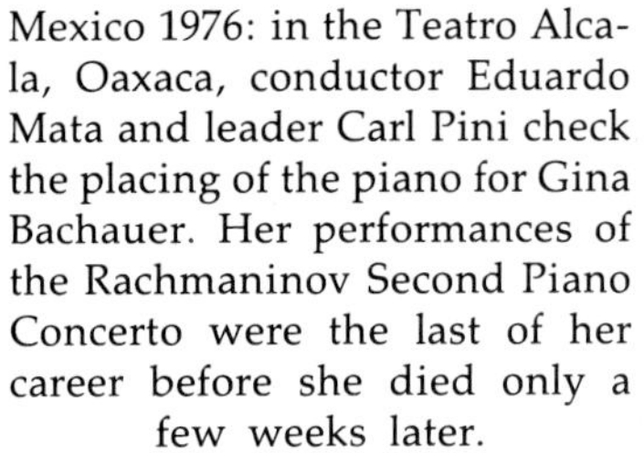

Mexico 1976: in the Teatro Alcala, Oaxaca, conductor Eduardo Mata and leader Carl Pini check the placing of the piano for Gina Bachauer. Her performances of the Rachmaninov Second Piano Concerto were the last of her career before she died only a few weeks later.

Jessie Hinchliffe (violin) the Orchestra's longest serving player, at the candle-lit crib of Jesus in the Church of the Nativity, Bethlehem, on the New Philharmonia's 1977 tour of Israel.

At the 1978 Barcelona Festival Don Luis Portabella Rafols presents the silver plaque of the Patronato to the Philharmonia Orchestra and Chorus 'in homage to their artistry'. Charles Spencer, Chairman of the Philharmonia Chorus receives his plaque and next to him stands Ian Stoutzker, the Orchestra's President, to acknowledge the presentation to the Orchestra.

The elaborate interior of the Palau de la Musica, Barcelona, with Kurt Masur conducting the Philharmonia Chorus and Orchestra in Mendelssohn's *Elijah*.

The Nottinghamshire At Home, May 1978: principal percussionist David Corkhill gives a master-class for young players as part of the Philharmonia's residency.

The Philharmonia were associated with the Wembley Conference Centre from the very outset and on 17 June 1978 Vladimir Ashkenazy is seen here directing the Orchestra in a Mozart piano concerto before a capacity audience.

Christopher Warren-Green, leader of the Philharmonia Orchestra since January 1981. At the age of 25 he was one of the youngest leaders in the history of the London Orchestras.

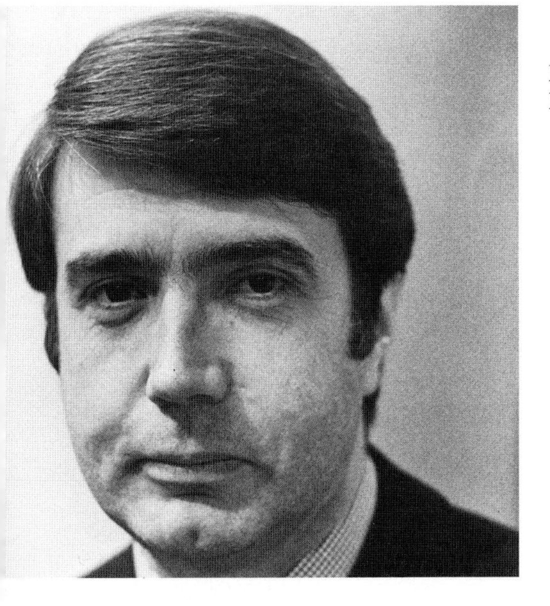

Martin Jones, Chairman of the Philharmonia's Council of Management.

Clem Relf, Philharmonia's librarian since 1946, pictured here in Kingsway Hall.

Left to right – Christopher Bishop (Managing Director of the Philharmonia), Elisabeth Schwarzkopf and Riccardo Muti at a reception held after the Philharmonia memorial concert for Walter Legge, on 3 July 1979.

HRH the Prince of Wales attended the Philharmonia's concert on 2 July 1981, his first since becoming the Orchestra's Patron. After the concert he met the players and here chats with Riccardo Muti and Signora Muti.

Sir William Walton's 80th birthday was marked by a gala concert in the Festival Hall on 29 March 1982, conducted by André Previn. Before the concert Sir William and Lady Walton were introduced to Princess Alexandra by Christopher Bishop.

Riccardo Muti conducts the Philharmonia in La Scala, Milan, in April 1982 as part of a major tour of Germany and Italy.

Giuseppe Sinopoli recording *Manon Lescaut* with the Philharmonia for Deutsche Grammophon in Kingsway Hall in January 1984, his first recording as Principal Conductor. Sadly, this was also the last recording to be made in the superb acoustics of Kingsway Hall before its takeover by the Greater London Council.

Philharmonia concerts would close the September cycle.

Klemperer had taken some persuading to conduct the Bonn concerts – his reluctance seemed to stem from his Jewish background – but McDonald tried to point out that he, and the New Philharmonia, had been selected by the German government; it was an honour that he could not refuse. When Klemperer still demurred, McDonald played his trump card: 'All right, Dr Klemperer, *we* will go to Bonn and play Beethoven 1 and 3, with Colin Davis.' That did it. Klemperer agreed to go, but he insisted on staying in Zürich and travelling through just for the concerts.

As in Japan, so in Bonn the New Philharmonia were in the company of the world's leading orchestras – the Berlin Philharmonic, the Vienna Philharmonic and the Amsterdam Concertgebouw. Any doubts by orchestra, conductor or public were swept away by the jubilant reception. To see Klemperer being helped painfully to the rostrum, one could hardly believe the evidence of eye and ear in the profoundly moving account of the *Eroica*, all achieved with the giant frame apparently carved out of granite, head bowed but eyes everywhere, even in the score. The critic of *Neue-Ruhr-Zeitung* had the temerity to ask Klemperer why, when everyone else seemed to manage without a score, he still used one. Back came the withering reply: 'I can read music!' The orchestra ringed him about on the platform and with a kind of priestly intuition he made the strings and wind achieve an absolute unity. The performance, to one listener at least, made an astonishing contrast with his 1955 recording, so very different yet with a new dimension. The Bonn performance was staggering – people in the audience were crying – but it was almost chamber music in its quality and an amazing change in only fifteen years.

At the end the audience rose in tumultuous applause. After Klemperer had given only the briefest nod, he left the platform, but the ovation went on and on. People crowded round the rostrum (someone even stole his baton), and the shouting went on for three-quarters of an hour. Most of the orchestra were back in their hotel when McDonald finally appeared, asked for quiet and said: 'He is very tired, he cannot come back – thank you so much.'

Back in London the decision was taken to engage Maazel as Associate Principal Conductor. Earlier discussions between McDonald and Maazel about some form of association for him with the orchestra had produced the reaction from Maazel that such a link should grow out of a firm basis of work with the orchestra. This seemed to the Council to be a sensible reaction, and it was felt that such an association was important to the future welfare of the orchestra. Klemperer's advice had been asked and he was in favour of the proposals, provided they did not impinge upon his own special position. His comment on Maazel was that 'The orchestra could not have picked a better man.'

The appointment of Maazel as Associate Principal Conductor, initially for three years, was announced on 23 November, the day following his appearance with the orchestra as both conductor and soloist in a Mozart violin concerto. While his performance as violinist did not quite take London by storm, there was a general welcome both within the orchestra and outside to the news of the appointment. The rest of the season was planned to include some exciting concerts under his direction and some recordings with Decca. One critic noted that, 'With Klemperer to take care of the orchestra's soul, Maazel will doctor the body.' Maazel's own comment on the appointment was: 'My plan is for the New Philharmonia to give superlative concerts. I would like it to be the orchestra that is expected to play just one notch better, and then I would like it to play better than people expect.'

Maazel was expensive: the Council offered him a guaranteed increase in fees from £500 to £750 per concert in 1971, and further to £1,000 from 1 January 1972. With ten such major concerts planned per year, this represented a large financial commitment, particularly when the self-promoted Festival Hall concerts did not pay for themselves, even with full houses. McDonald made this very point to the new Chairman of the New Philharmonia Trust, Ronald Grierson, Director of GEC Limited. The Trust now agreed on two urgent needs: to find a permanent home for the orchestra, costing in the region of £100,000, and financial help for new conductors at a cost of £15,000 per annum. This would help with the cost of Maazel, who also had promises of recording work from EMI – the Tchaikovsky piano concertos with Gilels and the Brahms *Requiem* with Janet Baker and Dietrich Fischer-Dieskau. The planned tour of the USA for November 1971 had the promise of good terms from impresario Sol Hurok and no less than £32,500 from the anonymous benefactor. The omens seemed more promising as the New Philharmonia faced 1971.

In the New Year Klemperer began to record Mozart's *Così fan tutte*. He had made the suggestion himself to record it, and the cautious enthusiasm with which the idea was apparently greeted only spurred him on. 'What do you want?' he protested, 'A posthumous interpretation?' The strain of the *Così* operation led Klemperer to cancel a Bach concert the following Sunday. The orchestra took the risk of engaging the twenty-five-year-old Michael Tilson Thomas for the first time. He kept one Bach item from Klemperer's programme, the Cantata No. 56, which was sung by Gerard Souzay, and replaced the rest with Mahler's Fifth Symphony. It turned out to be a little over-ambitious but Tilson Thomas's rapport with the New Philharmonia was established, and his flair for being able to bring off unusual mixtures of works was to lead to repeated engagements in the future, with great success. This particular concert brought an immediate invitation to devise and perform another programme the next season.

The new Queen Elizabeth Hall now offered possibilities for smaller-scale concerts, and a series of three in January, February and March 1971 presented a wide range of works by Telemann, Nielsen, Honegger, Wesley and Chaminade, and which featured the New Philharmonia principals in concertos and concertante-style pieces. At the opposite end of the orchestral scale was a performance of Mahler's Eighth Symphony, the so-called *Symphony of a Thousand*, in the Albert Hall on 21 April. Musically the work was daunting enough; financially, the burden was enormous: 'The Symphony of £13,000' as one newspaper dubbed it. The difference between box-office takings and the outlay on hall, soloists and orchestra was in the region of £8,500. The Royal Philharmonic Society put in £1,000, leaving the rest to be covered by the New Philharmonia Trust and the funds of the orchestra itself.

The financial loss for the year 1970–1 turned out to be a colossal £26,500. Lord Goodman had met the four major orchestras during May and suggested a formal meeting in September to discuss their future and the need for still closer co-operation on programmes and policy as outlined in the 1965 report. Goodman still supported *four* orchestras, but it was common knowledge that the Music Panel and the Music Director of the Arts Council did not. Further, the Royal Philharmonic Orchestra was in financial difficulties comparable with those of the New Philharmonia, and so the idea of an amalgamation between the two orchestras began to take shape in the minds of many closely associated with both bodies. The Royal Philharmonic were keen on the *idea*, and at a meeting between the two orchestras and Peter Andry of EMI there seemed to be a lot of enthusiasm to pursue the suggestion. McDonald had reservations about the Royal Philharmonic, however. They seemed to be pursuing the 'popular' market, they had a large deficit on their 1970 tour which they still had to clear, and they were inclined to work independently of the recording companies. McDonald therefore considered the merger unsuitable at present.

There were other problems, too. The leadership of the orchestra was under discussion again. Hurwitz was willing to continue, but he had the leadership of the Aeolian Quartet to fit into his work load, and he was very ready to step down in favour of one *young* leader who could give the time and energies the orchestra needed. McDonald had also received a letter from Giulini expressing his interest in renewing his collaboration with the orchestra from the 1973–4 season: this would take the form of a group of three concerts plus rehearsals grouped within the space of a fortnight. Giulini also confirmed two performances of Bach's B minor Mass for the July 1972 City of London Festival. It was all very promising but represented little progress in the conductor issue since Giulini was not interested in EMI's recording suggestions with the New Philharmonia, and his contract with them would expire in November 1971 anyway. The only recordings he had done for them recently had been with the Chicago Symphony.

About this time there came to the surface the issue of the use of the orchestra's name by an orchestra in the USA, although at this stage the matter concerned EMI principally and the New Philharmonia were kept in relative ignorance of the full facts. Since May 1969 the Camden Symphony Orchestra, conducted by Ling Tung, had presented its concerts in Philadelphia under the name 'Philharmonia Orchestra' to avoid the use of the word 'Camden' in the title as this was a slum area of Philadelphia. Camden had filed an application for the use of the name as a Federal registered service mark, in October 1969, for the purpose of giving concerts and making records. EMI had been aware of this since January 1970 and had begun legal investigations, initially, to avoid confusion by the use of the name by two organizations, but then the protection of their own pre-1964 Philharmonia Orchestra recordings became the main issue at stake. The problem was twofold: that Camden could stop EMI selling the Philharmonia Orchestra records in the USA which provided an annual income of some $1\frac{1}{2}$ million dollars, and that *if* Camden issued its own records under the name 'Philharmonia Orchestra'. Any benefit could only be to the newcomer in the market, Camden.

Until now EMI (owners of the 'Philharmonia' name and thereby receiving considerable currency on the US market) had not discussed the matter with the New Philharmonia, for it seemed likely that in the near future the New Philharmonia would disappear within the proposals for an orchestral merger and virtually become the EMI 'house' orchestra under a new name, or that in its present precarious financial state it would disappear altogether. But now, in March 1971, EMI obtained the agreement of the New Philharmonia to their trying to obtain a settlement with Camden to the effect that there would be no objection to the name being used by the Camden Symphony Orchestra for their concerts in America, but that they could not use the name under any circumstances for recording.

10 July 1971 brought a memorable visit to York as part of the city's 1,900th anniversary celebrations. Giulini was to conduct the Beethoven *Missa Solemnis* in York Minster, and the previous day he reaffirmed to McDonald his desire to return to an exclusive collaboration with the

New Philharmonia. York Minster was packed, with nave and aisles full to overflowing. Giulini, in morning dress, conducted without a score, and the performance was broadcast on BBC Television.

Prausnitz then followed a Prom performance with a recording for Argo of the Sessions *Rhapsody for Orchestra*, one of a series of recordings sponsored by the Calouste Gulbenkian Foundation. Directed by David Drew, this series was a response to a report dating from 1959 of a committee under Lord Bridges which was entitled 'Help for the Arts' and which noted that 'One of the least satisfactory features of the musical life of the country is that while it is fairly easy to fill a hall to hear a performance of the "repertory", the inclusion in such a programme of more than one item by a modern composer all too often has the effect of turning a small profit into a big loss.' One consequence of this was a continuing programme of recording sponsored by the Foundation and was initiated in January 1965 under the title *Music Today*. The New Philharmonia had played a significant part in this pioneering enterprise by undertaking these recordings with Argo; more were planned for early in 1972.

As if to underline the orchestra's financial problems, the London Orchestral Concerts Board met in July 1971 to review its policy of financial assistance to the four London symphony orchestras and to this end had asked the Board's secretary, T.E. Bean, to submit a paper setting out the relevant information and the issues that called for some decision. These seemed to be primarily: 1) Were the orchestras in fact solvent after six years' association with the Board? 2) Had the method of allocating subsidies in fact produced a rational and co-ordinated policy of concert promotion? 3) Had the subsidies provided stability of employment and improved the working conditions of the players? Bean used the period of three years ending 31 March 1970 as his basis, a period which for the New Philharmonia had become rapidly outdated in its reflection of the true financial picture, although some of the signs were already there. The New Philharmonia's reserves had stood at nearly £34,000, the largest of the four, but they had dwindled and the running surplus on the three years in question was in fact the second smallest, only just £4,500. Bean could foresee at least one orchestra ending up in the hands of the Official Receiver before the next three-year period was up. The present concert and orchestral structure allowed only two real alternatives: 1) to increase the grants to all four orchestras to allow adequate rehearsal and presentation of programmes which would result in the *solvency* of the four orchestras but have no correlative effect on the promotion policy, standards of performance or improved working conditions, or 2) to concentrate its resources on *two* orchestras rather than dissipate them on the ineffective subvention of *four*. The idea of a merger was one that therefore now had some support in important financial circles and would be reconsidered by the New Philharmonia, along with smaller ways in which money could be saved.

One such way was tried in August 1971 with the recording of Britten's *Young Person's Guide* and Prokofiev's *Peter and the Wolf* on the *Classics for Pleasure* label. The orchestra paid its own costs on the recording in return for a royalty payment – five per cent on ninety per cent of the retail price – which it was hoped would provide a good return on such a popular record. It was a long-term investment; it would take two years to repay, and the Trust helped out with a substantial loan to cover that period.

Klemperer returned for just one concert to open the autumn season on 26 September. Two standard repertory works were featured, Beethoven's Fourth Piano Concerto with the nineteen-year-old Daniel Adni appearing at Klemperer's invitation, and Brahms' Third Symphony. The concert opened with the Mozart K375 *Serenade for Wind* which Klemperer had just recorded at Abbey Road and which was to prove to be his last recording for EMI. The physical strain of taking sessions was now added to the limitations of his remaining usable repertoire.

McDonald discussed the recording problem with EMI in late September: the two most likely replacements for work with the orchestra had significant drawbacks. Maazel was very expensive on advance payments and royalties, and Giulini did not sell well, nor was he interested in EMI's repertoire suggestion. Maazel seemed the orchestra's best hope on the concert platform, although the same month as he was preparing for a three-week tour with the New Philharmonia of the USA he was appointed to Cleveland to replace the late Georg Szell, for a five-year term. The USA tour would be good publicity for him and for the New Philharmonia but not necessarily beneficial to the latter's long-term prospects with him as their Associate Principal Conductor.

The three October concerts that preceded the tour included seven of the works they were taking to the USA. The plan was to make up three separate programmes, with no soloist, which could be repeated and 'permed' over the sixteen concerts.

The cynics – and there were a good many of them – looked on the New Philharmonia's USA tour as a Maazel 'benefit' tour. The reviews of the concerts were full of praise for the orchestra: 'A dream of an orchestra, with glorious strings, tremendous brass and magnificent winds' was the *Washington Evening Star*'s comment. The New Philharmonia had been the first London orchestra to play in Washington's recently opened Kennedy Center for the Performing Arts; in Philadelphia, where they were the last of five London orchestras to reach the city, they were ascribed 'a quality the others lack – a distinctive sound, with a richness of strings that is not a mark of even the London Symphony Orchestra'. Maazel had the Cleveland appointment to live up to and was given a mixed reception by the Press. In Philadelphia his programme was accused of 'showing off the strengths of his orchestra without shaping up as a musical evening', and this was a regular comment, the result of opening programmes with such difficult works as Sibelius' Seventh Symphony or the *Adagio* from Mahler's Tenth Symphony. In the more extrovert pieces the emphasis was on 'dazzle' even when dazzle was not appropriate. McDonald wrote to Klemperer that the criticisms of Maazel, both implied and actual, were 'depressingly accurate. He annoys the players because he will not leave the music alone; he pokes at it'. Relations between Maazel and the orchestra became strained: there had been a row in New York which seemed to clear the air a bit, or at least, as Hurwitz commented wryly, 'The artistic affronts are now delivered with a smile rather than a scowl!'

Maazel's criticisms of the New Philharmonia dealt mainly with general discipline and section organization, which undoubtedly needed tightening up. He noted that players read books or played chess during rehearsals and were often ill-prepared in bowing and phrasing. At concerts the procedure for tuning and taking calls also needed to be more firmly directed, and Maazel summed up his proposals by asserting that, 'The survival of the orchestra and its acceptance as first among *the* equals in London and about the world is directly related to the conscientious maintaining of standards, and the presenting of a common front of keenness and discipline towards the public, the recording industry, TV producers etc.' There was no doubt in anyone's mind, except that of his sternest critics, that he had already had an effect on the alertness and playing standards of the orchestra, resulting in better performances than those with other conductors.

The musical and personal results were more controversial. On Maazel's appointment he had been encouraged to plan unusual programmes and had been given more rehearsal time but the public, the Press, the orchestra and to some extent the recording companies had serious misgivings. Attendances dropped badly, to an average of sixty-seven per cent houses in the Festival Hall, where even full houses lose money; the public were not sufficiently interested in Maazel. Perhaps the orchestra could persevere but it was reaching the point where it could no longer afford it. It was already estimated that the Maazel concerts from March 1970 to March 1972 would lose something in the region of £22,000: extra rehearsals cost money, and during the autumn of 1971 he had been allowed an average of 4½ rehearsals per concert, which he still regarded as inadequate. His own fees were now very high and his suggestion to limit the number of promotions to a few prestige events would lose them their administration grant immediately and would eventually forfeit the London Orchestral Concerts Board grant, as it was given for public service.

Maazel also wanted to limit his recordings to seven or eight top-quality items per year and felt that the New Philharmonia should be more selective in its overall recording policy – yet the orchestra needed a hundred sessions per year to survive. Maazel's relations with EMI were strained, with Decca just ticking over and with the remaining companies non-existent. The problem in 1970 had been gaps in the diary held open for Klemperer: the orchestra now had gaps held open for Klemperer and Maazel.

Finally, Maazel's views were of a New Philharmonia over which he had more control than its Council would be willing to allow. His wishes to limit his appearances to top promotions were just not practical. That kind of policy could cost in excess of £200,000, even if it did make any kind of artistic sense.

Before he replied to Maazel, McDonald asked two questions: 1) Does the New Philharmonia envisage that Maazel will become Principal Conductor in due course? If not, he should be told so now. 2) Who else is there? The answer to 1) seemed to be 'no' and McDonald therefore wrote to Maazel at great length and with the approval of the full Council as well as the principals of the orchestra. Maazel was booked to conduct a New Philharmonia Trust Gala concert on 21 March, and so McDonald contrived to delay despatch of the letter to arrive after that date – but he was overtaken by events.

Klemperer arrived in Britain on 15 January for a concert with the orchestra on the 21st, to be followed by a projected recording of Mozart's *Il Seraglio*. He was feeling very weak and saw his doctor, who found him to be apparently quite well. However, Klemperer withdrew from the Bruckner concert planned for that Friday and flew home to Zürich. On 20 January came the shock announcement that he had decided to retire from the concert platform. McDonald explained to the Press: 'He has a fantastic constitution, but he does now find the long periods of concentration in public concerts are too much. It is very sad.' Klemperer let it be known, however, that he intended to continue making records and would return in February for *Il Seraglio*.

The day after Klemperer's announcement, the orchestra's Council asked Gareth Morris to resign, both as Chairman of the Council and as principal flautist of the orchestra, a position he had held for twenty-four years. His departure had been imminent for some time and there was no row, no bitterness. The official reason given was 'irreconcilable artistic differences' but there were other factors involved, some of them deeper than just artistic intolerance from his colleagues. His stand over the Walton affair in 1966, his incurable habit of speaking his mind in a situation, however public, made him many enemies, while the burdens of Council affairs and the many years of threatened libel suits had drained his nervous energy. His highly individual style of play aroused some of the Press to mount a smear campaign on his performance, particularly over his intonation, and made him carry the blame for the entire woodwind section's shortcomings. Now that Klemperer was gone, with whom he had been closely associated for many years, the orchestra felt that they could ditch him, too. Morris, for his part, no longer felt he belonged in an orchestra where one played largely for safety and where his individuality was regarded as aggression. So he departed, having guided the New Philharmonia through eight very difficult years, with integrity and utter sincerity.

Lawrence Lea, No.8 first violin, was elected the new Chairman of the Council and soon found himself in the centre of a most interesting meeting. McDonald had been unable to keep his letter to Maazel back any longer, and it finally went on 23 February. On 1 March Council and Conductor met for discussions on the musical considerations of the European Tour, but the main business of the meeting was Maazel's relationship with the orchestra and its future. Maazel felt that the Council had been wrong in their thinking, and he could not accept their ultimate sanction to have the final say over programmes. He would withdraw from giving any advice about artistic policy in future and from identifying himself with the orchestra in this respect. He also took the opportunity to slate McDonald for the way he felt he had been badly treated. The Council listened patiently until he had finished. There was an interminable pause. Gwydion Brooke looked up: 'Mr Maazel, we all wish you well in Cleveland.'

Maazel resigned next day as Associate Principal Conductor.

In just six weeks the orchestra had lost the three principal obstacles to pursuing a new conductor and considering seriously the idea of an orchestra merger. Klemperer had retired from public concert life, and although his position as Honorary President gave him the privilege of veto on any proposals, it was no longer the position of strength it had been. Gareth Morris had gone, and with him his support of Maazel and the *status quo*. Now Maazel, too, had gone from a position of artistic policy-making. The way seemed open to pursue new policies of revival, but the end of the financial year was fast approaching and no one even tried to pretend that it would be anything but acutely depressing.

When the end of the financial year came, it made the need for *any* action very pressing indeed. The loss totalled £23,718, a staggering sum when one considers that the year's income included £10,000 from the anonymous benefactor. That same benefactor had given £32,500 to the USA tour but even that had still made a slight loss. The orchestra's reserves were now completely exhausted, and emergency action was required. A policy of survival for one year was devised, Bank and Trust loans were secured; even so, McDonald found himself at one stage covering a week's salaries for the players out of his own pocket. The New Philharmonia faced bankruptcy unless a miracle occurred.

11. *Recovery: Muti and Stoutzker, 1972-4*

During the Maazel discussions, McDonald had laid down his principles for a new conductor: he must be acceptable to the recording companies, acceptable to the public, musically acceptable to the orchestra and financially viable. Other conductors needed to be chosen to supplement the work and style of the main conductor, and with an eye to other recording companies. If these plans were successful, general acclaim would follow, including hired engagements, tours and commercial work. But above all, the orchestra must have a consistent, high standard and the willingness to work.

The short-list of possible conductors drawn up included four with whom the orchestra were not yet familiar and of whom they awaited first-hand experience – Sanderling, Masur, Muti and Levine. Of the British conductors, Andrew Davis seemed to be the most promising. He was young and could be suitable for an associate position. Opportunities would come during the coming months to consider many of the names on the list both in concerts and in recordings.

Towards the end of April 1972, Gerry McDonald had two separate invitations to consider long-term policy. The new Chairman of the Arts Council wanted a general discussion on the possibilities open to the major orchestras on the London scene and EMI wanted to discuss future plans as the New Philharmonia's current recording contract expired in July. During the last week of April, McDonald also met Walter Legge on a rare visit to London, and over lunch they discussed conductors. Legge proved most sympathetic, especially over the cost of Maazel, and made some recommendations of his own. They included David Oistrakh and a young Rumanian, Erich Bergel, but he had also seen a young Italian in Salzburg the previous summer, conducting *Don Pasquale*. His name was Riccardo Muti: Legge counted him the potentially the best Italian conductor since de Sabata and Serafin, and he had been recommended to Legge by Karajan. 'He is the conductor for you,' suggested Legge.

The EMI meeting took place on 1 May, and Peter Andry immediately revived the idea of a merger. The combination of the New Philharmonia and another London orchestra would form a new super-orchestra on the lines of the Berlin Philharmonic, using the best players from both orchestras. EMI favoured Barenboim as Musical Director as he was young and financially a good proposition for recording; Giulini and Karajan would be invited as outstanding guest conductors, Mehta, Haitink and Solti would also be invited to join the team. The orchestra would give sixty-five Festival Hall concerts per year and be assured of long-term recording prospects with a hundred sessions per year with EMI alone. Other plans included foreign tours, rehearsal premises of their own and a two-tier system of control, leaving considerable autonomy with the players but with the top Board accepting full responsibility for overall policy, finance, guaranteed continuity for an initial minimum period of five years, redundancy compensation and so on. It was all very ambitious and seems to have been based very much on enthusiastic optimism.

At this stage the discussions were very secret, even from the orchestra's Council. Only Ronald Grierson of the New Philharmonia Trust was involved, and McDonald confided his reservations about the scheme to him. They agreed that for recordings Klemperer and Maazel were not of real use to the New Philharmonia, Giulini had too small a repertoire, and young men like Muti and Andrew Davis would need time to build up a recording basis. EMI were at the time spending a substantial proportion of their budget on recording the Berlin Philharmonic with Karajan; they were interested in Barenboim, but he had designs on the Berlin Philharmonic himself. A merger on the lines proposed by EMI would have to be carefully costed, and even then there was no real hope of substantial financial backing. The orchestra to be merged with the New Philharmonia seemed most likely to be the London Philharmonic. The Royal Philharmonic had pursued its policy of diversification initiated two years earlier.

McDonald therefore got together with Eric Bravington (London Philharmonic), John Cruft (Arts Council) and Peter Andry to take the proposal a step further. The size of the proposed new orchestra would be 112 players, and Eric Bravington undertook to draw up a specimen budget. The choice of conductors in the second tier seemed well balanced, with Haitink and Solti on the London Philharmonic side and Giulini and Mehta with the New Philharmonia. There were problems: the new orchestra needed a name, and there was the New Philharmonia Chorus to be considered. John Morton of the Musicians' Union said that his chief concern was the provision to be made for redundant players and the opportunities for freelance players; otherwise he favoured the scheme. A further meeting was planned for September to consider the specimen budget and compare any further ideas.

EMI were so sure of the success of the merger scheme that they completed an agreement with the Camden Symphony Orchestra over its use of the name 'Philharmonia'. Signed on 9 June 1972, it gave Ling Tung permission to use the name 'Philharmonia' only for live concerts in the USA. Elsewhere a geographical designation would be necessary. EMI's freedom to sell recordings made by the original 'Philharmonia Orchestra' was safeguarded but on condition that EMI did not make use of the name 'Philharmonia' in future for the promotion of live concerts or the making of records. At the time this seemed safe enough. The New Philharmonia's present contract expired in July, and future recordings would be by letter agreement or as part of the new consortium, under a new name. The New Philharmonia were aware of the agreement with Camden over its geographical usage but they were not aware of the implications of EMI's recording limitation on the name 'Philharmonia'.

Giulini liked the consortium idea. When he conducted the New Philharmonia at the City of London Festival for two performances of Bach's B minor Mass, on 10 and 11 July, he talked with McDonald on the subject. He shared the view that radical changes were needed. The orchestra was playing well but was sloppy at rehearsals and lacked the spirit to put it back in the class of Berlin, for example, or Amsterdam or Chicago. He wanted no title himself with any London orchestra but would continue to work with the New Philharmonia exclusively, if they showed willing. It must be said that the orchestra did not need Giulini that much, but his views expressed to those in power in recording companies, festivals etc. would be vital to the orchestra's prospects.

Andrew Davis had conducted one of the planned Klemperer concerts on 4 June and strengthened his reputation as a possible regular conductor. His meteoric career dated from November 1970 when, newly appointed as assistant conductor of the BBC Scottish Symphony Orchestra, he had taken over from an indisposed Eliahu Inbal to conduct a performance of Janáček's *Glagolithic Mass*. He now had established a strong rapport with the New Philharmonia.

When, in August, Mehta recorded a complete *Tosca* with the orchestra, for RCA, McDonald took the chance to sound him out on the idea of a more permanent association with them, but Mehta felt that with his commitments to Los Angeles and Israel he could not give sufficient time to the New Philharmonia to warrant the title Principal Conductor until at least 1976. The merger scheme was discussed, and Mehta said he liked the New Philharmonia and would continue to work with them in London whatever happened. He added that, in his opinion, the London Philharmonic was not as good as the New Philharmonia.

Before the end of August Klemperer postponed his *Seraglio* recording yet again. It had been rescheduled for September and October 1972: now it was moved to January and February 1973. Klemperer added, in his letter to EMI, that he had lost a lot of feeling for the New

Philharmonia over their treatment of Gareth Morris and he felt that Walter Legge's assessment of the orchestra's future in 1963–4 had probably been correct; there had been a steady artistic decline since 1965–6.

The New Philharmonia now had a new leader. Hurwitz had left in December 1971, and since then various guest leaders had filled the gap until, in February 1972, Desmond Bradley took up his appointment. Bradley was no stranger to the orchestra, having been sub-leader to Hugh Bean before leaving the New Philharmonia in 1967 to go freelance. Like Hurwitz, he had a wide experience to bring to the leadership of the orchestra. He was a versatile musician, combining composition with his playing, and his own Violin Concerto was already scheduled for a Festival Hall performance in the 1973–4 season.

Plans for the approaching 1972–3 season included Mehta, who was booked for several concerts, as well as Kurt Masur, who had also promised his support to McDonald in the orchestra's future plans. Two guest appearances included Maxim Shostakovich on 20 November to conduct the British première of his father's Symphony No. 15, and Stokowski in the New Year to conduct and record some Beethoven and Rimsky-Korsakov. Both were expensive ventures, and extra rehearsals for the Shostakovich would be useful but costly. McDonald therefore followed up a suggestion from Council Chairman Lawrie Lea that he write to Ian Stoutzker, joint managing director of Keyser Ullmann, a prominent firm of City bankers. Lea had heard, quite by chance, that Stoutzker would be interested in some publicity for his company through programme advertising. McDonald was invited to meet Stoutzker on 8 September and asked him if he would consider a grant of up to £1,000 to cover extra rehearsals for the Shostakovich première, or towards the Stokowski concert. Stoutzker agreed to the extra rehearsals and then dropped a bombshell in McDonald's lap: as a close friend of Barenboim and his circle of friends (Zuckerman, Perlman etc), Stoutzker knew all about the proposed orchestral merger. Moreover, he not only would be interested in backing the project financially but would like to buy an orchestra outright.

McDonald discussed the idea with Stoutzker at length and learned a good deal about him. As well as being a top City banker, Stoutzker had played the violin, was a Fellow of the Royal Academy of Music and was a competent enough player to enjoy quartets with the Barenboim set, with whom he was extremely friendly. He knew the London orchestral scene intimately and had been on the Board of the Royal Philharmonic Orchestra briefly. He fully realized that the purchase of an orchestra meant anything from £2 million; money was clearly not a problem. He believed that Barenboim was the right choice for a principal conductor, not because he was the greatest conductor but because he was a fine all-round musician who would attract the best young conductors in the world to work with him. Stoutzker made just one condition for his own financial involvement: the orchestra might have its own governing body, but the overall control would be exercised by himself, together with the principal conductors and general manager. McDonald was understandably excited and agreed to send Stoutzker the draft budget and discuss the scheme again with him.

Meanwhile, the orchestra continued to look at the various options that were still open for a new principal conductor. Colin Davis seemed to offer several qualities that were attractive. He wanted to sever his BBC ties completely in the very near future, he could offer three months per year to an orchestra and would be living in London for another six months for his Covent Garden work. He was also the only British conductor always asked for by the big international festivals and other similar hirers. The New Philharmonia's Council had reservations about his relations with players and his limitations as a conductor but were willing to give him serious consideration.

McDonald had met Muti in Lucerne and invited him to conduct two concerts in December. He also discussed the idea of a permanent appointment with Ozawa, who wanted to work with the New Philharmonia and agreed to give them exclusive preference in London. However, with San Francisco, Boston and La Scala, Covent Garden, Berlin and Japan, he could not consider a major appointment.

The budget for the proposed super-orchestra was now ready, and on 10 October McDonald went with Lawrie Lea to EMI to talk it over. In simple terms the estimated costs prepared by Bravington came to a little under £800,000, of which just under half would be recovered from concert takings and recordings. A subsidy of over £400,000 compared favourably with that given to other orchestras: it represented about fifty-four per cent as compared with the Royal Liverpool Philharmonic's sixty per cent, the Scottish National's sixty-five per cent, Berlin and Amsterdam's eighty to eighty-five per cent. Stoutzker was prepared to meet at least half the subsidy, and both he and Peter Andry agreed on Barenboim as the principal conductor. They saw four conductors in the second tier: Giulini (EMI), Mehta (Decca), Ozawa and Haitink (Philips). The scheme was now ready for formal submission to a meeting of the Chairman of the Arts Council, the Greater London Council, the Trusts of both the London Philharmonic and New Philharmonia orchestras, and EMI; if the scheme was approved and the finance guaranteed in principle, it would be submitted to the members of both orchestras as a package deal.

At this stage discussions on the merger were still very confidential. Only the New Philharmonia Council knew of them, and at a meeting on

12 October they gave McDonald and Lea authority to continue with *discussions*; they were to report back regularly. The Council felt a little uneasy that the whole scheme was too much tied up with Barenboim and was hindering approaches to other conductors. Full agreement was reached on one important step, which was to offer Andrew Davis the position of Association Conductor as from 1 September 1973 for a period of three years. This would take effect whatever the outcome of the merger proposals or principal conductorship but it would not be announced to the public until a new Principal Conductor had been appointed. The Council's unease was not lessened when Mehta at last replied to a formal offer by McDonald; he said he was not happy with a scheme in which he would have to give up Los Angeles for a post with considerably less authority.

The Council seemed to value the independence of the orchestra more than anything else and the whole atmosphere at the time among the players was of cynicism and suspicion. Morale was very low, and with these considerations in mind, on 1 November, the Council told McDonald and Lea that they were not to pursue the merger idea any further.

McDonald turned to Ronald Grierson of the New Philharmonia Trust. The immediate concern was that the orchestra was already running some £6,250 above estimate losses. The orchestra badly needed a new principal conductor but it could not afford a top name; even if it could, the top conductors wanted too much say in the running of the orchestra. There seemed to be four courses of action open: 1) to continue as at present, making ends meet as best can for survival; 2) to appoint Principal and Associate Conductors and develop a policy with extra rehearsals etc. but on present strength, constitution and management; 3) the Stoutzker scheme i.e. an orchestra of ninety but a change of management structure; 4) the super-orchestra, which the Council had now ruled out.

McDonald had discussed these with Lea, too, before the 1 November meeting and already felt that Muti represented their best hope. He was relatively inexperienced but was likely to be quickly in demand for festivals and recording, and he would not want the management control asked for by Mehta and Barenboim, already having his own orchestra in Florence, where he could try out the repertoire for his London concerts. The only other name was James Levine, marginally a better bet as he was better known, but he was tied up for seven months of the year with the Metropolitan Opera in New York.

Stoutzker was still interested in the New Philharmonia, despite the collapse of the merger idea. He realized the immediacy of the orchestra's need when at the 12 November rehearsal in Morley College he heard

Maxim Shostakovich ask the agent Victor Hochhauser, 'Are they professional?' The day before the Shostakovich concert, McDonald and Giulini had discussed future plans. The meeting was not a happy one: when it was confirmed that the merger idea was abandoned, Giulini said that he felt he could no longer work with the New Philharmonia. He had faith in McDonald personally but not in the artistic management of the London orchestral scene generally. He would not work with any other London orchestra during the 1973–4 period either, despite some very persuasive talking by the London Symphony Orchestra, with whom he was recording in November. Everything now seemed to hang on the Muti concerts in December.

Riccardo Muti's programme for his début with the New Philharmonia at Croydon's Fairfield Hall on 2 December 1972 was very conventional – Beethoven's Overture *The Consecration of the House*, Brahms' Piano Concerto No. 2 (with Rafael Orozco) and Mussorgsky's *Pictures at an Exhibition*. For Muti it was just another engagement in a busy calendar that included the Vienna State Opera and the Orchestra de Paris in the New Year. It came as a surprise therefore when at the Croydon dress rehearsal McDonald asked him if he would be interested in accepting the post of Principal Conductor of the New Philharmonia. Of course he was interested, but he needed time to think. The concert gave orchestra and audience something to think about. A packed house in the Fairfield Hall produced an air of anticipation at the prospect of meeting the thirty-one-year-old Italian. They found him confident and energetic, able to communicate those qualities to the players. The performance showed he possessed an ear for sonority and detail and an innate musical intelligence. Above all, even the most carping critic noted that Muti succeeded in rekindling some of the spark from the players that had lain rather dormant recently.

On 8 December McDonald wrote to Muti making him a formal offer, and next day he went to see Stoutzker to discuss the matter. Stoutzker was still willing to sponsor an orchestra of ninety, preferably with Barenboim in control, but he could be open to alternative suggestions, including Muti.

While these discussions were in progress, Klemperer severed his last links with the New Philharmonia by writing to Peter Andry in December cancelling the *Il Seraglio* recording completely, on the grounds of ill-health, and to the orchestra asking that his name be removed from New Philharmonia notepaper and other publications. It was rather bad timing for EMI, who had to pay the orchestra considerable compensation for the lost sessions.

The last word on the whole Principal Conductor issue came from a source hitherto neglected. The orchestra's anonymous benefactor pressed for a decisive policy to be adopted as soon as possible, with a preference for Muti, or Mehta or Ozawa, rather than for Barenboim, unless as part of a team. The benefactor also felt that the Stoutzker offer should be accepted at least for a trial period of two years and that it would bring much needed financial expertise and influence into the orchestra in addition to the money. Unless something positive was done, the orchestra was in real danger of losing its valuable lifeline; on the other hand, the benefactor might be prepared to share with Stoutzker some of the money put up as guarantees. On 9 February the Council agreed on Muti.

The first days of February 1973 saw Muti conducting *Aïda* at the Vienna State Opera. In the audience was Gerry McDonald, in Vienna to make the final arrangements for Muti to accept the Principal Conductorship of the New Philharmonia. Later, at a meeting, McDonald persuaded Muti to accept the New Philharmonia, though he achieved this only after convincing Muti that it was the wish of the Council of the orchestra – that is, of the players – and not just that of the administrative staff.

Back in Britain, McDonald drew up the final details with Stoutzker and set about informing the orchestra of the proposals, in a letter dated 14 February 1973. After the orchestral rehearsal on Monday 19 February they had a chance to question McDonald about the proposals, and then after the Festival Hall rehearsal on Tuesday 20 February they were introduced to Ian Stoutzker.

The orchestra's backing was needed for a constitutional consideration. Stoutzker was offering to underwrite the general income and expenditure account of the orchestra for the two seasons 1973–4 and 1974–5, on the understanding that the anonymous benefactor continued support as before. Muti's appointment was designed to raise artistic standards, and Stoutzker promised a maximum of £40,000 per annum to give the orchestra the freedom to allow that to happen. Stoutzker felt that he could only be of the best use if he took an active part in the top management of the orchestra's affairs, as Chairman of the Council. The proposal was that from 1 April 1973 he would be appointed an Ordinary Member of the orchestra under Article 5B of the Constitution and then be elected Chairman of the Council. The seven elected Council members would still give the orchestra an absolute voting majority. Stoutzker was buying control of the New Philharmonia but in return was safeguarding the continued independence and rights of its members.

The orchestra agreed: it really had no alternative. Two or three of the players were utterly opposed to the idea of giving Stoutzker a central position. He was no fool and would be in a position to influence every aspect of the orchestra's activity. Having made their reservations, however, they bowed to the wishes of the majority of the players. At the Council meeting on 6 March, Lawrie Lea and Ronald Waller resigned as Chairman and Vice-Chairman as from 1 April; Stoutzker was elected Chairman, and Lea returned as Vice-Chairman. Stoutzker was also later appointed to the Trust in June.

However, Stoutzker soon found it difficult to attend every Council meeting, with the result that a new post was created, that of Deputy Chairman. In December 1973 Basil ('Nick') Tschaikov was elected to it – a man of long experience of such committees, through his work with the Musicians' Union. This election gave the players a representative whom they could trust. Most of them respected Stoutzker's money but not his artistic judgement – wrongly in Tschaikov's opinion. He did respect Stoutzker and had the unenviable task of persuading the players to recapture their faith in the democracy of which they were a part. The real power of a self-governing orchestra lies with the players themselves. In a company limited by guarantee they are the equivalent of shareholders. If they did not like the Council (the directors), they could call an Extraordinary Meeting and remove the Council.

What made Muti take on the New Philharmonia, where morale, technique and money were all at a low ebb? One of his first observations was that there was a potential that still lingered in the orchestra. The traditions of Karajan and Klemperer gave it a history and a culture that were exciting; to follow Klemperer would be a heavy responsibility. The Germanic sound and response that was an integral part of their playing could be built upon – Muti did not want to destroy the past, especially what was good in it. With an impeccable musical pedigree and already a considerable reputation, he offered high hopes for the artistic future of the New Philharmonia.

The biggest hope lay in his recording work. At the time only the London Symphony Orchestra recorded extensively with its Principal Conductor, André Previn, who had an exclusive contract with EMI and also with BBC Television. With the retirement of Klemperer, the New Philharmonia's work for EMI almost disappeared overnight. Muti's negotiations with EMI were well under way in the first months of 1973 and offered real progress in that direction.

On 6 July 1973 Otto Klemperer died, quietly in his sleep. The great giant had finally succumbed, losing a battle he had fought with such courage and determination for nearly forty years. From a brain tumour in 1939 to a second major hip fracture at the age of eighty-one, he had overcome the severest physical hardships to reign supreme as a great conductor of his time. Opera, twentieth-century music and, in his later years, the three Bs – Bach, Beethoven and Brahms: all had received his devoted and humble application of an intellect that was all-embracing in its simplicity and its genius. Almost to the last he never forgot the debts he owed to his many friends, among them Walter Legge who had given him a London audience and a supreme London orchestra, both of which loved and worshipped him with equal fervour.

On 29 August the 1973–4 season's plans for the orchestra were given at a press conference in the Festival Hall's Hungerford Room. Although it would be a while before the effects of a new conductor and financial security became apparent, there were already signs of renewed confidence in the orchestra. The five hundred working sessions booked for the year were a bigger total than any continental orchestra's, and about as many as an orchestra should undertake. Muti's appointment did not take effect until 1974 officially, but he had rearranged his programmes so that he could conduct four concerts this season. The 14 June 1974 concert would be repeated no fewer than three times in Milan, a daring move. The New Philharmonia Trust had commissioned two new works from English composers, one from Peter Maxwell Davies and Malcolm Arnold's Seventh Symphony, both to be given first performances by the New Philharmonia. Britten's sixtieth birthday would be marked by a special concert in November, and there were plans for a Klemperer memorial concert in January 1974. More immediately, Muti and Mehta were to conduct the New Philharmonia at the 1973 Edinburgh Festival.

There were obvious interests in the Muti concerts at this stage from audience and orchestra alike. Muti admits even now that he could be too demanding on players and that the New Philharmonia found him a hard disciplinarian and somewhat more distant than they were used to. Some even dubbed him 'the last disciplinarian': Muti does not like the word but he does believe that, with the hectic pace of British music-making, rehearsals have to be work in order to make music at all. He had been told that the New Philharmonia players read books and newspapers at rehearsals, that they even smoked, and that this was common among all the London orchestras. He could not believe this until he saw it happening for himself. At one Edinburgh rehearsal he noticed a woodwind player smoking. He glared – 'the death ray' as it came to be known – and the cigarette disappeared behind the player's back, the tell-tale smoke still drifting apparently out of the top of the player's head. Muti stopped and smiled. 'Please?' he asked, 'I do not understand the message you are trying to send.' The orchestra joined in the laughter, but the point had been well and truly made; no one smoked at Muti's rehearsals again.

The reactions to his choice of programmes was cool. The 1973 Edinburgh theme was French, and as Cherubini was an Italian and Franck a Belgian, both of whom happened to work in Paris, the choice of their respective *Requiem* (with the Edinburgh Festival Chorus) and Symphony in D minor seemed an attractive idea. The Usher Hall was not full, but reservations over the programme were outweighed by a definite realization of Muti's promising rapport with the orchestra. His second concert opened with Berlioz's *Waverley* Overture and showed up the work needing to be done on the orchestra's strings to give them a more polished and unified style, something Muti already had high on his list of priorities.

His recording contract with EMI had taken effect from 1 September 1973, although it was not signed until January 1974. The first work to be recorded was the Cherubini *Requiem* which he had conducted in Edinburgh. It was recorded just two weeks later, with the Ambrosian Singers. When producer John Mordler told Muti he had just one rehearsal with the chorus, Muti retorted 'You're crazy!' and demanded more. He got more, and the singers were delighted at a man who knew what he wanted and had such an ear for the right sound.

On 21 November Wilhelm Pitz died at his Aachen home. The 'father' of the New Philharmonia Chorus, he had been a father figure to the New Philharmonia Orchestra, too. He laid the foundations of a chorus that could still challenge the best in Europe. From the shattering Beethoven Ninth Symphony under Klemperer in 1957 until his reluctant retirement in 1971, his strict discipline and wise use of rehearsal time were the secrets of his success in London, as they were in Bayreuth. His creation of the 'Philharmonia sound' matched that of the parent orchestra, and his retirement had marked the end of an era. Now the mantle rested on Walter Hagen-Groll's shoulders to maintain the New Philharmonia Chorus as a permanent memorial to the man who had created it.

A Verdi concert on 12 February 1974 marked the Tenth Anniversary of the New Philharmonia Orchestra and Chorus, and the Trust saw a new goal on which to set its sights, to provide the orchestra and chorus with a rehearsal hall and recording studio of its own. On the night, Muti showed himself a superb Verdi conductor, controlling and judging each section impeccably. This was his first London concert as Principal Conductor of the New Philharmonia.

The financial benefits of such a gala night were excellent but within a month it had been eclipsed by a financial disaster which no one could have predicted and which could scarcely have been prevented. The New Philharmonia Orchestra and Chorus were booked for a tour of Lisbon and Oporto with Maazel from 26 February to 5 March. Previous visits to Portugal had been at the invitation of the Gulbenkian Foundation; on this occasion the invitation came from Sergio Varella-Cid, a pianist who had performed with the orchestra in the early 1960s and who had now booked the orchestra and chorus for five concerts. Part of the orchestra's fees, as agreed, was paid in advance, and they were told that the balance would be made out by banker's draft before the end of the tour. The chorus duly sang Beethoven's *Missa Solemnis* and Verdi's *Requiem* in Lisbon's Coliseu, were paid by Varella-Cid and flew back to Britain. The same day, Varella-Cid apologized that a banker's draft would not be available for the outstanding orchestra fees but said he would instruct his bank to make the necessary cash transfer to the New Philharmonia's bank.

The cash never arrived. A month later a telegram repudiated liability for the debt by virtue of political *force majeure*: on 25 April there had been a revolution in Portugal, and Varella-Cid now claimed that the tour had been financed by the 'pre 25 April Portuguese Government' and that since the *coup* the Ministries involved had denied all liability. The New Philharmonia lost £20,000 on the tour. It was a loss it could ill afford and which would take nearly two years to repay.

Another loss was that of Gerry McDonald, who suddenly, in May 1974, decided not to renew his contract as General Manager at the end of the year, having seen the New Philharmonia through four of its most precarious years, searching relentlessly for the two ingredients it needed for survival – money and a new principal conductor.

However, before retiring he had the satisfaction of seeing Muti achieve his first major triumphs with the New Philharmonia. In the second week of June, Muti felt sure enough to take the orchestra to Milan for three concerts in La Scala. The Scala Opera were in Moscow, and Muti had made his own arrangements for three performances of Mozart Symphony No. 34, Busoni's *Turandot* Suite and Tchaikovsky's Fifth Symphony. They were highly successful and reflected Muti's growing confidence that the orchestra was beginning to sound as he wished. One of his first priorities, after he had achieved the discipline he required, was the refining of the string sound to give the unified style which he regards as the basis for any good orchestra and essential for a world-class one. He took the string section apart and retrained them thoroughly, using such works as the Mozart symphony played in Milan which are a test for any string section. There had also been some sorting out of the desks of strings, the violins in particular, which had upset many players and had not been handled too diplomatically, but seemed to have the required effect on the quality of sound. In fact the recording of *Aïda* in July 1974 represented for Muti a landmark in his 'love-affair' with the New Philharmonia. In his own words: 'They already had a good, big sound – it came from Klemperer. A conductor and his orchestra are rather like two lovers. One gives what the other takes, and vice versa. If the Philharmonia likes you, then change is easy.'

Aïda was recorded in Walthamstow Town Hall, and the scene which perhaps best epitomized the success of the relationship between Muti and the orchestra was the recording of the big Triumphal Scene one hot summer afternoon. The main chorus was on the balcony, the soloists on a specially erected stage beneath the balcony, with the orchestra in front of them, and behind the conductor the chorus of prisoners and the priests. At the other end of the hall was the offstage band, flanked on either side by groups of trumpeters from Kneller Hall. Muti showed complete control of these dispersed masses around him but after the first take, recorded straight through without a break, was horrified that the playback sounded so lifeless. He went back into the hall to do it again in such a fury that his own excitement rubbed off on everyone and it was really thrilling.

In the weeks following McDonald's resignation the Council had looked for a suitable successor as General Manager. What was required was a young, go-ahead administrator with a flair for dealing with finance, perhaps someone from a record company or an artists' agency. Certainly no clear career structure existed for general managers of symphony orchestras.

For some time Ian Stoutzker had tried to interest Jasper Parrott in the job. Parrott ran a thriving agency which included André Previn and Vladimir Ashkenazy on its books, but felt too heavily committed to his artists to change career so radically. He had informal talks with Stoutzker, Nick Tschaikov and finally the New Philharmonia's Council. They were all impressed with his flair for organization, his world-wide contacts and experience, and when broad agreement was reached on policy, financial terms and the dual role as agent and General Manager, they offered him the post on 2 June. McDonald asked for his own term of office to end in July so that Parrott could begin on 1 July.

When Parrott began to work informally at the New Philharmonia offices in mid-June, opposition to the appointment was already in evidence. It came chiefly from two or three concert agents who felt that his appointment might in some way impair the engagement of artists from other managements if he continued as a partner in his own agency. The LSO were also concerned that Parrott would be acting both as agent for their Principal Conductor, André Previn, and as General Manager of the New Philharmonia, and feared that any advantage they received from him at present would soon disappear.

Both objections ignored the power held by the New Philharmonia's Council, not by its General Manager, over the choice of artists. If he engaged an artist who was not acceptable, the Council had the power to prevent him. The Press also made a great deal of mileage out of the affair, especially when on 10 July the New Philharmonia decided to delay Parrott's formal appointment until the whole matter had been fully resolved. Their worry stemmed from the considerable pressure that was being applied to the London Orchestral Concerts Board and the Arts Council by outside interests opposed to Parrott's appointment. The LOCB indicated that it might review its future grants to the orchestra if approval for the appointment had not been given. The right of the LOCB to interfere in such an appointment at all was hotly contested but the New Philharmonia clearly faced the prospect of a full-scale collision with the LOCB and the Arts Council which could only mean the curtailment of funding in the very near future.

By late September Parrott realized that his own position was an impossible one and jeopardized the future of the orchestra. Early in October he formally resigned from the post he had never really held. He had received considerable personal support from Ian Stoutzker, Nick Tschaikov and the whole Council throughout, and the break was a wholly amicable one.

On 16 September there had been an important gala concert to welcome the Russian cellist Rostropovich, and his wife, Galina Vishnevskaya, at the London début of their two-year stay in Britain. Rostropovich was also making his British début as a conductor with the New Philharmonia, an occasion welcomed by a full hall and the glaring lights of the television cameras. His technique was unorthodox but had all the fire of his cello playing – too much fire for the woodwind, perhaps, in a very brisk *Silken Ladder* Overture. Rostropovich played and conducted Haydn's Cello Concerto in C, his wife made a brief appearance with Tatiana's Letter Scene from *Eugene Onegin*, a work Rostropovich had already recorded for EMI Melodiya, and the concert ended with a fine account of Tchaikovsky's Sixth Symphony.

The season proper opened with concerts to celebrate the centenary of the birth of Holst. The opening Fairfield Hall concert, 21 September, actually marked the date, and had his daughter Imogen conducting her father's *Marching Song* to open the concert. Andrew Davis conducted the *Perfect Fool* Suite, and there were also performances of Mozart's G major Flute Concerto, with Jean-Pierre Rampal, and Mahler's First Symphony. Four days later, the Royal Philharmonic Society chose the New Philharmonia, conducted by Sir Charles Groves, to play a whole concert of Holst's music for their celebration of the centenary. The long-neglected double concerto for two violins was a delight, not just for its intrinsic musical merit but that it brought onto the platform two former leaders of the orchestra, Hugh Bean and Manoug Parikian. The *Hymn of Jesus* found the New Philharmonia Chorus below their best but the familiar *Planets* Suite received an outstanding performance.

The winter season was very short on recording work, although some help came from a Denham Studios film recording for *Great Expectations* and BBC Television's production of the *Yeomen of the Guard*. The concerts provided ample interest if not the same financial rewards. For his second season with the New Philharmonia, Muti chose to introduce some new works to the orchestra's repertoire or revive some from the past. Hindemith's *Concert Music for Strings and Brass* and some rare Vivaldi were joined by a concert *Divertimento* fashioned by Stravinsky from *The Fairy Kiss*. It revealed an affinity between Muti and the music of Stravinsky that many felt should be explored further, and the playing of the orchestra encouraged the optimism that had been growing since Muti's appointment. Muti's own confidence in the renewed quality of the orchestra inspired him to play the early Mozart G minor Symphony No. 25.

12. *Young Blood, 1975-7*

There was no longer a question of the orchestra's mere survival, but it needed direction and it needed work. Ian Stoutzker and Keyser Ullmann parted company in July 1975, and although Stoutzker made promises of personal financial support, there were no longer the unlimited funds for extra rehearsal time and the orchestral diary was looking rather bare. The orchestra had a new conducting team, but Muti still had to prove that he could draw a public on a long-term and dynamic basis. It needed something of the popular appeal that the London Symphony Orchestra was attracting under Previn but with the emphasis very much on 'master-concerts' with great artists. Such was the task that faced Gavin Henderson when he became General Manager in May 1975.

Aged only twenty-seven, Henderson had managed his first orchestra while still at school and had founded an Arts Festival at Brighton College to bring together the town's Sixth Formers after the summer examinations were over. By the time he joined the New Philharmonia he had managed theatres, ran the York and Portsmouth Festivals and for several years served on the Arts Council's music panel, opera sub-committee, experimental projects committee and performance art committee. Despite his youth, Gavin Henderson therefore brought a considerable breadth of involvement which was coupled with a firm belief in a national role for the New Philharmonia in the musical life of Britain.

At the helm of a major London orchestra he found a number of pressures and problems from within the New Philharmonia in addition to those ideas he wished to impose on it himself.

Within a week of starting work in the office, Henderson found the orchestra off on a visit to Barcelona for two concerts with Frühbeck in the Palacio della Musica. On their return they began a recording of Elgar's *Dream of Gerontius* with the eighty-seven-year old Boult and the London Philharmonic Chorus. In deference to his age and because of his ability to do only one session per day, producer Christopher Bishop spread Boult's sessions out into July. The results, however, showed no signs of either age or fragmentary recording.

Bishop also recorded Beethoven's *Missa Solemnis* with Giulini in May 1975, and, together with Boult's *Gerontius*, it reflected the attitude of EMI to the New Philharmonia Orchestra and showed something of the role of the New Philharmonia Chorus at this time. There is no doubt that Bishop regarded the London Philharmonic as the prime London recording orchestra at that time. Boult who was President of the LPO, was unable to use it for *Gerontius* as during July it would be taken up with Glyndebourne, so he contented himself with the London Philharmonic Choir and the New Philharmonia Orchestra. Giulini could, and did, use the London Philharmonic Orchestra in May for the Beethoven but preferred to use the New Philharmonia Chorus which frequently worked with other orchestras. There were signs that Giulini might be prepared to return to the New Philharmonia, and Henderson made it his personal mission to try to win him back. Giulini's loyalty to the LPO meant that there would have to be a patient wait and a long period of applying gentle pressure on him.

One of Henderson's principles that he wanted to further through the New Philharmonia was that no orchestra should be dependent on recording for its main income or reputation. In fact, no orchestra could really survive without it to a certain degree, but the ratio was wrong between the Philharmonia's recording sessions and its live concerts. He could not achieve the new balance alone, and so the first task he set himself was to build up a strong team as soon as possible.

The first addition to the staff was Fiona Grant, appointed Assistant General Manager in mid-May. She had excellent credentials: a pianist and cellist she had assisted in the running of recent Edinburgh Festivals and had worked as an artists' agent. Her knowledge of singers filled that gap in Henderson's experience.

The very day Fiona Grant started at the New Philharmonia, 15 May, Muti had pulled out of that night's concert. Orchestral standards were improving but audiences were still poor, and Muti was still not really settled. *Aïda*, recorded the previous summer and issued in February 1975, had seen a marked improvement and established his reputation on disc as a superb interpreter of Verdi. Also in February he had recorded Tchaikovsky's First Symphony which was planned as the first of a complete Tchaikovsky cycle of recordings; there were also plans for a Mendelssohn symphony cycle to begin in the autumn of 1975. In June and July 1975 Muti recorded Verdi's *Masked Ball* and again showed the warmth and precision he had recaptured from the strings and his real sense of the theatre in his handling of the singers.

For the third year running, Andrew Davis conducted the orchestra's Prom performances. Muti was still not totally confident in Davis's position with the orchestra, but Davis himself was not only fulfilling the early promise he had shown but now in May 1975 he demonstrated further progress with an important recording contract with CBS. It was a sign of faith by CBS in the upturn in the New Philharmonia's fortunes that they not only took on Andrew Davis but began to interest themselves in Maazel.

Amid the general rebuilding of the orchestra, the first violins, in particular, had undergone much re-shaping. The so-called 'wedge', the vital second desk of first violins, had been a major issue and was still creating some considerable ill-feeling among those players who were moved back, but it had to be done. Desmond Bradley had resigned from the leadership by letter on 12 March and left in May, just before Henderson arrived. The position now needed someone younger, with some personal flair as well as a fine technique, someone who would be prepared to be firm on decision about seating and auditions.

A new leader was soon apponted to begin work with the orchestra in the autumn of 1975. Carl Pini brought experience of leadership not only of the English Chamber Orchestra but also of the Boyd Neel Orchestra (later the Philomusica) and his own chamber orchestra, the Sinfonia of Sydney. He had the personal flair and style that Stoutzker wanted and the orchestra needed. The Council offered him the job at the end of May and his appointment, and that of the chorus's new chorus-master, Norbert Balatsch, was announced to the Press at a reception on 20 June.

Pini had already in June been approached by Decca about forming an ensemble similar to the Academy of St Martin in the Fields for the purposes of recording. This fell in nicely with a similar idea that Gavin Henderson had proposed on his appointment, and Pini seemed the ideal person to carry it out. In his first months with the orchestra, Pini set about organizing the wind and string principals into just such a group, using the Schubert Octet's instrumentation as a basis. It would be the autumn of 1976 before their first engagement but there was the perpetual problem of accepting engagements a year or more ahead and then finding that the full orchestra was booked on the same day. It was a real pity that the Ensemble, a fine showcase for the orchestra's principals, never really got off the ground for that very reason.

The orchestra also needed new oboe, trumpet and horn principals. The last had been found in Michael Thompson, who was appointed in April 1975, just before Henderson joined. Michael Thompson had been the youngest principal player in the country when at eighteen he had been appointed principal horn to the BBC Scottish Symphony Orchestra. Still not quite twenty, he was very much the 'baby' of the New Philharmonia but as the months went by there was apparent a remarkable talent and a fine section leader.

A new principal oboist started with the orchestra on 1 November;

Gordon Hunt was no stranger to the New Philharmonia, having played with them for the 1971 USA tour with Maazel, his first professional engagement, at the age of twenty-one. Then came six months with the BBC Symphony Orchestra and three years with the BBC Welsh Symphony Orchestra. He was a young player of rare calibre who would provide the lift that the woodwind section needed.

Even before the new principals had time to settle in, the Press soon began to notice that the orchestra's standards were creeping up again. The *Financial Times* commented as soon as October 1975 that, 'Mr Muti and the New Philharmonia Orchestra are providing some of the choicest orchestral playing to be heard in London.'

As part of his policy to create a clear musical and social strategy for the New Philharmonia, Gavin Henderson pursued an involvement between the orchestra and local and regional schemes. There were a number of benefits to be gained from this: 1) it would underpin the financial and public support for the New Philharmonia, whose identity was still rather precarious and ill defined; 2) it would help to broaden the traditionally narrow vision of the orchestral musician; 3) it would spread the opportunity of taking major artists to other venues than the Festival Hall; 4) it would provide a staple body of work to protect the orchestra against the vagaries of the commercial world. This stability, combined with the orchestra's own rehearsal facilities, would help to attract and maintain the greatest international artists.

On 27 November, twenty-three members of the New Philharmonia went to test the acoustics of the newly opened Arts Centre auditorium in the University of Warwick. (The university shared the same anonymous benefactor with the orchestra.) The acoustics were tested with a variety of effects, including gunshots and then there was a concert, directed by Carl Pini, of Copland's *Quiet City*, Bach's D minor Violin and Oboe concerto, the Trumpet Concerto by Richard Mudge, Wagner's *Siegfried Idyll* and Schubert's Fifth Symphony. However, it would be another five years before the complete Warwick scheme would be realized with the addition of a larger concert hall.

More immediately, there were important new developments with the London concerts that November. An excellent Beethoven Ninth Symphony introduced the New Philharmonia to an exciting new conductor, Jesus Lopez-Cobos: not only was he charming and well liked by the orchestra but he had a very promising technique and a clear, firm beat. Conducting without a score, there was no exaggeration, no fuss.

On 20 November a very attractive concert brought together Eduardo Mata and veteran pianist Gina Bachauer in glittering performances of Mahler's First Symphony and Beethoven's Fifth Piano Concerto. Mata also had a very clear beat, the clearest since de Sabata, according to one player in the orchestra, and had enjoyed a week's work with the New Philharmonia recording works by Revueltas for RCA. In fact, Mata had enjoyed the work so much that he immediately set about trying to arrange a tour of Mexico with the New Philharmonia in the immediate future. He had friends in the Mexican Ministry of Education, and through them he managed to get a contract for the tour which was planned for August 1976.

Just before the close of 1975, Muti accepted the offer of the post of Principal Guest Conductor of the Philadelphia Orchestra, thus cementing the growth of a long association. The post was a major step towards succeeding Ormandy there when he eventually stepped down, and Muti liked the conditions in Philadelphia, the challenge of taking an orchestra with an established quality of sound and playing as compared with the New Philharmonia which he was still reshaping.

At this stage one must not underrate the role Maazel played in the reshaping of the New Philharmonia. He had lost much of the 'flash' approach that had dominated his earlier work with them, and the plans for two long spells during the winter of 1975–6 promised a rich continuation of the big Romantic works such as Bruckner's Seventh Symphony and the Brahms *Requiem*, as well as some novelties, notably the British première of Druckmann's *Windows* and Liszt's *Dante* Symphony. Unhappily, Maazel injured himself badly in a fall at his Cleveland home that winter and was ordered by his doctors not to conduct for at least four weeks. This led to some frantic rescheduling of a very tight programme of engagements for the last few days of February 1976.

An important début on 15 February was that of Simon Rattle, the youngest conductor ever to appear with the New Philharmonia. In a Festival Hall performance of Shostakovich's Tenth Symphony, he conducted from memory – something that does not impress every professional player, but when in the middle of the performance Gwydion Brooke came in with a bassoon entry that was mistimed, Rattle took him through it and steered the whole section out of disaster. It was a masterly triumph for the young conductor.

The end of February 1976 proved to be exceptionally hectic. The orchestra and chorus were due to go to Barcelona with Maazel at the beginning of March for performances of Beethoven's *Missa Solemnis* and the Brahms *Requiem*. The same works were to be played a week previously, on 21 February at the Fairfield Hall and on 22 February in the Festival Hall. Lopez-Cobos was available to replace Maazel for these two, performances of Bruckner's Seventh Symphony on 26 and 27 February and the Barcelona tour. There were problems with his agent and it turned out that Cobos could do only the Bruckner concerts.

For the two choral concerts and the Barcelona tour, which were clearly 'tied' together, Fritz Rieger was engaged.

Back home there were preparations for another new venture initiated by Gavin Henderson. The medium of radio for the presentation of music was important on both a local and a national scale, and it was discovered that under the terms of a new agreement between the Musicians' Union and the Independent Broadcasting Authority, a percentage of Capital Radio's advertising revenue had to be spent on live music broadcasting. Peter James, one of Capital's producers, was approached, and it was agreed that the New Philharmonia should launch the scheme. Between them a suitable programme was chosen for the first concert, which was recorded for later broadcast from the Fairfield Hall on 16 March 1976. The concert was conducted by Kurt Masur and included Roger Woodward playing the world première of the Brahms D minor Piano Concerto in the earlier first version before Brahms revised it. Capital found the experiment very encouraging, with numerous telephone calls from those who wanted to know when the concert was to be broadcast and later from satisfied customers saying how much they had enjoyed it. The success of the first broadcast prompted Capital to plan another relay from Croydon, this time with Muti conducting Tchaikovsky and Dvořák on 1 May.

When Henderson joined the New Philharmonia there was already a scheme under discussion for an arts centre based on Chelsea College as part of their building expansion programme. Stoutzker had joined the Council of Chelsea College in August 1974 and had interested himself in the scheme. The funding would be divided equally between Chelsea College itself, Wandsworth Council and the New Philharmonia's Benefactor, if the orchestra were to become involved. The scheme came to nothing as the new hall would not really be adequate for a symphony orchestra, for rehearsal or for recordings, and the local authority interest was unstable. The subject of a permanent home for the orchestra was to reappear in several guises during the next few years. The Henry Wood Hall in Southwark was the kind of venue being sought but linked with the community in a more active way. The Henry Wood Hall, too, was much in demand by the London Symphony and the London Philharmonic Orchestras.

The kind of project that Henderson had in mind became possible at Riverside Studios in Hammersmith. There were opportunities for youth involvement, supported by Hammersmith Council, open rehearsals, a substantial commitment to new music and composer workshops, a permanent rehearsal home and perhaps recording hall, all coupled with popular concerts at the Odeon Cinema. The Benefactor was interested in this, too, but there were problems with acoustics and outside noise which made it useless as a recording venue. London seemed to offer little promise at this time but there were new halls and festivals opening up in the provinces which needed the support of a top London orchestra. If the New Philharmonia could become associated with one or more of these it would give it a much-needed national identity and provide regular work. Riverside would also have made possible direct funding by the Arts Council.

The appointment of a new General Manager had encouraged Malcolm Tibber, long a supporter of the original and New Philharmonia Orchestras, to write in and offer his help in the formation of some kind of supporting club. Henderson's response was enthusiastic, and the Philharmonia Club was launched in July 1976. There was no money in the bank but the Trust helped with the generous offer of a combined grant and loan. A committee was formed, and within a year over four hundred members were to join. Members enjoyed a priority booking facility with a ten per cent reduction on most of the Festival Hall concerts. Rehearsal passes were negotiated as well as a reduction of up to one third off the price of all the orchestra's recordings. Monthly meetings brought speakers both from within the orchestra itself and from the music world generally, and soon there were moves to make arrangements for members to travel with the orchestra on tour, at home and abroad.

In May 1976 the New Philharmonia planned a major tour of Germany and Austria with Muti, their first trip abroad with him since the La Scala concerts in June 1974. Before they left, Muti gave three concerts, the first of which, on 25 April, was the first complete performance in the United Kingdom of Prokofiev's exciting cantata *Ivan the Terrible*, culled from his score for Eisenstein's film. The cast included Irina Arkhipova of the Bolshoi Opera, and Prokofiev's widow came to the concert. *Ivan* was an adventurous undertaking and lost a good deal of money. The Trust underwrote losses up to £4,000, and EMI were persuaded by Muti to plan a recording for 1977 as part of a possible complete series of Prokofiev recordings with Muti and the New Philharmonia.

EMI also undertook a splendid promotional campaign throughout the May tour. The programmes for this were considerably less adventurous – just four works, Mozart Symphony No. 36, Tchaikovsky Symphony No. 5, Beethoven Symphony No. 7 and Britten's *Sea Interludes*. It was a gruelling tour, with thirteen concerts in fifteen days, beginning in Mainz on 12th May and finishing in Berlin on 26 May. It did not get off to an auspicious start when they arrived for the first concert in Mainz to find that the Beethoven symphony was billed instead of the Tchaikovsky that they were expecting to play. There were those who also suggested that playing Mozart in Vienna's Musikverein was dangerous if not impertinent, but the reception from the audiences said otherwise. The Viennese critics applauded the 'silky polish of the strings' and an 'ensemble of virtuosi' which 'exhibited fabulous precision'. *Wiener Zeitung* claimed that, 'With this concert musical life in Vienna reached a remarkable peak.'

Maazel was fit again to return in June for a series of concerts. For some time now, Stoutzker and Henderson had been keen on a closer association between him and the New Philharmonia. With the success of the June concerts and the promise of major recordings, the time was now ripe to act. CBS had also succeeded in securing a three-year recording contract, and so on 9 July it was announced that Maazel had been offered and had accepted the invitation to become Principal Guest Conductor of the New Philharmonia with an exclusive three-year contract.

The CBS connection provided a major boost to the New Philharmonia. They no longer depended so much on EMI, who behaved a little patronizingly towards the orchestra in general and, with regard to Muti in particular, were recording works such as Stravinsky's *Firebird* with the Philadelphia Orchestra. Now Maazel and others were signed up for CBS with the New Philharmonia, EMI became decidedly more interested.

The summer of 1976 was filled with some exciting major recordings, including four complete operas. There was also a new development: a huge video recording project with Unitel, a vast film production and distribution organization, specializing in sales to the German television networks. Puccini's *Tosca*, conducted by Bruno Bartoletti, gave the orchestra nine sessions at very large fees – and it was a significant artistic success too.

The tour of Mexico in August was also a huge success. The Mexican Government had organized everything superbly well and the orchestra received VIP treatment. Soloist was Gina Bachauer in what were to be her last public concerts, for she died only a week after the end of the tour, on 22 August.

Immediately before leaving for the 1976 Edinburgh Festival, Muti conducted a Prom with the orchestra on 4 September. The first half of the concert, Mendelssohn's Fourth Symphony and Mozart's *Sinfonia Concertante*, with Carl Pini and Csaba Erdelyi as soloists, was televised. In the Usher Hall the New Philharmonia were that year in the company of the Leipzig Gewandhaus and the Vienna Philharmonic Orchestras but Muti's 6 September concert, with Weber's Overture *Ruler of the Spirits* and Stravinsky's *Firebird* Suite, brought out an astonishing best from the orchestra. Muti also partnered Radu Lupu in Beethoven's First Piano concerto and forged an artistic partnership that has proved a fruitful and a lasting one.

Next evening Muti conducted Schumann's Fourth Symphony, which he was to record with the New Philharmonia for EMI as soon as they were back in London, and showed ample evidence of thorough preparation and total musicality. Writing of the concerts in the *Glasgow Herald*, Malcolm Rayment commented: 'There was a time when no British orchestra would relish having to follow in the footsteps of the Vienna Philharmonic Orchestra but it is doubtful whether the New Philharmonia Orchestra gave any thought to this. Nor was there any need to do so, for it is decidedly better equipped in the woodwind and brass departments, while even the strings – the glory of the Vienna orchestra – are comparable.' This was vindication indeed for the recruitment of players such as Carl Pini, Gordon Hunt, Michael Thompson and the trumpeter John Wallace, and the influence they had on their sections. (John Wallace had been principal trumpet since August when Muti had approved his appointment after a trial period.)

Still in festival mood, the New Philharmonia helped Capital Radio to celebrate its third birthday on 14 September with a concert in the beautiful Plaisterer's Hall in the City of London. That summer Capital Radio had already widened its interest in classical musical broadcasts by promoting its own concerts before invited audiences. Simon Rattle had conducted a live broadcast from the Henry Wood Hall on 4 July with an appropriately American programme of works by Gershwin, Copland, Ives and Sousa, which the orchestra had enjoyed immensely but for which they had been rather poorly paid. The 14 September celebration included a dinner and a rather more cosmopolitan programme with Alan Civil playing a Mozart Horn Concerto and works by Elgar, Debussy and Haydn.

The Philharmonia Chorus and the New Philharmonia Orchestra joined forces in the third week of September 1976 for two of the three concerts in the Flanders Festival. Andrew Davis conducted an orchestral programme in St Nicklaas in Brussels and then a stunning performance of Mahler's Second Symphony in St Baaf's Cathedral in Ghent. Both concerts drew standing ovations, and the Mahler was hailed by many as the most exciting concert ever given in the nineteen years that the Festival had been in existence. It was also an auspicious start to a proposed complete Mahler cycle with the New Philharmonia in Flanders over the coming years. Elgar's *Dream of Gerontius* on 22 September in St Peter's, Leuven, was the first performance of the work in the Low Countries – appropriately during the sixtieth anniversary year of the Battle of the Somme – and it, too, received a rapturous ovation.

Gavin Henderson had campaigned to change the New Philharmonia's pattern of work for the BBC, taking the opportunity of tackling repertoire that the orchestra could not afford to do in its own promotions and taking it outside the studio. A chance came to combine this with a more formal relationship with the GLC in a joint promotion of four concerts to celebrate the centenary of the birth of the composer Havergal Brian. Henderson received enthusiastic support from Robert Simpson at the BBC, and Ray Few of the GLC was pleased to offer Alexandra Palace as the venue for three of the concerts. The fourth, the Centenary Concert proper, was held in the Royal Albert Hall. The concerts were spread over the period 24 September to 10 October and were conducted by four British conductors – Harry Newstone, Stanley Pope, Vernon Handley and Sir Charles Groves. Many first performances were included, notably of Symphonies 20, 26 and 30, and the *Preludio Tragico*. The Albert Hall concert paired Part 1 only of the vast *Gothic* Symphony (with Brian's blessing) and the Berlioz *Symphonie Funèbre et Triomphale*. Large venues had been essential for the scale of the works being performed, and at times the players outnumbered the audience in Alexandra Palace, but the Albert Hall audience was more encouraging, the equivalent of an eighty per cent house at the Festival Hall in actual numbers. The players had not been over keen but it did represent good income in orchestral fees at quite short notice.

For the 1976 autumn season the public could look forward to Maazel's complete Beethoven cycle in November, the orchestra's first such cycle since the legendary ones with Klemperer. The New Philharmonia Trust was trying to raise £20,000 and aiming to find five sponsors, asking for £4,000 from each. An approach was also going to be made to British American Tobacco in this connection, an interesting contact that would prove significant to the orchestra four years later.

At a September Council meeting, Ian Stoutzker had reported to the members the progress that had been made in trying to regain the 'Philharmonia' title for the orchestra. Since 1974 he had made enquiries through EMI about the possibility of getting the name back and had been authorized by the Council to pursue the Camden Orchestra on the subject. Stoutzker now made the point that the New Philharmonia had an outstanding team of conductors, headed by Muti, some excellent new principals and rank-and-file players, and a sound financial footing, and yet the public still did not come in the way they had in the old days. What was needed, and the players felt this too, was a return to the original name. What only now became apparent, almost by accident, was the fact that, in their 1972 contract with the Camden Symphony Orchestra, EMI had signed away any entitlement to the future use of the name 'Philharmonia'. Ling Tung seemed more than willing to sign a new agreement releasing the use of the name in return for a number of important concerts with the New Philharmonia in London. It seemed a small price to pay, and by September Stoutzker could report that EMI had traced the relevant papers. Ling Tung's contract had been signed on 8 June and was on its way.

Some discussion took place over the best time to revert to the old name. There were three obvious choices. Maazel's coming Beethoven cycle seemed the most appropriate but might cause offence to Muti. There were two further opportunities, with the next publicity brochure (i.e. at the end of January 1977) or at the beginning of the 1977–8 season. The last option was to prove the most convenient, with some modifications, as the final paperwork took some time to complete. It enabled the orchestra to give its first concert under the new title with its Principal Conductor and would also involve Giulini's return to open the 1977 Festival Hall Season.

October 1976 turned out to be an exceptionally busy month for the orchestra with two major new projects in hand. The first came from an invitation to the New Philharmonia to go to Nottinghamshire for a number of days, in residence, to give five concerts with the full orchestra, ensemble performances, master classes, lecture recitals and school visits. As always the obstacle was money. No direct subsidy was available to the orchestras for concerts outside London, and yet it seemed grossly unfair that people should be penalized for living where they did.

The money was found to finance *four* days in October 1976, and the forces were used to the full. On the first evening, wind and string principals combined in a library in Worksop to play a wide range of chamber works; the rest of the strings, conducted by double-bass player John Steer, gave a popular programme in Mansfield and included a *Concertante for Strings* by another member of the orchestra, Ray Premru. The Brass Ensemble made its début in Nottingham and also included a 'home-grown' piece, this time the first performance of Leslie Pearson's breezy march entitled *Trip to Jerusalem*, written as a tribute both to real ale and to the ancient pub hewn out of Nottingham Castle's walls. The next two days were filled with master classes, all over-subscribed, and rehearsals for two concerts. The second of these, conducted by Vernon Handley, was the first major concert to be held in the dome of Kelham Hall, Newark, where seven hundred people gave the New Philharmonia and soloist Henryk Szeryng a rapturous welcome. The Eastern Authorities Orchestral Association together with East Midlands Arts generously supported the whole enterprise with a grant and a guarantee. The orchestra found the project a valuable chance to become really involved with a community, and it was some indication of the public service an orchestra should be able to offer if properly funded. It certainly fired enthusiasm for a repeat visit, and a week in May 1978 was soon set aside.

Just a few days later the orchestra went to Swansea for three concerts in the extraordinary Brangwyn Hall as part of the Swansea Festival. The last of these was what some regarded as a coals-to-Newcastle exercise, taking the New Philharmonia Chorus for a performance of Elgar's *Dream of Gerontius*, conducted by Christopher Seaman. The response was tremendous, and there and then plans were laid for the New Philharmonia to become the 'house orchestra' of the Swansea Festival.

Muti's contract with the New Philharmonia had come up for renewal in August, and the Council had unanimously agreed to proceed with the drawing-up of a new contract as soon as possible. There was a chance to discuss the details with Muti while he was in London in late October for two Festival Hall concerts and a recording of Vivaldi's *Gloria*. This latter caused some stir among critics. Muti used the ample numbers of the New Philharmonia Chorus and gave rise to the comment that it was a 'distinctly backward-looking approach to Vivaldi', the charge being that it was too Romantic. Muti used Malipiero's edition rather than the better known Casella edition made for the Siena Festival just before the War. He probably had the better text; the size of his choral forces reflected his willingness to temper his enthusiasm for textual purity with a wish for a warm, full-blooded sound. Not all the *Gloria* was completed in October and some more sessions were planned for November. On the day of the last of these, 25 November, a press reception was planned at the Royal Overseas League to mark the signing of Muti's new contracts with both the orchestra and EMI. His contract with the New Philharmonia was for three more years and would expire on 1 August 1979.

Maazel's Beethoven cycle began on 2 November in the Festival Hall. It had the help of sponsorship from Guinness and Overseas Containers Limited and the concerts were well received by orchestra and public alike. The comparison with Klemperer was inevitable, but Maazel's cycle stood up exceedingly well. His pianist was Rudolf Serkin, and one of the supreme moments of the whole Festival was Serkin's performance of the Fourth Piano Concerto; the chorus found the performance of the Ninth Symphony highly emotional, too. Maazel worked well with the New Philharmonia Chorus and stayed loyal to them when other conductors were preferring to use professional bodies. He recorded the Brahms *Requiem* with them that November, a project that he had been forced to postpone from earlier in the year through his accident.

At the end of the 1976 Ian Stoutzker's first term as Chairman of the New Philharmonia expired. The Council decided not to renew the agreement: much as they and all the orchestra had valued his financial support and business acumen, there was a growing feeling that they no longer had effective independent control over their own affairs. Stoutzker had time to be in the office and to involve himself in matters that they felt were not his business. He also referred to the Philharmonia as 'my orchestra', which the players resented as unjustifiably possessive.

Many wanted to be rid of him completely but, as Nick Tschaikov pointed out, it would be very wrong to throw out the man who had given so much in time and money to them. Tschaikov proposed offering him the Presidency of the orchestra, a title that Klemperer had once held. This was a different situation; it would enable Stoutzker to retain an *ex-officio* place on the Council but prevent him from being involved too directly in the running of the orchestra. It would make Gavin Henderson's position easier as it was a constant difficulty balancing Stoutzker's executive role with the independent thinking of the players.

The offer of the Presidency to Stoutzker created a good deal of tension at first. He suspected Henderson as being the agent for his total removal as Henderson had stated that he would not continue if the executive role of the Chairman were to be maintained. Stoutzker's reaction was to see Muti, Maazel and the anonymous benefactor's representative in turn, and try to persuade them all to withdraw their support from the orchestra. Tschaikov and Henderson had already seen all three to consult them over the original decision; Tschaikov had to now go round all three again and persuade them of the orchestra's honesty and integrity. After much talking the matter was smoothed over, and on 4 December 1976 Tschaikov was elected Chairman of the Council and Stoutzker took up his new title of President.

The last major musical venture of 1976 was an extension of the idea started in Nottinghamshire. With the support of the Musicians' Union, a pilot scheme for involving young musicians was devised to link up with a concert in Chatham. On 27 November seven of the orchestra's principals initiated an experimental 'workshop' for a unique talk-in, teach-in, play-in with the Medway Youth Orchestra, which comprised about 150 youngsters of a wide range of abilities and ages. By the end of the day two large groups – a symphony orchestra under Carl Pini and a wind band under Nick Tschaikov – produced very creditable performances of such pieces as Berlioz's *March to the Scaffold*, Haydn's *Clock* Symphony and a Mozart Flute Concerto. Then in the evening a large party from the Medway Youth Orchestra attended the New Philharmonia's concert in Chatham's Central Hall, conducted by Maazel.

Concerts in Swansea and Aberystwyth in January 1977 marked the first concert appearance of the pianist Vladimir Ashkenazy as a conductor of the New Philharmonia. 'The orchestra has always been my passion,' he stated, soon after his Welsh début. 'I always wanted to be a conductor. It's just that I played the piano.' Ashkenazy praised the indulgence of the New Philharmonia to his conducting. 'They are very friendly and help me a great deal.' He also relished the full and warm sound of the New Philharmonia strings: 'In the intense, lush passages of

Tchaikovsky they are so good you don't need to do anything, don't need to ask anything from them.'

The New Philharmonia visited Israel for a week in March 1977, at the invitation to the Israel Philharmonic Orchestra, with Frühbeck as conductor.

The first concert was in the Frederick Mann Auditorium in Tel Aviv and was followed by a reception given by the Israel Philharmonic in the Artists' House. Frühbeck had chosen works that were easily understood, Falla's *Amor Brujo* and Dvořák's Eighth Symphony framing the Britten *Serenade*, a novelty to Israeli audiences.

The British Council gave a reception after the Jerusalem concert, attended by the President, and at once began to apologize for the general lack of publicity and some unfilled halls on the tour. The Jerusalem concert had been packed, but there was no sign of the box-office receipts; it was claimed that there was no surplus. True, blocks of tickets had been bought by the Israel Arts Council for offer to students, the Army etc, at reduced prices, but the hall had not been full of students and soldiers. The players were sun-tanned and happy but the tour had made a large loss. Nevertheless, Israel has produced so many fine musicians who have nourished London's musical life that it was good to be able to do something in return. The New Philharmonia Orchestra was the first British symphony orchestra to do so for ten years.

At the 1977 Barcelona visit, Gavin Henderson was able to make more progress in his attempts to woo back Giulini to the New Philharmonia. The President of the Patronato Pro Musica, Don Luis Portabella Rafols, pointed out that the Festival had never had a performance of Beethoven's Ninth, and Henderson at once suggested Giulini. He was already booked to conduct the orchestra again in the autumn of 1977 to coincide with the reversion to the original 'Philharmonia' title. Henderson took a chance and rang Chicago and caught Giulini only minutes before he was due to go on to conduct. A quick look at his diary and he happily agreed to conduct in Barcelona in 1978.

Despite the losses on the Israel tour the financial year 1976–7 ended with a surplus of £56,000. By March 1977, too, the final contractual details had been settled over the agreement between the orchestra, EMI and Ling Tung over the change of name. In a contract dated 16 February 1977 the New Philharmonia now had the right to use the name 'Philharmonia Orchestra' for concerts and live recordings; EMI were released from the restrictions of the June 1972 agreement, and the Camden Symphony Orchestra agreed to use the name 'Philharmonia Orchestra' for live concerts only with a geographical designation. In return, the New Philharmonia agreed to offer Ling Tung concerts with them at the Festival Hall once a season for three successive seasons, beginning on 10 April 1977.

The effect of this change was twofold. All appearances of the orchestra on or after 1 September 1977 would be billed as 'Philharmonia Orchestra', omitting the prefix 'New', and all recordings made on or after 17 February 1977 which would be released on or after 1 September 1977 would also be billed as by 'Philharmonia Orchestra'. The same situation applied in each case to the Chorus, which would also drop the 'New' from its title. The second point is that the change was over the use of 'Philharmonia Orchestra' as a business name and its subsequent registration. The company would have to remain 'New Philharmonia Limited' for the moment, as 'Philharmonia Limited' was still owned by EMI; they agreed to seek the registration of another name in due course.

The resumption of the old name was also a suitable time to launch one of Fiona Grant's schemes, the production of the first Orchestra Year Book, a combination of information and interest, lavishly illustrated – another useful vehicle for bringing the quality now associated with 'Philharmonia' before the public. The Year Books have continued ever since with high consistency of quality.

13. *Name and Fame Regained, 1977-9*

The artistic balance sheet looked even rosier than that at the bank. The orchestra had in the year ended March 1977 obtained its highest critical acclaim for many years. The reviews could be summed up in a report by Alan Blyth in *The Times*, who said: 'The New Philharmonia at the peak of its form provided my most enjoyable occasion at the Festival Hall all season, and I do not exclude distinguished visitors from Vienna and Berlin.'

Nevertheless, the financial success was still one to be savoured. On the subject of foreign tours, Gavin Henderson made the point in a programme note in May 1977 that while public subsidy for the arts was being slowly strangled in Britain, those who held the public purse-strings might care to ponder that the New Philharmonia actually generated more money into the economy than it took out in subsidy. Like any successful business, the orchestra needed investment to keep ahead in an international market, and if foreign tours ceased, Britain would be the poorer not just artistically but also financially. The New Philharmonia were just about to leave for a week at the Lausanne International Festival to give three concerts in six days. The first concert there was to bring an invitation to return on an annual basis but at a fee no greater than that charged by one of the major European orchestras. Henderson was making the point that foreign orchestras were heavily subsidized for touring abroad whereas the New Philharmonia had to charge considerably more for a foreign engagement than, say, the Berlin Philharmonic or the Orchèstre de Paris. The fee varied, too, according to the number of players required, the number of extra rehearsals needed and the nature of the programme performed. The invitation to Lausanne had come from Pedro Kranz of the Caecilia agency in Geneva. The opening concert on 7 May marked the début with the orchestra of the young Swiss conductor Charles Dutoit. He accompanied Nathan Milstein in the Mendelssohn Violin Concerto very competently with a very fluid style and established an excellent rapport with the orchestra in Stravinsky's *Petrushka*. The Palais de Beaulieu was packed, as it was two days later for the return of the veteran Yugoslavian Lovro von

Matačić. Now seventy-eight years old Matačić conducted a splendid *Eroica* Symphony.

Muti continued his Tchaikovsky cycle in June by performing and recording the Third Symphony. In an interview at the time, he spoke of his recording work, notably the complete series of Tchaikovsky, Schumann and Mendelssohn symphonies, all with every repeat and no tampering with the score. He spoke too of the New Philharmonia: 'It's wonderful – there's a fabulous atmosphere of work and they're playing very well at the moment.' Muti spoke too of Philadelphia, where Ormandy and the orchestra were keen to cement his ties still further by naming him co-conductor, but this was a decision he wanted time to consider. The attraction of the Philadelphia Orchestra itself ('the best strings in America, I think') and the chance, with a subscription audience, to programme more adventurously, was a strong temptation. To allay anxiety over his future with the New Philharmonia, he said: 'There's the New Philharmonia and the whole European tradition – a warmth and spontaneity which the more virtuosic American orchestras can't quite manage.'

Before the end of July 1977 and the Proms, Muti recorded Prokofiev's *Ivan the Terrible* for EMI. In a coupling that linked it with Prokofiev's *Sinfonietta*, it proved a useful addition to the catalogue as neither work was available on record. Muti's Prom, on 29 July, rounded off a packed schedule for him in London. He had conducted six performances of *Aïda* at Covent Garden on top of the *Nabucco* and *Ivan* recordings; his way of working with opera meant his being present from the very beginning in the theatre with producer, singers, orchestra and technicians. He also liked to take the first piano rehearsals with the singers, too. His Prom concert included Mozart's *Paris* Symphony and Shostakovich's Fifth Symphony.

That same month the first details were sent out to announce the orchestra's Corporate Membership scheme. Fiona Grant had found that there had been repeated requests from companies for regular seats at the Philharmonia's Festival Hall concerts. For quite a small outlay, companies could enjoy priority bookings of seats for their own use and to use as hospitality for clients. It also gained them wide advertising in the programmes, and there were other benefits, such as discounts on recordings, rehearsal passes and affiliation to the Philharmonia Club.

The 1977 Edinburgh Festival concerts – three – were all with Giulini, and the reunion was an emotional one. The orchestra had great respect and affection for him, as he did for them, although he confessed that he recognized only about a dozen faces from his last appearance with them. The Edinburgh concerts on 22 and 23 August were all-Mozart; the *Linz* Symphony and the *Requiem*, while 25 August had just one work,

Bruckner's Eighth Symphony.

The first London concert under the new name was an Albert Hall programme conducted by Muti and featuring Sviatoslav Richter in Beethoven's Third Piano Concerto. Richter and Muti followed the concert with a recording of the work for EMI. It was Muti's first recording of a piano concerto, and it was particularly appropriate that it should be with Richter. As Muti said: 'Richter has been with me on all the big occasions of my musical life, like my first concert in Salzburg in 1971.'

The Philharmonia had regular connections with the Flanders Festival and for the twentieth year of the Festival two performances of Mahler's Eighth Symphony were booked for 25 and 26 September, conducted by Frühbeck. This huge work involved the Philharmonia Chorus, the Choir of the Düsseldorf Musikverein and the Schola Cantorum Cantante Domino. A very complicated rehearsal schedule had been carefully worked out. What made it still more complicated was that Frühbeck fell ill: the only available replacement was Michael Tilson Thomas.

At the Brussels performances, in the Palais des Beaux Arts, there were immediate staging problems. The platform was too small, and a very shaky large extension had been built out. In St Baaf's Cathedral in Ghent the space was perfect, and a suitable touch of drama was added by the soprano Arleen Auger insisting on singing the 'Mater Gloriosa' from the top of the choir screen, some forty feet above the ground. What she had not anticipated was that daylight would finally fade just as she reached the poignant solo and that she would have to sing it surrounded by bats which had awoken from their perches high in the roof and begun to flap around her. Some comic relief also came from Hugo Dalton, who insisted on waiting for his mandolin cue before walking solemnly onto the stage while the performance was in progress.

It had been the twentieth year of the Flanders Festival, and appropriately it was also the twentieth anniversary of the Philharmonia Chorus. Many of them had signed a note to the orchestra for the Beethoven Ninth performances with Giulini. The Philharmonia Trust planned the 2 October concert in the Festival Hall as a gala to celebrate both the Chorus anniversary and the restoration of the old titles. The programme also included Mozart's *Sinfonia Concertante* for Wind which highlighted four of the orchestra's wind principals.

The concert raised £7,000 for the Trust and the promise of two or three more donations of £1,000. The reunion with Giulini was a happy one and a further step towards a more permanent association again. Gavin Henderson got on very well with Giulini and little by little was countering the pressure put on Giulini to stay with the London Philharmonic Orchestra by their manager Eric Bravington. Giulini was too much the gentleman to make an abrupt break with the London Philharmonic, but he was obviously impressed with the progress that had been made in rebuilding the Philharmonia since 1972. He accepted a proposal by Henderson that he give an extra concert, on 1 October, in the Fairfield Hall. Giulini's allegiances to Chicago and Los Angeles were still very strong, and he had the 1978 Edinburgh Festival already booked with the London Philharmonic Orchestra. He would wait and see how the orchestra continued to shape up before making a firm commitment. Meanwhile, he accepted a proposal to record Britten's *Les Illuminations* with the Philharmonia as a coupling for a Britten *Serenade* recording in Chicago.

At a Trust meeting early in November, Gavin Henderson reported that for the last few months the Philharmonia had been the only orchestra in London with a stable principal conductor. The orchestra was busy and successful, and for the first time for several years there were almost no vacancies; the only dissatisfaction lay in the viola section, where a change of principal seemed necessary, and this was under discussion. Muti's contract with the orchestra was to be extended, and they would soon be discussing new links with Mehta and Ozawa. It also seemed likely that the Philharmonia would be the next British orchestra to play at the Salzburg Festival.

Work continued with the regular conductors – Frühbeck, Maazel and Ashkenazy. Frühbeck conducted Haydn's *Creation*, in German, on 13 November and then recorded it with EMI. His gift for choral work and his happy relationship with the Philharmonia made both projects very successful. They were deeply moving performances, a continuing tribute to the flexibility of the Philharmonia Chorus and their chorus-master, Norbert Balatsch, at a time when there had been some concern over the chorus's general standard and suitability for recording and the level of attendance at rehearsals on concert days.

In late January 1978 there was an interesting collaboration with the Italian conductor Claudio Scimone in the performance and recording of four symphonies by Clementi. By a series of accidents the manuscripts of these symphonies (numbering nearly twenty in all) had been lost or scattered since Clementi's death. Some pages fell into private hands, some went to the British Museum and the Library of Congress, and one stave was even found written out at the bottom of a page from a piano sonata. Scimone had worked closely with Pietro Sparda who had recently published a reconstruction of the first four symphonies in Milan. Even so, the individual parts were not complete or the cuts and repeats all corrected, and Scimone found himself still copying out bits furiously by hand on the train down to Hastings where the concert performance was to take place, on 20 January. The recordings were made in the Henry Wood Hall for Erato (RCA), for whom Scimone had already made over seventy recordings with his Solisti Veniti. His first rehearsal with the Philharmonia had worried him as he was not sure how they would react to his requests for special bowing and articulation. He admitted afterwards that he need not have worried: 'They were so open to suggestion,' he said, 'and so ready to co-operate that it was really a pleasure to work with them.' The recordings of the Clementi symphonies were an important piece of musical documentation.

Another important landmark was the long-awaited world première on 2 February of Peter Maxwell Davies' Symphony. The Philharmonia's interest in the promotion of significant new works found an ideal subject in Maxwell Davies, whose music was keenly supported by Gavin Henderson and for which there was keen competition. Philharmonia double-bass player John Steer had been the prime mover in persuading the Trust and the Arts Council in 1973 to commission an orchestral piece from Maxwell Davies, who asked specifically that Simon Rattle should conduct it: Rattle described it as a colossally difficult work that even the Philharmonia could only just play, but it was one he was convinced would survive. The players seconded Rattle's opinion; many reckoned it was about the hardest piece they had ever played. On the day of the première, some six hundred people crammed into the Festival Hall's Waterloo Room to hear the composer describe how the work had come to be written and something about its programme; many were turned away, such was the demand. For the concert itself, Rattle's idea was to follow it with Mahler's *Das Lied von der Erde*. He conducted both from memory, without the slightest arrogance or affectation, not putting a foot wrong throughout. The symphony was hailed as one of the most outstanding works to have emerged since the War.

It would have been useful to follow this London première with a number of subsequent performances around Britain had sufficient subsidies been available. As it was the cost of preparing the symphony for just one London concert had resulted in a subsidy of £150 per paying customer. Relatively little extra investment would have exposed the work to many more people and helped the performance to mature. There was some compensation in that the work would be heard again at the 1978 Proms and at the Flanders Festival in September.

Rattle's fine work with the Philharmonia prompted some to consider offering him the Associate Conductorship of the orchestra, now that Andrew Davis no longer held the title. Muti was not happy about extra titles: Maazel was already Principal Guest Conductor, and the question was further complicated by the orchestra's relationship with Giulini and Ashkenazy, and possibly with Ozawa, Svetlanov and Levine.

At a Philharmonia Trust meeting early in 1978 Charles Spencer, chairman of the Chorus, glumly reported that for the first time in twenty years the Orchestra was not in a position to fill the chorus's calendar: the Philharmonia Chorus now had to face the future without the support of the Philharmonia Orchestra. He was speaking in general but there was a particular issue under consideration at that time which exacerbated the problem. On 14 February Muti and the Philharmonia were booked to perform the Verdi *Requiem* in the Albert Hall. Early in 1977 the Philharmonia Chorus had been engaged for the concert as well as the EMI recording that was to follow. Muti, concerned over the Philharmonia Chorus' general standard at the time and its suitability for recording, had asked for some professional stiffening for both the concert and recording, about sixty extra singers in all. At this stage Equity entered the scene and tried to insist that there should be a ratio of at least one professional to two amateurs and that the professionals (the Ambrosians) should be titled separately. The question of cost was undoubtedly one concern but the chief worry in Charles Spencer's mind was that separate titling of the professionals would imply to the public that there was something wrong with the Philharmonia Chorus. The Chorus itself also stood to lose money on the recording and wanted a guarantee that no fewer than a hundred of their singers were engaged. By mid-November 1977, when rehearsals were due to begin, the position was virtually stalemate.

By now Muti, who was not a great supporter of the Philharmonia Chorus, offered to donate his own fee if it would help the financing of the professionals. The Chorus flatly refused to accept double titling, and so the Orchestra and EMI now considered very seriously the possibility of doing both concert and recording with the Ambrosians. It was with 'immense regret', according to Gavin Henderson, and the Chorus was seething with indignation. By raising the top ticket prices and with Muti's fee donated, the potential deficit would be about the same as using a mixed chorus and charging the present ticket prices. Help, in the form of a guarantee from an outside source, was promised, and so the issue now rested solely between Equity and the Philharmonia Chorus. The deadline for the Albert Hall's publicity was fast approaching and a decision was needed. Neither side would yield, and so the Ambrosians were engaged.

At stake was not only one concert and recording but the future of all choral concerts and recordings in London, for there was a growing demand for work among the professional singers, and the costs of engaging amateur choruses were increasing. The Albert Hall concert did not really justify the upset; the performance lacked sparkle and did not live up to Muti's or the work's reputation. The soloists were an uncomfortable mixture of talents, and the recording needed twelve sessions to solve just this problem of achieving a satisfactory blend of voices. The last of the sessions was not completed until June 1979, which did not make for the unity of style which was needed to seal this important enterprise in Muti's career.

The most exciting venture on the immediate horizon was a visit to Barcelona with Giulini – the first of six major tours in 1978: the Philharmonia was breaking a personal record as one of the most widely travelled of British orchestras. In Barcelona there were two concerts, Mozart's *Requiem* and Symphony No. 36 on 28 March and Beethoven's Ninth Symphony on 29 March, both in the extravagant Palau de la Musica. Don Luis Portabella had arranged for the orchestra and chorus each to be presented with the Plata del Patronato. The silver plaque of the Patronato is their highest honour and only five had previously been awarded in a long and distinguished history. The presentation was 'in recognition of their constant and magnificent co-operation and in homage to their artistry'. In return, the Philharmonia made Portabella the first non-playing honorary member of the orchestra, an honour he deeply appreciated.

The orchestra flew home for rehearsals with Muti for a Festival Hall concert on Sunday 2 April and the European tour which began on Monday. The programmes for the two-week tour of Switzerland and Italy were relatively standard repertoire – three overtures (*Semiramide, Romeo and Juliet, Leonore* No. 3), three symphonies (Mendelssohn's Fourth, Tchaikovsky's Fifth and Prokofiev's Third) and Stravinsky's *Firebird*. This last was for the Italian section of the tour and meant that the extra players needed would fly out later to join the orchestra in Basle on 8 April.

The Philharmonia had been lucky in obtaining generous sponsorship for the European tour with substantial help from the Trust. The tour was to start with a concert in Paris on Monday 3 April for which the promoter was paying exactly twice what he was paying for the Vienna Philharmonic under Bernstein. In Switzerland and Italy the Philharmonia would be the most expensive orchestra to have toured there. EMI were mounting a big promotion campaign in Paris with copies of the Philharmonia Year Book available and Muti's picture and story splashed over just about every Paris magazine. In fact, it was only EMI's large interest that persuaded Muti to do the Paris concert. There had been a mistake over the hall booking, with the result that very few tickets had been sold, but EMI promised more money and Nick Tschaikov persuaded Muti to show Paris what the Philharmonia could do, even if only a few Parisians were there to witness the fact.

The Monday of the Paris concert was a total disaster. A ban on all charter flights from Heathrow and Gatwick was the first obstacle and although a crew of senior staff was found who would fly them out it was agreed that to fly out at all would only aggravate the strike. Paris was abandoned and the orchestra would be flown direct to Zürich. Muti was waiting patiently in Paris and was understandably furious at the cancellation after the trouble to persuade him to go at all. He met the orchestra at last in Switzerland and this section of the tour went exceptionally smoothly.

In Venice, however, it was pouring with rain. Two of the three hotels were on the Lido; they had been closed all winter and now were damp and cold. There seemed little or no co-ordination of the water-taxis, the guide got lost and most of the disgruntled orchestra had to change at the hall. Next stop was Naples, Muti's home town, but transport strikes prevented the players from reaching it until half an hour after the concert starting time. In the beautiful Teatro San Carlo, with its superb acoustics, the Philharmonia played like angels, the audience were wildly delighted and Muti was evidently pleased and relieved.

The boat journey across to Sicily was unbelievable. In a Force 9 gale it was one of the worst seas anyone, including the crew, had ever seen. In fact, the crew seemed to have vanished, nearly everyone was violently sick and the boat spent more time out of the water than in it. Finally, about midnight, there was huge explosion as if a mine had gone off amidships. A seaquake had erupted almost directly under the boat, creating an alarming tidal wave. With all this behind them, the concert in the beautiful Basilica di Monreale was a splendid occasion – with the clergy enthroned on their ornamental chairs and the Mafia leaders everywhere.

There was still much work to be done. The orchestra faced its second, Nottinghamshire residency in the first week of May. This was a more substantial and ambitious visit than the October 1976 one, which had been looked on as something of an experiment. Three British conductors, Nicholas Braithwaite, Edward Downes and Simon Rattle, were to conduct a range of programmes which included Haydn and Sibelius symphonies, Prokofiev and Tchaikovsky, while soloists such as Cherkassky, James Galway, Marisa Robles and the Philharmonia's own Michael Thompson featured in concertos. Local interest was strengthened by the financial involvement of the Broadmarsh Shopping Centre Tenants' Association and was repaid by the Philharmonia Brass Ensemble playing a lunchtime concert on 3 May in the centre itself. Positioned between the Co-op and British Home Stores, they entertained shoppers with arrangements of the *Sugar Plum Fairy*, the *Pink Panther* and Ray Premru's own *Blues March*. The concert, the first to involve the whole of the Philharmonia's brass section, was recorded for transmission by Radio Trent.

On two mornings, some of the orchestra's principals gave master-classes to music students in local colleges, with tuition in technique and the technical aspects of playing. The highlight of the week was, undoubtedly, the first public performance of George Lloyd's Eighth Symphony, in Southwell Minister. Lyrita planned to record it later in the year, and in many ways the symphony première encapsulated the whole idea of the residency – orchestra, composer, conductor and the local community, all involved in the construction of an event.

Gavin Henderson had made tentative plans for two major recording projects during April 1978. One was an idea to record for Argo a substantial selection of works by Stanford. The Philharmonia's principal clarinettist, John McCaw, had wanted to record the Clarinet Concerto and Argo, with the help of Alan Suttie and some sponsorship from a tobacco company, were ready to offer twelve sessions at the end of the year. Another idea arose out of discussions with Maxim Shostakovich and Douglas Pudney of EMI about the possibility of a long-term project to record all the Shostakovich symphonies and a group of other orchestral works, spread over the next three years. Both ideas were welcomed enthusiastically by the Council but both foundered. The Stanford project lacked a big name conductor and secure sponsorship and EMI put a damper on the Shostakovich idea as they felt they were too busy with their main artists to consider such a major project. Out of this and a plan for all the Borodin symphonies with Svetlanov, EMI promised only a recording of the Tchaikovsky Violin Concerto with Spivakov and Svetlanov. It was indicative of the beginnings of a recession in the recording industry as a whole, not just for EMI, with a steady decline in the number of sessions.

On 24 May Gavin Henderson was happy to present the Tenth Anniversary Gala Concert for the Martin Musical Scholarship Fund. In the Queen Elizabeth Hall, an orchestra made up of twenty-eight former Martin Scholarship players was led by Nigel Kennedy and conducted by Anthony Ridley. The cello section alone was worth a concert – Colin Carr, Rafael Wallfisch, Robert Cohen and Julian Lloyd-Webber were just four of them. A wide range of diverse works was performed by Martin Scholarship winners, and they all signed a souvenir poster to present to Gavin Henderson after the concert. But on 25 May Henderson handed Nick Tschaikov a letter addressed to the Council in which he requested that his resignation from the post of General Manager be accepted. He had been growing restless in his job and had already, in early March, been to Australia to discuss an appointment with the Adelaide Festival. He wanted to travel more, and felt that it might be possible to combine the work with his Philharmonia post and realize a long-felt ambition to take the orchestra to Australia and New Zealand. It unsettled the orchestra, and Nick Tschaikov advised Henderson to reassure them with a statement that he intended to stay. The Council also agreed to consider revised terms of employment – a better salary, travel allowance, a car and the title of Managing Director. The offer was tempting but Henderson still felt that the staff had been badly treated by the orchestra. A lot of the criticism for the Italian trip had been levelled at Fiona Grant, which was unfair and he told the Council so, insisting that they take a different view of Fiona's work generally, which was exceptionally good. In his heart, however, he felt he could count on little support from the Council, from Ian Stoutzker, who was still equivocal over his own removal as Chairman, or from Muti. The time had come to move on and the Council accepted his resignation 'with regret'.

Gavin Henderson's contribution to the Philharmonia Orchestra had been appreciable. The orchestra now had a very stable conducting team, and discussions were well in hand for future work with Ozawa, Levine and Haitink. He had seen through the promotion of regional festivals in Wales and Nottinghamshire and he had been an ardent champion of much neglected and unfashionable music, notably Havergal Brian in the 1976 Festival. He had also been closely concerned with the Philharmonia Club and the move to new offices in New Cavendish Street. Many future plans were still to be realized, notably an Elgar Festival, a Mahler cycle with Maazel and concerts at Wembley that would include a Beethoven cycle with Sanderling in January 1980.

On 1 June Maazel began recording *Madame Butterfly*. It was one of no less than five operas recorded by the Philharmonia that summer, but not quite all the recording work was operatic. Ashkenazy began to record the Mozart piano concertos for Decca on 20 June, beginning in Kingsway Hall with the E flat concerto K482, and Muti continued his Tchaikovsky cycle with the Fifth Symphony. Muti also repeated the Nottingham performance of Mozart's Flute and Harp Concerto with soloist James Galway in the Festival Hall on 29 June.

The Philharmonia Chorus had long been associated with the annual Festival at Orange, in Southern France, held in the town's great amphitheatre. Now they were to be joined by the orchestra for the Brahms *Requiem*, with Frühbeck on 29 July. All went well on that occasion, but on 5 August the audience of twelve thousand actually booed the producer of Verdi's *Macbeth*.

After a trip to Barcelona and their usual appearance at the Proms, there was yet another tour abroad before the autumn concert season started; it was really two tours in one, an invitation to the Bruckner

Festival in Linz on 9 September and three concerts at the Flanders Festival from 11 to 13 September. Tilson Thomas conducted a very routine programme in the Brucknerhalle in Linz, and at the second of the two concerts in Ghent's Opera House he gave just a single work, Mahler's Third Symphony, with Ria Bollen and the Philharmonia Chorus. In a performance supported by finance from the British Council, Simon Rattle conducted the first performance outside Britain of the Maxwell Davies Symphony: with such difficult notation, much of which the performer may have to improvise, no two performances are identical anyway. Frühbeck closed the Flanders visit with the Brahms *Requiem*, again with the Philharmonia Chorus but this time in St Peterskerk, Leuven. The musical schedule was complicated enough, but with such a variety of programmes there were no fewer than three outward flights – one to Linz and two directly to Brussels, and then one direct from Linz to Brussels and two back from Brussels to London.

Muti's first Festival Hall concert of the autumn season was an all-Schumann programme, the Piano Concerto with Gilels and the First Symphony. The EMI recording that immediately followed the concert marked the end of Muti's Schumann series with the Philharmonia. The last session finished an hour early, a good example of his economical use of time. Always with a watch on his stand, he never wastes a minute in unnecessary effort. This means a great tension at recording sessions but the results are impressive. He prefers live performances but enjoys recordings for the extra time it gives over and above the normal rehearsal time for a concert, time to get inside the music. A recording following a concert also allows the performance to mature until it is ready for the permanence of a record.

Muti likes long takes rather than a 'patchwork' recording but sensibly realizes the need for certain short passages to be remade. His fanatical desire for precision will lead him to correct something in the fifteenth bar before A, for example, in a passage that is being re-recorded to correct something in the *tenth* bar before A. The Schumann recording illustrated an aspect of Muti's art in the quality of sound that he drew from the Philharmonia Orchestra. The 'Muti' sound? 'No!' Muti says. 'There is a *Verdi* sound, a *Schumann* sound ...' This flexibility has been built onto the warm, romantic sound of the Klemperer era and was part of the immense pride and self-respect the Philharmonia had regained during their years with Muti – 'pride, not arrogance', as Muti himself is quick to point out.

The same day as the completions of the Schumann, there was a Philharmonia Council meeting at which it was decided to offer Muti the title of Music Director to coincide with the renewal of his contract the following summer. It was early yet, but it could not be very long before

Philadelphia offered him something more permanent, and the closer his ties with the Philharmonia, the better the chance of keeping his first loyalty to London. A draft contract was to be worked out for discussion with Muti when he returned for his next concerts and recordings in January.

The Philharmonia Brass Ensemble acquired a new name in November 1978, when trombonist Peter Goodwin was asked to fill in a concert date in the Ashcroft Theatre in Croydon. Goodwin already ran an *ad hoc* brass group called the Equale Brass which he had formed in 1974 to accompany early Baroque choral performances by the Monteverdi Choir. Their title is derived from three peices for four trombones by Beethoven, *Drei Equale*, the implication being that the constituent parts making the whole are of equal importance.) For the Ashcroft Theatre concert Goodwin invited the Philharmonia Brass Ensemble to appear at the Equale Brass, and the title became permanent. It had a good pedigree, and if a player eventually left the Philharmonia, it would not mean he had also to leave the ensemble.

The first half of November 1978 was devoted almost entirely to a costly project planned by Gavin Henderson, the beginning of a complete Mahler cycle conducted by Maazel. The 1978–9 season's most striking feature was a number of such series and cycles, devoted to specific composers or themes and beginning with Muti's emphasis on Schumann. The performance of all nine Mahler symphonies and *Kindertotenlieder* was to be split into two halves, all the odd-numbered symphonies being given in late 1978 and the even ones in June 1979. They in turn would be followed by a Tchaikovsky cycle, conducted by Muti in July 1979.

Maazel took immense trouble over the Mahler symphonies; it would be the first complete cycle in London, and he was anxious to do the subject justice. To everyone's delight he did more: Edward Greenfield wrote of the Fifth that, 'Whether on record or in the concert hall, I cannot remember another performance which in its individual way was more illuminating.' Maazel's skill in controlling large orchestral forces and his impeccably accurate stick technique were of paramount importance, but he added an interpretative dimension that staggered even the orchestral players. The first movement of the Third Symphony had a demonic quality that they still remember with a shudder. The Ninth, very much associated with Klemperer, was very well done: according to one critic: 'Maazel does much. He has the ability to recreate composers' thoughts in a manner unburdened by earlier interpretations.'

The Mahler Ninth had been on Tuesday 14 November, and two days later the orchestra were off to Japan for a two-week tour. It was their first visit there since the 1970 Expo tour, and it was interesting to note that the Japanese were to pay substantially more for the Philharmonia's concerts than the orchestra received in total annual public subsidy. Despite this, the tour would have been impossible without generous support – from the Rank Organization in particular, as well as the British Council and a number of other sponsors. In Japan the tour was being promoted by the Japanese broadcasting corporation, NHK, and two of the Tokyo concerts were to be broadcast on television and radio. Frühbeck, who had worked a good deal in Japan, was conductor for the whole trip. Two programmes (repeated throughout the tour) were 1) Maxwell Davies' *First Fantasia on an In Nomine by John Taverner*, Mendelssohn's Violin Concerto with soloist Pierre Amoyal and Brahms' Second Symphony, and 2) Delius's *Walk to the Paradise Garden*, Debussy's *La Mer* and Berlioz's *Symphonie Fantastique*.

The first two concerts, in the NHK Hall in Tokyo, were televised, and this was something of a mistake. Even after forty-eight hours in Japan, the effects of jet-lag had still not worn off and the performances were not the best of the tour. The second concert had its share of light relief when, in the middle of *La Mer*, the tubular-bell player, who was hidden in the dark behind the stage, lost his footing and grabbed the frame as he fell, pulling the entire set down on top of him with a tremendous clatter.

14. *Bishop's Moves, 1979-80*

In January 1979 Nick Tschaikov resigned as Chairman of the Philharmonia's Council. His work with the Musicians' Union had mushroomed since August 1977 with the setting up of a Working Party for Advanced Orchestral Training, and he was now busy with the preparations for the opening of the National Centre for Orchestral Studies, due to open at Goldsmiths' College in September 1979. His place as Chairman was taken by Martin Jones. One of Tschaikov's last duties was to confirm the appointment of a new General Manager for the orchestra – Christopher Bishop, chief recording producer for EMI's International Classical Division.

When Muti had flown out to Philadelphia in October 1978 it was to spend a week recording Stravinsky and Beethoven with Bishop as producer. During the sessions, Muti took Bishop out to dinner and asked him if he would be interested in managing the Philharmonia. Bishop was very surprised and very flattered but said 'No.' He had a secure job, a comfortable home and a family, and he knew the precarious nature of orchestral managership. Nevertheless he was intrigued; he had already begun to think that all was not well with the record industry and, at forty-four, perhaps he needed a change before a move became impossible. At least he would meet the Council.

He was very impressed by Chairman Martin Jones and it seemed that he and the Council agreed on the general aims for an orchestra like the Philharmonia. He also admired and worked well with Muti and so the chemistry seemed right; as General Manager, he would be able to get on well with both the Principal Conductor and the Chairman of the Council, two key figures in the structure of an orchestra. Bishop accepted the job and the appointment was announced to the Press on 12 March 1979. It would take effect from 1 June.

The early months of 1979 were bringing to fruition some of the more pioneering enterprises both in the concert hall and in the studio. Before the Elgar Festival there was a Lyrita recording of William Alwyn's opera *Miss Julie*. It was Lyrita's first complete opera recording and celebrated twenty-one years of their unique work in the recording field. It was conducted by Vilem Tausky, long experienced in opera but rarely heard on record. Benjamin Luxon played Jean, the manservant, a part he had played for the opera's first performance on BBC Radio 3 in 1977, and Jill Gomez featured in the title role. It was an unusual but outstanding addition to the catalogue and exceptionally well performed and recorded, although the public had to wait until December 1983 before it was released.

Andrew Davis always received notable acclaim for his performances of Elgar's music with the Philharmonia, and February 1979 brought the realization of an idea conceived by Davis and Gavin Henderson, a cycle of concerts devoted entirely to Elgar. No such series had ever been given before in London, but plans went ahead, the Festival Hall was booked for three evenings and a Sunday afternoon, and the Queen Elizabeth Hall for a concert of Elgar's chamber music to be played by the Philharmonia Ensemble with Davis at the piano. The brown and orange posters had appeared late in 1978, a single programme book with notes for the entire cycle was written by William Mann, and the Elgar scholar Jerrold Northrop Moore was invited to give a series of pre-concert talks in the Festival Hall's Waterloo Room. The series brought a response and a commitment from the players that was on a very deep and convincing level, and Davis was paying modest tribute to a composer by his totally dedicated conducting. The cycle made a deep impression on the public, too, and was a convincing demonstration in standards of performance and attendance levels of the value of this kind of concert series.

Muti conducted Orff's *Carmina Burana* on 1 March and then recorded it for EMI. Although he entered the market with stiff competition from Previn and Frühbeck, the new recording with the Philharmonia was an outright winner, certainly as a performance to thrill its listeners. Muti also received a letter of congratulation from Orff himself, which pleased him immensely. His conducting of contemporary music was always selective. sometimes done out of a sense of duty but always of works with which he could identify. (Nick Tschaikov chose the last day of recording *Carmina Burana* to leave the Philharmonia for his new appointment. It was a great musical occasion, orchestra and chorus working well under their Principal Conductor, and Tschaikov felt it was a good time to leave.)

While Muti was in London in March, the Council took the opportunity to discuss the position of Ling Tung and the Philharmonia. They had already agreed that he should not be engaged again for Festival Hall concerts, tours or concerts in major cities. The discussion was now whether, after a contracted pair of concerts on 24 February and 11 March, together with a recording of Berlioz's *Symphonie Fantastique*, the orchestra would work at all with him in the future. The solution of the issue was delayed by Ling Tung's offer to raise the funds himself for a tour in January 1981 of Korea, the Philippines, Tai Wan and Hong

Kong, with Frühbeck sharing the conducting, but taking the *major* share. Muti agreed to this but not to the inclusion of China in the tour as well. This was to be investigated as a possibility for Muti himself.

A relationship that was continuing to flourish was that of Ashkenazy as conductor/soloist. From 10 to 13 May he took the Philharmonia on a Welsh tour, playing the Mozart Concertos in F and C minor and conducting Sibelius's Second Symphony and Tchaikovsky's Sixth. Both the concertos were recorded immediately for Decca, followed by the Tchaikovsky symphony; the Sibelius was left until the autumn. The intensity of Ashkenazy's rehearsals and recording sessions with the Philharmonia gave the lie to the myth that for him conducting was just a hobby. Score abandoned in the control room, he revealed an intimate knowledge of the music.

The final rehearsal for the Welsh tour, on 9 May in Brent Town Hall, brought the news that Gwydion Brooke's bassoon had been stolen from his home the previous evening. It was the only instrument he possessed. It had cost him only £30 and only *he* knew his way around its unique 'plumbing', making it unplayable by anyone else. His woodwind colleagues knew just what the loss of the instrument would mean. Brooke was one of the oldest members of the Philharmonia, and yet it was too soon for retirement. The Trust offered a £500 reward for its recovery, but sadly, it never was found, and on 12 June 1979 'Gwyd' Brooke tendered his resignation from the orchestra. The Philharmonia lost not only one of its oldest and wisest players, a true professional, but a kindly man with a dry sense of humour and the author of countless witty asides, timed to perfection and at the expense of many great conductors.

In May 1979 the newspapers carried the long-expected news that Muti had been approached to succeed Ormandy as Music Director of the Philadelphia Orchestra. Ormandy intended to retire in 1980, and Muti's contract was for an initial period of three years beginning with the 1980–1 season. As he told the Press, he had every intention of remaining Principal Conductor of the Philharmonia and of the Maggio Musicale, although it was evident that his loyalties would be divided, or at least tested, and his time at a high premium. The need to renew his Philharmonia contract and confirm the new title of Music Director of the Philharmonia Orchestra was paramount and was one of the first items on Christopher Bishop's list when he arrived in his office on 1 June.

His arrival came in the middle of the second half of Maazel's Mahler cycle and Muti's recording of *I Pagliacci*. The Mahler concerts had begun with a reading of the *Adagio* from the Tenth Symphony that the *Guardian* found 'one of the finest realizations I have ever heard'. Throughout the remaining concerts, culminating in the *Symphony of a Thousand* in the Albert Hall, comparisons were drawn with such great

Mahler interpreters as Bruno Walter and Klemperer, alongside whom Maazel should clearly now be placed. Maazel's own delight at the standard of the Philharmonia's playing was reflected in his dropping one scheduled rehearsal, and he gained special pleasure from the attendance of Karajan at the Albert Hall performance. Karajan was in London for two Berlin Philharmonic concerts and was much impressed by what he heard.

Muti's recording of *I Pagliacci* and, very soon after, of *I Puritani* broke his rule of doing only one opera per year. *I Pagliacci* and *Cavalleria Rusticana* (which was scheduled for recording in August) had been postponed because of the illness of singers, hence the crowded schedule for 1979.

Muti believes that the improvement in the Philharmonia's standards came to a considerable extent from their work together on the opera recordings. 'Playing for opera,' he said, 'everybody in the orchestra has to learn to make his instrument sing every note. During the rehearsals of an opera I sing all the time, all the parts, in full voice, which I believe helps the players to catch the feeling of the music.' His adaptability to different recording conditions with the Philharmonia is well exemplified in the *Pagliacci/Cavalleria Rusticana* recording. *I Pagliacci* was recorded in Kingsway Hall and *Cavalleria Rusticana* in Watford Town Hall, and yet there is no feeling of a jarring change of atmosphere but a well-judged sound suitable for each.

June 1979 had seen the Philharmonia's second visit to Lausanne, for three concerts with Kondrashin, Frühbeck and Leinsdorf. Then there was a Tchaikovsky cycle of concerts with Muti which orchestra and conductor had unanimously agreed to dedicate to the memory of Walter Legge, who had died on 22 March, not quite seventy-three years old. Since that day in March 1964 when he had suspended the orchestra he had nourished, Legge had lived almost entirely abroad, producing his wife Elisabeth Schwarzkopf's records and giving master-classes with her all over Europe and in the USA. He had maintained slight interest in the orchestra, visiting them only a few times and even then keeping very much in the background.

The main concert season extended well into July 1979, nearly a month longer than usual. It had been a busy and profitable season: the financial year had ended in a comfortable surplus of £21,000, chiefly through the earnings on foreign tours. During the time that Fiona Grant had been acting General Manager, the office had at various times been without a finance officer, personnel officer and publicity officer. It meant that everyone else working at full stretch, seven days a week if necessary.

At the Council meeting on 12 July Christopher Bishop was able to report that Muti had written to accept the position of Music Director. The appointment would be announced at the Edinburgh Festival in August. He had also accepted a three-year contract with the orchestra, with two further one-year options rather than a five-year contract, and he was also discussing a similar renewal of his EMI recording contract. Muti laid down two conditions: 1) consultation and the right to approve all programmes for Philharmonia-promoted concerts, and 2) to approve players' full membership of the orchestra. With his new Philadelphia appointment confirmed, the Council felt that they should give him these powers, but a new title now gave him more commitment to the Philharmonia and he should try to allocate more time for consultation. In addition, the orchestra would be losing Maazel as Principal Guest Conductor from 1980, when he took up his appointment with the Vienna State Opera, but he was willing to stay for the 1979–80 season.

Despite the rosy report on the finances for 1978–9, the future looked less secure. Cuts in local authority spending and Arts Council funds were making themselves felt, and the imposition of fifteen per cent VAT on concert tickets was a further blow. In the coming season there were still some gaps to be filled, notably during late December 1979 and January/February 1980. Everyone agreed that further sponsorship must be attracted as soon as possible.

July 1979 did offer a large number of recording sessions, which continued into August and included Muti's recording of *Cavalleria Rusticana*. In the middle of August there was a short British Council tour to Dubrovnik for two concerts with Del Mar. Both programmes for 14 and 15 August contained works by British composers, Delius and Britten for the 14 and Elgar for the 15. Del Mar also conducted a Prom a week later, the first of two Philharmonia Proms that summer, with an interesting programme that ranged in scale from Mozart's *Haffner* Symphony to *Also Sprach Zarathustra* by Richard Strauss.

The 1979 Edinburgh Festival was the scene for Muti's début as Music Director of the Philharmonia. Under the glare of the television lights, the programme was at times harsh in its rather oppressive excitement, especially in Mussorgsky's *Night on the Bare Mountain* and the accompaniment to Accardo's playing of the Tchaikovsky Violin Concerto. More beauty of tone appeared in the second half, with Ravel's *Rapsodie Espagnole* and Falla's *Three-Cornered Hat*, as it did in the following evening's *Les Préludes* by Liszt and Mozart's Symphony No. 24. Muti had included Penderecki's symphony, too, which received the superb comment in *The Scotsman* that, 'The strange thing about Penderecki is that the actual noise is such fun for the listener. If you say that the opening sounds like dementia in the jungles of Borneo with Stravinsky crashing about at times in the undergrowth, who am I to contradict you?' The third concert in Edinburgh was conducted by

Rattle, who partnered Sir Clifford Curzon in Mozart's *Coronation* Piano Concerto and closed with a rollicking account of Poulenc's *Les Biches*, while Cobos closed the Philharmonia's 1976 contribution with Mussorgsky's *Pictures at an Exhibition* on 1 September.

Muti's second Prom, on 13 September, had just two works – the Penderecki symphony and Schubert's Ninth. The latter was recorded for EMI later that week but was never issued. The four sessions pencilled for 17 to 19 September had been for Muti to record the Tchaikovsky First Piano Concerto with Richter, but Richter was seriously ill and cancelled on 10 September. Muti was willing to record an orchestral work, and so three of the sessions were used for the Schubert; the fourth session, was postponed until November and used to record some Rossini overtures. At this time Muti seemed to drive some performances hard, and Schubert's Ninth Symphony is such sheer hard physical work for the strings that it is difficult to achieve a satisfactory artistic unity, even with the benefits of editing.

The same day as the first Schubert session, 17 September, saw the Philharmonia's annual press conference. Christopher Bishop's theme took up the points made at the July Council meeting, particularly the need for private sponsorship as an attractive alternative to State support, if only because it brought with it a refreshing lack of artistic interference. He also pointed out that the Minister for the Arts, Norman St John-Stevas, had promised tax relief similar to that operating in the USA to be available to private industrial sponsors. The year's work ahead, however, already promised 115 concerts, three television programmes and 140 recording sessions. The Philharmonia's youth projects would also continue, with the usual master-classes and coaching by the orchestra's principals.

A further Nottinghamshire residency had had to be cancelled but there was soon an opportunity for regional involvement and help for young musicians when the Philharmonia made its regular visit to the Swansea Festival in October. Three concerts were shared between Kondrashin, who had a series of concerts with the orchestra in early October, and Ashkenazy, who was to take the orchestra on a tour of Germany later that month. The Philharmonia was now very much the 'house' orchestra of the Swansea Festival. Their association had begun in 1977, with Ashkenazy, and they were booked now as far ahead as 1981, again with Ashkenazy much involved.

The German tour with Ashkenazy lasted two weeks, from 23 October to 7 November, and included twelve concerts. It was Ashkenazy's first major tour with the Philharmonia and he was to play Mozart concertos in seven of the concerts; the soloists for the others were Wilhelm Kempff in Beethoven's Fourth Piano Concerto in Freiburg, Nuremberg and Frankfurt-Hoechst, and Itzhak Perlman in Tchaikovsky's Violin Concerto in Munich. The tour was well received by the public, but Ashkenazy found difficulty in learning how to pace a hectic foreign tour.

December 1979 saw some reorganization and rationalization of the orchestra's management structure. Ian Stoutzker, President of the Philharmonia for three years, was informed that his contract would not be renewed after the end of the year. There was no feeling of ingratitude on the orchestra's part. Stoutzker had been a lifeline in the doldrums of the early 1970s and a staunch ally ever since. His methods and manner of working were not agreeable to everyone, and it was that which prompted his removal. There was some bitterness, quite understandably, but Stoutzker remained on the Trust until 1984.

The same month, Christopher Bishop became Managing Director and Fiona Grant was given the new title of Administrator. The paperwork was completed on 10 December for the company title of the orchestra to become 'Philharmonia Limited'. EMI still owned the title by virtue of their holding of Walter Legge's shares. They now registered a new name – 'EMI Hesketh Limited' – thus releasing 'Philharmonia Limited' for the orchestra to register with Company House.

During three weeks in January 1980 Kurt Sanderling conducted a Beethoven cycle at the Wembley Conference Centre. The series was financed by Brent Council and the London Orchestral Concerts Board, the first to be so financed at Wembley, much to the annoyance of the other London orchestras. There had been fears over the financial viability of the series which were not allayed by very poor attendances at the three Wednesday concerts; the three Sunday concerts were better attended but only the last – the Ninth Symphony performance on 27 January – came anywhere near to filling the large hall. The fault lay partly in Wembley's location: for anyone south of the Thames and for many others it was a difficult venue to reach and return from for a weekday concert.

From the first concert, on 9 January, a similarity to Klemperer's approach was apparent. Indeed, Sanderling thought highly of Klemperer's work himself, and one critic felt that his *Eroica* performance was the finest he had heard in London since Klemperer's first performance with the Philharmonia in 1948. At rehearsals in Brent Town Hall, the Philharmonia players gradually grew accustomed to Sanderling's rather schoolmasterish approach, but as he pointed out: 'Performing a Beethoven symphony nowadays is devilishly difficult, because it is usually such a routine job. The players know the notes backwards and approach their task with bored resignation.' He had asked for three rehearsals per concert, although he cut several of them short. 'I have never known an orchestra do this in such a small time he commented in praise of the Philharmonia's quickness to adapt. The series was complemented by John Lill's piano playing in the five concertos and the *Choral Fantasia* which preceded the Ninth Symphony.

The big financial losses on the Wembley Beethoven cycle and the earlier Mahler cycle were very much on Christopher Bishop's mind when he attended one of a series of seminars in January by the American subscription expert Danny Newman. At the time, audience figures had dropped significantly, and it would need a bold step to remedy them. Bishop convinced the Council that the right decision was to offer the Festival Hall season on subscription: its success was such that by mid-July over one third of the seats available on subscription had already been sold. Also in January the seeds were sown for major sponsorship of the Philharmonia. Christopher Bishop had been telephoned by an ex-pupil, Andrew Newton, who was now a young director of an advertising agency. They met for lunch and Newton came straight to the point: could the orchestra use some major sponsorship? Bishop was indeed highly interested and Newton arranged for him to meet Gordon Watson, Director of the UK Market for British American Tobacco Limited, who was interested in the idea of sponsoring a symphony orchestra in association with a then undisclosed brand of cigarette. Watson proved to be a lively and keen contact. He knew and admired the work of the Philharmonia under Muti and was anxious to link his company with such an orchestra, giving it financial stability and the resulting confidence to widen and deepen its interests. The talks continued throughout the early part of 1980 and it seemed that before the end of the current season a definite agreement could be reached.

In February 1980 the great violinist Accardo returned to appear in a Brahms concert at the Festival Hall and then join the orchestra for a repeat performance at the Barcelona Festival two weeks later. In the Palau de la Musica the Philharmonia violins were rehearsed by Muti in the Beethoven *Pastoral* Symphony with unrelenting toughness. The acoustics made it hard for one side of the orchestra to hear the other, and Muti had the first violins repeating a high phrase time after time. It was near sadism, but entirely in the pursuit of perfection; if other London orchestras would not allow themselves to be subjected to such vigorous discipline, it perhaps explained why their strings did not produce the rich, resonant sound that the Philharmonia could carry over even in the Palau de la Musica.

It was Maazel's last season as Principal Guest Conductor, and his fiftieth birthday fell on 6 March. He chose to celebrate it with the Philharmonia Chorus and Orchestra in a performance of Beethoven's

Missa Solemnis, but with typical generosity he gave it in aid of the Beethoven Fund for Deaf Children.

The Philharmonia Trust were working harder than ever to match the new initiatives of subscription and sponsorship. For concerts, they had had underwritten a substantial deficit on the Japanese tour in December 1978, supported a visit by the Philharmonia Chorus to Düsseldorf in November 1979 to give three performances of Mahler's Eighth Symphony as part of the Nordrhein-Westfalischen Mahler cycle, and were now busy organizing support for the tour of the USA by Muti and the Philharmonia, planned for the autumn of 1980. On the capital expenditure side, they had made grants to the orchestra to buy new timpani, xylophone and glockenspiel; now in March 1980 they saw the final touches put to a set of eight matching double-basses they had commissioned for the orchestra.

Gerald Drucker is principal bass and principal photographer of the Philharmonia. In his younger days he studied instrument-making, and after playing for ten years on a Pöllmann bass, he wanted to improve his section's assorted conversions for the lower notes by acquiring a matching set of five-stringed instruments. He went to Günter Kramer's Pöllmann workshop in Neumarkt St Veit in West Germany to supervise the choice of woods, some of which had been drying for thirty years. The instruments duly arrived in London after months of painstaking work by hand; Drucker tuned them each up to pitch, and after some minor adjustments they went into use with the Philharmonia bass section. They were soon noticed and admired by the London critics who could distinguish 'a fine clarity as well as resonance' and 'a new dignity'.

In May Bishop turned his energies to two further important matters. The Philharmonia had no funds to call on in the event of unforeseen hardship or tragedy among its members, whereas the other three major London orchestras had set up such schemes years before. The idea of a Benevolent Fund had been on the Council agenda since 1978 but was never taken up until now. Bishop engaged the services of Laurie Watt, the London Philharmonic Orchestra's solicitor who had done outstanding work to save the London orchestras from problems arising through their tax status. With the able help of Hugh Davies from the Philharmonia's violin ranks who was also a qualified solicitor, Watt drew up a Trust Deed, and a Festival Hall concert on 20 May was earmarked as a gala event in aid of the new fund. The Philharmonia Club sponsored the concert, and Muti and Ashkenazy, who were conductor and soloist for that evening, gave their services in aid of the fund. The new Trust Deed was able to bring together several sources of income. For more than four years, money had come in steadily to the Philharmonia from foreign royalties on record sales of recordings made many years before and which were now not able to be credited to the individual musicians who had played in the relevant sessions. More than £2,000 also came from the proceeds of the Royal Concert on 20 November 1979 for which the players had given their services but on which the orchestra would otherwise have had no claim.

The Philharmonia had never had a patron, and Christopher Bishop had pursued the idea enthusiastically. It would be prestigious for the orchestra's image, coming at a time when their fortunes were significantly on the upturn. The London Symphony and Royal Philharmonic Orchestras both had royal patrons, so Bishop now thought of the Prince of Wales. He took the advice of Lady Fermoy, a member of the Philharmonia Trust, and wrote to the Prince's Private Secretary. It was with great pride that at the 20 May rehearsal Martin Jones was able to announce to the players that the Prince had agreed to become the first Patron of the Philharmonia Orchestra. His patronage was a great morale booster for the players, too, for he was to take his duties very seriously.

Muti conducted the last concert of the season on 3 July with Sir Clifford Curzon in Mozart's last B flat Piano Concerto. Muti then began a recording with the Philharmonia of *La Traviata*. It was his fifth Verdi opera recording with them and one of the two Verdi operas he felt to be the most difficult; the other was *Falstaff*. His speeds for the music were on the fast side: since Toscanini's 1946 version there had been a reactionary vogue for slow tempi. Muti returned to a more urgent pace, arguing that 'The whole opera has a feeling of urgency, even feverishness. Also, there are few slow markings in the entire score.' The digital sound made the urgency seem at times aggressive to the point of unreality but it gave great clarity to the playing.

The season's concerts with Simon Rattle had been exceptionally fine, from his 1979 Edinburgh Festival appearance to a brilliant Janáček *Glagolithic Mass* on 23 June. In August 1980 he was due to take up his appointment as Principal Conductor and Artistic Adviser of the City of Birmingham Symphony Orchestra and just one month later planned to take a sabbatical year's study leave. Before doing either, the Philharmonia were able to secure from him a five-year exclusive contract among the London orchestras, with the exception of the London Philharmonic at Glyndebourne. He was also due to conduct the Philharmonia's first 1980 Prom, on 10 August, but this began to look increasingly unlikely. In February 1980 the BBC had proposed drastic cuts involving the winding-up of five of its orchestras; the Musicians' Union reacted strongly to the loss of jobs, and on 1 June the BBC Symphony Orchestra went on strike. The Proms became the battleground of the dispute, and the Managing Director of Radio,

Aubrey Singer, said that they would not take place if the dispute could not be settled. Long and delicate negotiations continued until a solution was finally reached in the early hours of 24 July, six days into the Prom programme. The BBC Symphony Orchestra began the delayed season on 7 August, and Rattle was able to conduct his Prom three days later, with Iona Brown the soloist in Bartók's Second Violin Concerto.

The final contract with British American Tobacco for major sponsorship had now been signed and the details were announced to the Press at a reception at the Savoy Hotel on 14 August. The brand of cigarettes that was to be linked with the sponsorship was du Maurier, and the terms of the contract were very generous indeed, in fact the largest sponsorship sum given to an arts organization in Britain. No less than £300,000 per year, for an initial period of two years, was on offer, almost exactly the figure paid by the London Orchestral Concerts Board. There were very few specific restrictions placed on the use of the money: £220,000 was to sponsor Philharmonia-promoted concerts in the Festival Hall for the whole season apart from the period January to March which would be kept for existing sponsors. £40,000 was set aside for tours and special events: these were later to include two du Maurier Proms, a *Music of Today* series, specific commissions and short tours in Britain to enable the orchestra with its top soloists and conductors to be heard in the more distant parts of Britain. The remaining £40,000 was to be used specifically for out-of-town concerts to offset the difference between the money put up by the local promoter and the total cost of the concert. Examples would be appearances at the Malvern Festival and Leeds Castle's open-air concerts.

The du Maurier money was very timely as it helped to boost finances just as the orchestra was embarking on its subscription scheme, whose administration was very costly. It helped to turn a deficit on the 1979–80 season into a surplus. The money represented twenty per cent of the orchestra's yearly income and was, in Christopher Bishop's words, a 'lifeline'.

The uniqueness of the deal, and its size, attracted a great deal of comment and interest. After all, sponsorship of the Arts on this kind of scale was comparatively new. Surprising acerbity came from no less a figure than the Secretary General of the Arts Council, Sir Roy Shaw, who suspected the Philharmonia would now live in luxury for two years and then be as impecunious as before. Christopher Bishop was quick to point out that the Philharmonia had not voted itself an increase in fees but was investing the money by building audiences through subscription and by increasing the amount of rehearsal thus raising standards of playing which would continue even if the du Maurier money ceased after two years.

The Philharmonia performed four concerts at the 1980 Edinburgh Festival, two with Muti and two with Andrew Davis. Muti opened the Festival on 17 August, when Schubert's Ninth Symphony at last got a reading in which everything fitted, not over-driven but full of excitement and with well-planned nuances. Andrew Davis' programmes included Elgar's First Symphony and a well-paced, lyrical Dvořak Eighth Symphony.

Just one week later, the same conductor, orchestra and symphony were in the Plaza Porticada in Santander. This festival was a new venue for the Philharmonia; the performances took place on one side of the large square with a huge tarpaulin slung high above the stage. The local authorities were most helpful in closing the square to traffic for the concert but this did not extend to the rehearsal, which took place with cars and vans roaring past, only feet from the nearest players! The highlight of the first concert, at 11 p.m. on 28 August, was the appearance of Lucero Tena to play Balada's *Concertino for Castanets.* Very dramatically the soloist chose her castanets from a velvet-lined box that was placed on stage and then proceeded to clack her way through a part which Davis later said bore little resemblance to the score he had in front of him. The audience went wild with delight; to be fair, they also went wild with delight the following evening at John Wallace's performance of the Haydn Trumpet Concerto, which was superb. Ending with Beethoven's Fifth Symphony, it was a programme that was unashamedly popular in appeal.

Normal Del Mar was the conductor for the third and last Philharmonia Prom, on 10 September. Giulini and Itzhak Perlman then recorded the Beethoven Violin Concerto for HMV and a video was produced of the sessions. The following two or three days were spent preparing for a short tour of Germany built round the Bonn Beethoven Festival and the Berlin Festival. In Bonn, the Philharmonia gave two out of the seventeen concerts in the 1980 Beethovenfest: it was the same programme twice over, the Overture *Leonora* No. 3, the Third Piano Concerto with Radu Lupu, and the Seventh Symphony, all played in the lovely modern Beethovenhalle.

Only a few days separated the orchestra's return from Germany and the long-awaited tour of the USA and Canada, also with Muti. For most of 1979 Ronald Grierson and the Trust had laboured mightily to raise money for the tour. It was the most ambitious foreign tour undertaken by the Philharmonia for many years and turned out to be the biggest money-raising operation ever mounted by the Trust. A subsidiary charitable trust was set up in the USA to handle the sponsorship from the American side, and thanks to a generous donation by the new Chairman of the Board of GKN, Sir Trevor Holdsworth, the entire £140,000 needed was raised before the orchestra flew out from Heathrow for Boston on 29 September. Part of the help, in the form of £10,000, also came from the orchestra's anonymous benefactor who still provided a vital lifeline to the Philharmonia's finances.

It was almost twenty-five years to the day since the Philharmonia first visited Boston with Karajan in 1955. On 1 October Muti conducted just two works in Symphony Hall, Mozart's Symphony No. 41 and Schubert's Ninth. The 1955 Karajan tour had covered a wide area; the 1980 Muti tour was within a much smaller sphere, with eleven concerts in the two weeks. Muti had the sense not to over-rehearse, even programmes like the gruelling second night in Ottawa's National Arts Centre which had Tchaikovsky's *Romeo and Juliet*, Stravinsky's *Firebird Suite* and the Third Symphony of Prokofiev. The Prokofiev was in fact one of the most successful items of the tour, with some memorable performances.

After Cleveland and Chicago there were two concerts outside the regular concert circuit, two consecutive nights at the Reynolds Coliseum in Raleigh, North Carolina, a huge basketball stadium seating over eleven thousand.

The last three concerts were in Washington and New York and for the last, in Carnegie Hall, Muti relented and gave the first encore of the tour, the little overture to Verdi's *Joan of Arc*. The tour had taken the USA by storm in much the same way as the 1955 Karajan tour: the Philadelphia Orchestra's manager was at Carnegie Hall and was heard to comment, 'Man, we have got to do something!' In Cleveland one man was heard to say, 'We've got Maazel's grave dug!' in the heat of the moment. Even in the cool light of dawn the *New York Post* put the seal on the triumphs of the visit by writing: 'I would venture to say on the basis of the concert last night at Carnegie Hall that England's Philharmonia Orchestra is one of the most polished and responsive in existence.'

15. *The Smoke of Success, 1981-2*

It was for Andrew Davis, recording Sibelius's First Symphony, that Carl Pini led his last Philharmonia session. He had always fancied conducting, and he now had an offer to lead the Hong Kong Philharmonic Orchestra, where he would have the opportunity of forming a chamber orchestra of his own, conducting and working with his quartet again. Since he joined the (New) Philharmonia in 1975, the strings had developed an outstanding quality under his leadership. He was very much a chamber music player and brought that feeling for ensemble and an ability to listen in his section. He also led by sheer hard work: he was the ideal link man for Muti and imposed a terrific discipline on the whole orchestra. Muti described him as a 'very intelligent musician', and Pini never sat back or gave a concert with less than a hundred per cent of his energies. It was typical of his concern for the future of the orchestra that before he left he had found a suitable replacement, the twenty-five-year-old leader of the BBC Welsh Symphony Orchestra, Christopher Warren-Green.

Christopher Warren-Green's first major engagement with the Philharmonia, before his appointment had been confirmed, was to lead for the recording of the complete Beethoven symphonies with Kurt Sanderling, in January 1981. It was a very concentrated period of work, with two sessions per day spread around three different halls, and the producer was Beatrix Musker who had worked with Christopher Bishop at EMI and who in 1984 was made Administrator of the Philharmonia. Four overtures and all the symphonies were fitted into the period from 4 January to 6 February, but Sanderling found the challenge exciting and stimulating. In this first digitally recorded Beethoven cycle he was anxious to rediscover the emotions of the music felt when it was first written and favoured long takes to give the architectural span of whole movements where possible.

Du Maurier had helped finance that venture and also widened their scope of help by sponsoring an international concert series at Wembley between November 1980 and March 1981. Muti conducted two Festival Hall concerts in January and then travelled with the orchestra to open the new Warwick University Concert Hall on 26 January. The choice of the Philharmonia Orchestra to perform at the opening concert and of Muti to unveil the commemorative plaque was largely due to the fact that much of the money for the new £1 million Hall came from the same anonymous benefactor who helps the orchestra itself. The Philharmonia had helped test the acoustics of the Arts Centre auditorium in November 1975, and the new Hall, which would double as a concert auditorium and a multi-purpose space for university functions, was the result of many consultations between the orchestra, university and contractors. The man responsible for raising the greater part of the finance for the Hall and who, since 1965, had administered the anonymous benefaction to the orchestra was Phil Mead. An accountant by profession, he took a keen interest in all the Philharmonia's activities and particularly those which involved young people, through the Martin Scholarship Fund for example. He was tragically killed in an accident in May 1984 and not only the Philharmonia lost one of its most loyal friends but many other organizations mourned the loss of a staunch ally, among them Coventry City Football Club, Warwick University and the Royal College of Music.

On 9 February the orchestra were delighted to welcome Bernard Haitink, formerly Principal Conductor of the London Philharmonic Orchestra, working with the Philharmonia for the first time. His two programmes were Bruckner's Ninth Symphony and *Te Deum*, with Mahler's Third Symphony a week later. Bruckner also featured in Matačić's second set of concerts that winter, this time the F minor Mass on 8 March. Matačić was less steady on his feet than he had been in November, but he still refused a chair on the rostrum.

Both Haitink's and Matačić's concerts had been with the Philharmonia Chorus, and it was both orchestra and chorus that Matačić then took to Barcelona on 10 March, where he repeated the Bruckner. He also conducted Mozart's C minor Mass, which Muti had given at the Festival Hall in January, and Haydn's *Bear* Symphony, the like of which some of the chorus who were on stage had not heard since Beecham. In the choral works he also evoked nostalgic memories of Klemperer in the way he shaped and moulded phrases.

Since September 1980 the Philharmonia Chorus had been trained by Heinz Mende, for Norbert Balatsch had left in the spring of 1980 because of growing commitments in Vienna and Bayreuth. Mende brought patience, a meticulous attention to detail and dedication that won him respect and acclaim from chorus and from the Barcelona audiences. He was even beginning to learn a little English!

Capital Radio continued its association with the Philharmonia by relaying a Maazel Festival Hall concert on 19 March. The most interesting item in the programme was Ray Premru's Symphony, which was receiving its world première, just two weeks after its completion. After the Philharmonia's performance of his *Concerto for Orchestra* in December 1977, they decided they would like a piece of their own, and so with the help of the Arts Council they commissioned a new work. Premru was delighted at being able to write specifically for his own orchestra, and Maazel gave it a strong and dramatic first performance. It was a very approachable work that also reflected Premru's other self as co-director of a jazz orchestra.

In March 1981 the Friends of the Philharmonia came into being, to help the orchestra increase the number of ticket subscribers by personal introduction.

The subscription scheme had proved an outright winner and the du Maurier money had made its operation financially viable. From a position where Philharmonia audiences had been the poorest of the big four orchestras, sixty per cent paid attendances in 1979–80 compared with the average of seventy-three per cent between the other three orchestras, the average had now risen in early 1981 to a staggering eighty-five per cent, and Muti's Festival Hall concert in January had been the twelfth consecutive sell-out; by the end of the season twenty-two out of the thirty-four concerts would be sold out. This meant that while the LOCB subsidy for the last ten concerts of the 1979–80 season had been £2.87 per seat, for the first ten concerts in the autumn of 1980, because of subscription, the subsidy was only £1.60 per seat. Public money was thus being made twice as effective. The improved audience figures and healthy financial state were good news at a time when London audience figures were showing an overall decline. New increased rates of pay, effective from 1 April 1981, also had to be met and there had been a recession in the recording industry, resulting in a drop in the number of sessions offered to all the big London orchestras.

If Dennis Brain had lived, he would have been sixty in May 1981, and the orchestra with which he had played only hours before his fatal car crash in September 1957 chose to commemorate the anniversary with a Fairfield Hall concert on 2nd May, conducted by his friend Norman Del Mar, an appropriate choice as Del Mar had begun his own musical career as a horn-player beside Dennis Brain in both the Philharmonia and the Royal Philharmonic Orchestras. The programme was framed by two works that use the horn most evocatively, Elgar's Overture *In the South* and Strauss's *Till Eulenspiegel.* Ian Partridge and the Philharmonia's own Michael Thompson gave a cogent performance of the Britten *Serenade* which Dennis Brain had premièred in 1943 and for whom it had been specially written. Michael Thompson also played the

Third Mozart Concerto, not Dennis's own favourite No. 2 but a very shapely, dedicated performance.

The actual anniversary of Dennis Brain's birth was 17 May, and it was perhaps appropriate that on that Sunday in 1981 the Philharmonia was remembering Andrew Newton; also in his mid-thirties, Newton had died in a car accident in January, plunging eight floors to his death in a multi-storey car-park. He was one of the best friends the Philharmonia ever had, for it was he who had made the introduction that led to the du Maurier sponsorship of the orchestra. Because his own love of music had been awakened by singing, Mendelssohn's *Elijah* was chosen to dedicate to his memory, as a thanksgiving and as a message of sympathy to his family and friends. Frühbeck conducted the work he had long made his own in the only appearance he made that season with the Philharmonia.

In the long history of Philharmonia tours the orchestra had never visited Scandinavia, but in the first week of June 1981 Ashkenazy took them to the Bergen, Oslo and Tivoli Festivals on a tour sponsored by the British Council. The latter's backing meant the obligatory inclusion of a British composition, which was Tippett's Double String Concerto. Ashkenazy was both soloist and conductor in Mozart's last Piano Concerto, and there were two Fifth symphonies, those of Sibelius and Tchaikovsky. In the second of their two concerts, Christina Ortiz joined the Philharmonia for Ravel's G major Piano Concerto and so delighted the audience that she had to give them an encore, a little Brazilian piece written by Villa-Lobos for Rubinstein. The tour was completed on 8 June with a concert in Paris, where the Champs-Elysées audience, normally very reserved over British performances, positively raved over Ashkenazy and his performance of Tchaikovsky's Fifth Symphony.

The rest of June was dominated by Seiji Ozawa, who was returning to the Philharmonia for the first time since 1974. Since then he had worked regularly with the Boston Symphony Orchestra and had toured Japan with them in March 1978. His repertoire was now very wide and included all Schoenberg's orchestral music, all the Mahler symphonies and most of Bruckner's.

His Mahler Second Symphony, on 21 June, was controversial but made audiences who felt that they had been recently over-exposed to the work sit up and take notice of a search for new detail; Jessye Norman was certainly stunning as soloist.

Before conducting the last four concerts of the season, featuring Radu Lupu in all the Beethoven Piano Concertos, Muti recorded Gluck's *Orfeo* for EMI with the Philharmonia. He also continued his Tchaikovsky recording cycle with the *Manfred* Symphony immediately following a Festival Hall performance on 2 July.

This concert was also the first to be attended by the Prince of Wales since he had become Patron of the orchestra. After the performance he shook hands with every member of the orchestra backstage and talked with them at some length. They were delighted by his interest in orchestral matters. The Philharmonia were included in the Prince's wedding service on 29 July as well as members of the two other orchestras of which he is Patron, the Orchestra of the Royal Opera House and the English Chamber Orchestra. John Wallace was especially honoured to be chosen to play the solo trumpet in Handel's 'Let the Bright Seraphim', sung by Kiri te Kanawa. His playing was flawless. As a memento of the occasion, the Prince and Princess sent wedding cake to the Philharmonia.

The 1981 Proms cemented two important friendships with leading conductors. After Haitink's Mahler Third Symphony in February, *The Times* wrote: 'Let us hope that this partnership has more Mahler performances in store for us,' and Edward Greenfield wrote in *Guardian*: 'Haitink's first ever collaboration with the Philharmonia was everything we could have hoped.' It was Mahler's Third Symphony that Haitink conducted at the Prom on 19 August, with the same soloists too – Alfreda Hodgson, the Southend Boys Choir and the Philharmonia Chorus. Happily Haitink was booked for more concerts during the next season that included Beethoven's *Missa Solemnis* and Walton's First Symphony. The second Prom, on 23 August, was with Giulini. After long discussions he had at last decided that apart from visits with foreign orchestras he would in future conduct the Philharmonia exclusively in Great Britain. At the Prom concert, also with the Philharmonia Chorus, he conducted Rossini's *Stabat Mater* and then recorded it with them for Deutsche Grammophon over the next two days.

The Philharmonia Chorus had seen a change of Chairman; after seventeen years of hard work and dedicated leadership, Charles Spencer now stepped down and was replaced by John Chumrow. Like Spencer, Chumrow sang in the basses of the chorus; also like Spencer, he served on the Philharmonia Trust, and one of his first moves was to sit down with Christopher Bishop to discuss a closer working partnership with the orchestra, which he felt would serve the best interests of both parties concerned. There had been only six choral concerts when the orchestra had used the chorus during the 1980–1 season; as a result of the discussions ten were now planned for the 1981–2 season, and there would be twelve the following season.

Muti conducted two of the Philharmonia's three Edinburgh Festival concerts that year. An exciting performance of Berlioz's *Romeo and Juliet* on 29 August was followed by a Schumann and Tchaikovsky orchestral concert. The soloist in the Schumann Violin Concerto was the Latvian

Gidon Kremer who dispelled some of the dullness of the work by standing on tiptoe for the high notes and crouching for his low ones, playing the entire polonaise with his mouth open. Kremer and Muti repeated the Schumann on a short Philharmonia tour abroad in mid-September. Mendelssohn's Fourth Symphony, Schubert's Ninth and Tchaikovsky's Sixth were the principal items for three concerts, one sponsored by Radio France in the Théâtre des Champs Elysées in Paris, and two as part of the Flanders Festival in Brussels and Ghent. Even after Edinburgh there were four three-hour rehearsals in the Henry Wood Hall of all the works during the three days leading up to departure. The Paris concert was a live broadcast of the Schubert and Mendelssohn; next morning the orchestra travelled by train to Brussels, where they were met by the extra players required for the Tchaikovsky that evening in the Palais des Beaux Arts. The next day, 15 September, coaches took the Mendelssohn and Schubert players to Ghent, where the concert was again broadcast live from the Opera House.

The Philharmonia had been invited back to Leeds to play for the two final concerts of the International Pianoforte Competition in September, conducted in Leeds Town Hall by Sir Charles Groves. The winner, Ian Hobson who had been fourth in 1978, overcame any unease in his playing of the Rachmaninov Second Concerto and was able to repeat the success of that night in two further performances with the Philharmonia, the following Monday at the Hexagon in Reading and a week later in Croydon's Fairfield Hall.

On 23 September the Philharmonia began a new series of concerts in association with du Maurier to promote the music of living and recent composers, with the title *Music of Today*. It had long been felt that a fresh start was needed on the problems of presenting contemporary symphonic music. Hitherto the London Orchestral Concerts Board had made a small amount of money available for the inclusion of contemporary music, but that money was to cease from the beginning of the 1981–2 season. Promoters faced the dilemma of including new works alongside Beethoven's Fifth Symphony and pleasing no one, or putting on whole concerts of new music to which only a dedicated few came. Smaller concert-halls were therefore chosen for the first three du Maurier-sponsored concerts at which the pieces, although already prepared, would also be rehearsed and discussed at the concert before being performed. Du Maurier's involvement followed long and persuasive talking by Christopher Bishop and meetings between du Maurier and the Council. They agreed that part of the £40,000 set aside for tours and special events could be used to promote the new venture.

Simon Rattle was deeply interested in the project and undertook to offer general advice. An informal 'think-tank' was also set up to generate and filter ideas for future concerts; three outsiders, composer Oliver Knussen and critics Bayan Northcott and Norman Kay, were joined by five members of the Philharmonia, David Corkhill, James Ellis, John Miller, Michael Harris and John Wallace, together with Christopher Bishop. The 23 September concert was in St John's, Smith Square, with Witold Lutoslawski conducting his shattering Second Symphony. The three-hour morning rehearsal had broken the back of the thirty-five-minute work, and the evening performance was preceded by a short open rehearsal. Lutoslawski proved to be outstanding at establishing a good rapport with a full house which gave the series a promising start. Michael Tilson Thomas and Simon Rattle would conduct the remaining two concerts in March and May the following year.

The Master of the Queen's Musick, Malcolm Williamson, celebrated his fiftieth birthday in November 1981, and the Philharmonia had been invited to help in the celebrations with a concert on 11 October that included his *Mass of Christ the King*, a work that had been written for the 250th anniversary of the Three Choirs Festival and dedicated to the Queen on her Silver Jubilee; this was in fact its third performance but its first on the South Bank. Williamson's music had been played by the Philharmonia as early as the 1950s, and when Horenstein had performed Stravinsky's *Symphony in Three Movements* in June 1958, the pianist on that occasion had been the thirty-six-year-old Malcolm Williamson.

Haitink continued his association with the Philharmonia with Mahler's Seventh Symphony on 30 October and then Walton's First Symphony, which he immediately recorded. It was a challenge to try the Walton but one which Haitink brought off supremely well. The Festival Hall performance lacked some of the necessary tension, and even in the recording the first movement was not quite up to Previn's superb 1966 version with the London Symphony Orchestra, but the rest was colossal. Haitink's approach was deeply thought out from first to last. Much of this came from his approach to recording. Here he likes to perform and becomes irritable when asked to repeat short passages for 'patching'. Nevertheless, the sessions were immensely enjoyable, and the record was a valuable addition to the catalogues, made almost thirty years to the day after Walton himself had recorded it with Walter Legge's Philharmonia.

Wolfgang Sawallisch, who had not conducted in London since 1968, returned in November 1981 to conduct a Brahms cycle with the Philharmonia. His return had been mooted since the summer of 1978 as part of a general plan to attract back many of the conductors who had worked with the Philharmonia in the 1950s. Giulini, Matačić and now Sawallisch formed a significant part of this plan. Four concerts were to include all the Brahms symphonies, the Violin Concerto and the Double

Concerto with Accardo and Lynn Harrell; there would also be a performance of the *Requiem* in the Albert Hall with Julia Varady, Dietrich Fischer-Dieskau and the Philharmonia Chorus. The series began on Remembrance Sunday with the *Tragic* Overture. Sawallisch's problem in London had always been a cool response from the public – he was a musician's conductor, the orchestra loved him and he knew his job superbly well but in the past he had lacked that something extra, that extra fire that could make the audiences feel that they were involved.

The Brahms cycle did seem to have some of that missing fire at last. For Noel Goodwin of *The Times*, the First Symphony was 'an experience, a sense of symphonic proportion which makes the music convincing, in presenting it absolutely free of accrued tarnish.' It promised well for the Beethoven concerts in the spring of 1982.

However, before the end of 1981, the news had broken in the London music world that Muti intended to give up his post of Music Director of the Philharmonia when his present contract expired in July 1982. Christopher Bishop had almost talked him into staying at least one more year, until 1983, when he would have completed ten years as Principal Conductor, but in a letter to Bishop dated 1 December he declined, saying that he no longer had the time to justify such a position. He did not want it to be said at a later date that his professional conduct had been anything other than correct. There was no question of a total severing of all ties. The Council had agreed to offer him the title of Conductor Laureate, and Muti now indicated his willingness to accept a title that would demonstrate his continuing exclusivity to the orchestra. The lure of Philadelphia was undeniable. It had been the prize for which he had been seeking for several years and it now offered him an orchestra in first-class condition on which he could impose his stringent discipline one hundred per cent. It also had a long tradition of subscriptions which gave a wide freedom of repertoire. When he discussed the move with me some two years later he was able to look back more coolly and observe that he had given the Philharmonia nearly ten years and built it into a first-class ensemble, with a high level of achievement both in concert and on record. They had been 'ten beautiful years, but an orchestra and conductor need fresh air and fresh water; a conductor must have new experiences'.

In October Ashkenazy had been offered the position of Principal Guest Conductor, and he accepted. He was booked for a long period of work with the Philharmonia in the early weeks of 1982, including a tour of Japan fixed for the period 19 to 30 January; a visit to Manila had been talked of but had to be abandoned because of the very high travel costs involved. Instead, a Paris concert was fixed for 13 January, and du Maurier had been persuaded to sponsor a short tour of the Midlands and

North of England in the days before departure. In the bitter cold the orchestra toured Buxton, Sheffield, Newcastle upon Tyne and Nottingham, playing works from the Paris and Japan programmes. The Paris concert repeated the success of the previous June, although Ashkenazy was a little on edge, perhaps knowing that his friend and colleagues Daniel Barenboim was in the audience.

On the orchestra's tour of Japan, Ashkenazy put into practice all he had learned about touring. Under the banner of Toshiba's prestigious Aurex hi-fi system the Philharmonia's concerts were the first to be sponsored by the Corporation. They were received with wild acclaim and, so the British Council commented, attracted the largest audiences in Tokyo for many years.

If one adds together the du Maurier tour, Paris, Japan and three Festival Hall concerts on their return, Ashkenazy in fact conducted the Philharmonia in twenty consecutive concerts in just one month. Such a long continuous period of work with one conductor can be *too* long, but now the chemistry seemed just right, as demonstrated in the recording they now made of Beethoven's *Pastoral* Symphony and Mozart's C major Piano Concerto K503 for Decca. The *Pastoral* was felt by the critics to be one of the most relaxed and the best for sound of all recent issues of the work. Then Muti returned to launch a unique series of concertos, beginning on 25 February, with the violinist Salvatore Accardo. October 1982 would mark the bicentenary of the birth of the legendary Nicolo Paganini, and to celebrate this Accardo was to play all the six Paganini concertos in London during the year. 25 February launched the series with the First Concerto in D. It was the first time in musical history that such a cycle had been undertaken. Accardo was the obvious choice as his name had become synonymous with that of Paganini, and he had already made musical history by recording all the six concertos.

Du Maurier had been so pleased with the success of the 1981 Beethoven symphony recordings that they tried a second major recording cycle, this time the complete Tchaikovsky ballets – *Swan Lake*, *Sleeping Beauty* and *Nutcracker*. 'Complete' meant just that: not the usual suite arrangements nor even the customary cut versions but every single note of the scores, even to the extent of some orchestrations of small numbers left unfinished by Tchaikovsky himself. EMI organized the project on behalf of du Maurier this time, booked the Philharmonia and set up the recordings with their own producer, John Fraser. They began on 1 March, and the sessions were conducted by John Lanchbery, whose authority was undisputed and was based on over thirty years experience in ballet all over the world. It would be $3\frac{1}{2}$ months and thirty-one sessions before every note was recorded.

Lanchbery enjoyed the sessions: he found the Philharmonia 'a crack orchestra' and tremendously 'exhilarating', and the players in their turn conveyed a sense of fun and excitement in the new sections which were often quite challengingly difficult. Christopher Warren-Green played the violin solos with all the qualities of a great leader and in his stockinged feet. For perfect balance he was required to stand on a podium in the middle of the orchestra, but it creaked noisily while he wore shoes, so off they came. His complete professionalism was put to the test when in the middle of a take no one remembered to creep up and turn his music for him and he found himself playing an entire page of difficult solo completely from memory.

The Tchaikovsky set, complete with notes by Dame Margot Fonteyn, sold even better than the Beethoven symphonies. Sanderling came to London again on 9 March to conduct Shostakovich's Fifth Symphony, and approaches were made to du Maurier about the possibility of recording the Brahms symphonies with him. Sanderling's success with the Beethoven symphonies made such a venture look highly feasible but du Maurier did not take up the suggestion, nor a later one to record a film music set with Carl Davis.

Far from standard fare was offered in St John's, Smith Square, on 27 March in the second of the du Maurier *Music of Today* concerts in Morton Feldman's *The Viola in My Life, No. 4* and the first London performance of Jonathan Lloyd's *Everything Returns*. These scores were dauntingly complex but Michael Tilson Thomas handled them with total mastery.

These concerts were gaining credibility with the public and the Press alike. Already the *Music of Today* concerts had been hailed as 'a breakthrough' and 'enlightened', and du Maurier's whole approach had been reorganized by the presentation on 25 November 1981 of the Association for Business Sponsorship of the Arts Award, made jointly with the *Daily Telegraph*, for the Best First Time Sponsor in the Arts. Gordon Watson received the award from the Duchess of Gloucester; it was he who had taken the initiative of responsibility and it was appropriate that his work should be so recognized.

On 29 March 1982 Sir William Walton was eighty, and the Philharmonia Orchestra and Chorus took part in a gala concert in the Festival Hall to celebrate the occasion. The concert had originally been arranged by the London Symphony Orchestra but they could not take it on during their Barbican season, and so it was open for offers. Christopher Bishop secured it for the Philharmonia and agreed to take Previn to conduct. Walton's own connections with the Philharmonia dated from its very earliest days, and it was appropriate that the concert should open with his own special arrangement of the National Anthem that he had made for the Philharmonia's first USA tour in 1955, later adapted for use with the Philharmonia Chorus.

After the National Anthem the programme opened with the *Anniversary Fanfare*, written in 1973 for EMI's seventy-fifth anniversary and specially designed to lead into *Orb and Sceptre*, the 1953 Coronation March for full orchestra. Kyung-Wha Chung then played the Walton Violin Concerto. Her recording of the work with Previn in 1972 had given it a youthful intensity; ten years later it had a maturity and poise that were astonishing. Thomas Allen and the Philharmonia Chorus joined the orchestra for *Belshazzar's Feast*, and it received a tremendous birthday performance. The total effect of the evening was undeniably moving, and the admiration and affection in which Walton was held were demonstrated by the numerous standing (and singing) ovations given him by the audience. The veteran composer stood to acknowledge the applause several times, visibly moved.

The applause had scarcely died away before the Philharmonia had to be at Gatwick Airport for the 9.00 a.m. flight to Frankfurt to begin a ten-day tour of Germany and Italy with Muti. Schubert's Ninth Symphony and Liszt's *Les Préludes* feature largely on the German programmes. The audiences showed some of the usual German reserve but the Press showed how much the artistic quality of the performances came over. Frankfurt's *Allgemeiner Zeitung* felt that the performances put the Philharmonia 'into the front rank of the world's orchestras', while in Munich 'The orchestra's playing was simply heavenly.' The Italian audiences went wild even before the performances began. The excited buzz would settle, and then someone would call out 'Riccardo Muti, you are the greatest!' and it would start all over again.

André Previn conducted two performances of Beethoven's Ninth Symphony in April after the Philharmonia had returned from Italy. He then gave the first performance on 22 April of a new work by Michael Berkeley. The piece, scored for orchestra and entitled *Gregorian Variations*, had been commissioned by du Maurier in another extension of their involvement with the Philharmonia and new music. Berkeley regarded the commission as a 'considerable step forward for contemporary music' and was rewarded with an outstanding performance and a tremendous ovation from the Festival Hall audience.

Michael Tilson Thomas's conducting of Debussy was very impressive during the early days of May 1982. He recorded *La Mer* and the three *Nocturnes* for CBS at the same time and found the experience very rewarding: 'We're finding different ways of developing an even closer understanding,' he commented. 'The Philharmonia is a community. I am amazed at how much commitment and spirit they put into performances, frequently after a really demanding daily schedule. They really want the concerts to go well. It's so wonderful to work with an orchestra that wants to work with you and arrives at something magical.'

Simon Rattle was heavily committed to the City of Birmingham Symphony Orchestra but he worked very well with the Philharmonia. His programmes were adventurous but always well thought out from an inexhaustible mind. He was equally at home with Stravinsky and Mozart, and on 4 June, for example, he combined the former's *Symphony of Psalms* with the latter's C minor Mass, to great artistic effect. It was his task to conduct the last of the three du Maurier *Music for Today* concerts on 13 May, on this occasion an open rehearsal and performance of David Matthews' Symphony No. 2. The success of these concerts was already sufficient to encourage du Maurier to consider repeating the experiment during the next season.

The du Maurier sponsorship was also very timely. On 11 May Simon Rattle had conducted the world première of Peter Maxwell Davies' *Black Pentecost* in a concert that was one of eight given under the heading of *Music of Eight Decades*, supported by the London Orchestral Concerts Board and broadcast by the BBC. The hall was two-thirds full on 11 May, the fullest of the eight concerts in the series, but the concerts exhausted the Arts Council's funds that were available for new music. The Maxwell Davies work had grown out of his First Symphony, and the commission was taken over by the Philharmonia from the London Symphony Orchestra, who found the work too sombre for their seventy-fifth anniversary.

Du Maurier also sponsored two 'du Maurier Proms' over the Whitsun Bank Holiday, with Sawallisch conducting two all-Beethoven programmes on Saturday 29 and Monday 31 May. Youri Egorov played the *Emperor* Piano Concerto which he and Sawallisch also recorded and then Sawallisch himself played the piano for the *Choral Fantasia* as well as conducting the Philharmonia Chorus. In the parts and scores Sawallisch noticed that Klemperer's markings were still preserved and insisted that they be left in, with anything that he wanted put below.

The Klemperer Beethoven sets were just part of the vast library of music the Philharmonia Orchestra and Chorus had built up and which was now owned by the Trust, who looked after its replacement and additions to it. The Trust had also recently put up generous funding towards the provision of a computer to handle the subscription bookings. The success of the subscription scheme had steadily increased each season since its introduction and some way had to be found to cope with extra demand without employing more full-time staff, who would not be required at every time of the year.

A feasibility study was carried out on the advantages of a computer, and on the strength of the results an Encotel Televideo 816 was ordered at a cost of nearly £20,000. No longer would thousands of papers and tickets have to be stored and monitored over a period of months. The computer would give instant information on available seats, progress of selling for each concert and an immediate reply to a caller about a subscription application. The Philharmonia could print its own tickets and only those it was actually going to sell; despatch and handling were also much simplified. Finally, the computer could look back over a season and analyse the success of concerts, individually and as a series, and produce weekly reports.

The Beethoven emphasis begun by Sawallisch in May was continued in mid-June by Ozawa, who conducted the Violin Concerto with Isaac Stern and the Seventh Symphony. He also conducted Haydn's *Creation*, which surprised those who thought it outside his normal repertoire and who found it a very beautiful performance. The last four concerts of the season were Muti's, as he approached the end of his contract as Music Director. Gidon Kremer joined him in the Schumann Violin Concerto which he now recorded with Muti together with the Sibelius Concerto. All four concerts received high praise from the Press as closing one of the most successful season in the Philharmonia's history, both financially and artistically. Perhaps the best tribute – after the final concert – came from Robert Henderson in the *Daily Telegraph*: 'Yet again,' he wrote, 'it confirmed the Philharmonia's supremacy among the various London orchestras.'

Later that day, also at the Festival Hall, Christopher Bishop outlined to the press the plans for the next season. In a period of deep recession the Philharmonia was on average playing to a twenty-five per cent larger audience than the other London orchestras, helped enormously by the success of the subscription scheme. Two seasons of consistently full houses had been a great boost to morale. July 1982 marked the end of the initial period of du Maurier's sponsorship but they had promised their continuing support until December 1982 at least. This would include two more *Music of Today* concerts, this time in the Barbican; the Arts Council refused to make grants available to orchestras other than the London Symphony to appear at the Barbican, and so du Maurier were also opening up a new concert venue that would have been otherwise unavailable for the Philharmonia's own promotions.

The decline in recording work coincided with a useful revival of the orchestra's connection with the film industry. There had been occasional film recordings over the years, but very few, certainly when compared with the large number of film scores recorded by the Philharmonia in the late 1940s. In July 1982 they were engaged to record the music for the Monty Python award-winning film *The Meaning of Life*. Only twenty-five strings and a harp were required but the sessions at Britannia Row studios under John du Prez earned these players £110 per session, nearly three times the usual rates. Three more films were booked for later in the season. It was good financially, and it also meant the beginning of a useful new aspect of the orchestra's activities.

The Philharmonia also had four Prom concerts in the summer of 1982. They opened on 19 July with Giulini conducting the Mozart *Linz* Symphony and Bruckner's Seventh Symphony. It was the first time Giulini had conducted the Bruckner in London, and in the *Financial Times* Dominic Gill wrote: 'Monday's Prom was a paradigm of the best kind of Giulini concert: cultivated and refined in every aspect, relaxed and magisterial in its command. It was no small advantage for Maestro Giulini either, to have at his artistic direction the orchestra which is, just now, far and away the most rewarding of London's five: warm-toned, fine-tuned, alert, vigorous and responsive.'

Soon after joining the Philharmonia, Christopher Warren-Green had revived the Philharmonia Ensemble begun by Carl Pini as an offshoot of the main orchestra. There were not frequent opportunities to perform but an important engagement was at the English Heritage Concert series on 14 August in Bath. Seventeen strings, with oboist Gordon Hunt and harpsichordist Leslie Pearson, gave a programme of Bach, Handel, Elgar, Mozart and Samuel Barber in the famous Pump Rooms. Christopher Warren-Green directed the works from his leader's desk, something he enjoyed greatly and did extremely well.

The Philharmonia had not been to the Lucerne Festival for fourteen years when, in late August 1982, they returned.

The theme of the Festival was Britain's place in music, and Kennedy's performance of the Elgar brought him back to the stage eight times. Even then, he was not allowed to go before he had played an encore – his own Opus 1, a short, jazzy piece which was received exceptionally well. Next day, the concert should have been conducted by André Previn and included Vaughan Williams' *London* Symphony, but Previn was out of action with a damaged back; his late withdrawal left insufficient rehearsal time for Ashkenazy to rehearse the Vaughan Williams, and Sibelius's Fifth Symphony was substituted for the morning concert.

Sir Clifford Curzon had collapsed at a rehearsal in Lucerne and had to withdraw from the opening concert. On Wednesday 1 September, while the Philharmonia were preparing to leave for Edinburgh, he died, and so Simon Rattle dedicated their first Usher Hall concert to his memory. Curzon had been a frequent and much-loved soloist in Edinburgh, most recently accompanied by Rattle himself. The Fauré *Requiem* was chosen, one of the least sensational works, and was most movingly sung by Jennifer Smith, Dale Duesing and the Edinburgh Festival Chorus, a fitting tribute to one of the most musical but least sensational of pianists.

Later in the month, in Lyon, Marek Janowski was the conductor for three concerts: the Overture *King Lear, Herminie* and the *Te Deum* (with Grace Bumbry, Arley Reece, the Berlioz Festival Chorus and the Coro Caso) were performed twice in the Auditorium Maurice Ravel and on 20 September in Les Halles de Côte St André, the birthplace of Berlioz, just an hour's drive away near Grenoble. This latter was an open-air concert with performers and audience packed into the large square with its sides roofed in, still with the original beams and tiles.

Ashkenazy opened the autumn Festival Hall season with a programme that revealed yet another side of his versatile genius. It was the first public performance of Mussorgsky's *Pictures at an Exhibition* in his own new arrangement. Ashkenazy justified his own audacity at re-orchestrating a work that had become so popular the world over in Ravel's version by his observation that Ravel had not followed Mussorgsky's original dynamics and intentions. 'I don't think he was intent on bringing out Mussorgsky's spirit, very dark and Russian.' he said. 'In Mussorgskian terms it sounds wrong.' Ashkenazy's version certainly sounded darker, and the results in concert and on record were well received. Decca had recorded the piano version already and planned to couple it with the new orchestral version, which Ashkenazy and the Philharmonia recorded the day after the concert, but in the event they were issued separately.

Muti's first concert of the new season had the second performance of *Alexander Nevsky*, the Prokofiev cantata he had first performed in March 1977. The concert on 2 November was being broadcast when suddenly a group of demonstrators left their seats and began to shout. Some grabbed the microphones and began protesting 'How could we listen to the Soviet Union sing when Anatoly Scharansky is dying in a Russian prison?' This came in the middle of Irina Arkhipova's solo 'Field of the Dead', and she tried to start again – three times. Muti wanted to go off but was persuaded to continue; to abandon the performance would allow the demonstrators to have their way. The BBC surprisingly had not broken off their recording of the concert as soon as the trouble had started, nor did they later edit out the disturbance from the tapes. Irina Arkhipova, visibly upset and in tears, sat patiently until the commotion had subsided and continued; the agitators seemed to have lost all advantage but it had been very disturbing for all.

Andrew Davis conducted a Gala Concert on 7 December, the second of two performances of Elgar's *Dream of Gerontius*. The concert had been offered to the Prince of Wales as a wedding present the previous year; the Prince is also the Patron of the Elgar Foundation and he asked that the proceeds of the concert, which he and the Princess were delighted to attend, should go to the Elgar Foundation's appeal for the Elgar Birthplace. The soloists, conductor and orchestra all responded to the Prince's generosity by donating their own fees for the concert to the appeal. Du Maurier also contributed to the occasion by not only sponsoring the concert but providing a reception for the royal couple to meet the orchestra and other guests afterwards.

The concert also marked the twenty-fifth anniversary of the Philharmonia Chorus, and the particularly happy relationship between chorus and orchestra was reflected in the fact that twelve of the season's concerts already featured them jointly. To mark the jubilee the chorus had produced a handsome souvenir booklet, and there had also been a party on 26 November in the Ironmongers' Hall, to which not only the chorus, some of the orchestra (the rest were busy recording *Pineapple Poll* with Sir Charles Mackerras) and many distinguished visitors came, but also Mrs Erna Pitz, widow of the first chorus-master Wilhelm Pitz, sealing the occasion by presenting to the chorus her husband's scores of Beethoven's Ninth Symphony and, appropriately, the *Dream of Gerontius*.

Since its formation in March 1981, the Friends of the Philharmonia, under the Chairmanship of Hazel Westbury, had flourished in its support for the subscription scheme. Several recitals and talks had been given; the very first yielded over eighty subscribers. The second, in mid-November 1981, was held in the elegant reception rooms of the Fishmongers' Hall and in addition to the 185 new subscribers there had been sixty-eight students who had taken up the new schools' subscription scheme. Directors of Music from several schools had attended their recitals, and through them and their subscribers came about the Young Friends of the Philharmonia. Through this some fourteen schools eventually joined and could subscribe at half the box-office price. Young Friends could also attend lectures and orchestral sessions, and at their May 1982 meeting Christopher Bishop announced that there were plans for an orchestra of gifted young musicians to be drawn entirely from the schools subscribing to the Young Friends scheme. Principals of the Philharmonia were to coach the orchestra during the day and then join it for a public concert in the evening.

On 18 December over a hundred young players met in the Royal College of Music. They were trained as sections in the morning and then rehearsed as a full orchestra in the afternoon by Jacek Kasprzyk, who conducted a concert in the evening of a remarkably high standard. The success of the programme, Tchaikovsky's *Romeo and Juliet* Overture and Dvořák's Eighth Symphony, was such that plans were immediately laid for a repeat of the exercise in December 1983.

16. *Sinopoli and the Future, 1983-5*

As 1983 opened, the concert agents were all wooing the Philharmonia with suggestions for a new Principal Conductor, but the Council would make no definite approaches yet.

For 13 February 1983 Christopher Bishop had engaged a young Italian to conduct Mahler's *Des Knaben Wunderhorn* and Schumann's Second Symphony.

Giuseppe Sinopoli was just thirty-six, Venetian born, and raised in Sicily. He saw himself as a late developer musically, since he had qualified as a doctor of medicine in Padua, but he had studied music since he was twelve and continued his lessons throughout his medical course. In 1972 he was appointed Professor of Contemporary and Electronic Music at the Venice Conservatory and soon afterwards moved to Vienna to study conducting under Hans Swarowsky. During the 1970s Sinopoli continued to teach in Siena, Darmstadt and Paris and received a number of commissions to compose. He steadily developed a fine conducting career that began with an outstanding *Aïda* at the Teatro La Fenice in Venice in 1976, continued with a sensational new production of *Macbeth* at the Deutsches Oper in Berlin in February 1980 and included numerous guest appearances with major orchestras in Berlin, Los Angeles, New York and Israel. He settled in Austria and made a few recordings for Deutsche Grammophon of contemporary music by Bussotti and Maderna, a Brahms *Requiem* and *Nabucco*. His concerts he limited to fifty a year, half orchestral and half operatic. His London orchestral début had been with the London Symphony Orchestra, on 27 May 1982, conducting Mahler's Sixth Symphony. It was a performance that induced ardent rage from staunch Mahlerians as much for his extravagant platform manner as for the eccentricity of his approach to the music. It was also a performance that Christopher Bishop heard and he had been very impressed.

Sinopoli had very definite views on the relationship of conductor and orchestra: 'The relationship between an orchestra and a conductor should begin as an encounter and end as a fusion. If they form two separate poles standing apart from one another then there is failure. The first need is to eliminate the distance between those poles: once that is achieved there is the chance of making great music. What fascinates me is making everyone, singers and players, perform *above* their ability.'

When Sinopoli first rehearsed the Philharmonia in Kingsway Hall for the 13 February concert there was fusion.

At the concert the consensus of critical opinion was that here was a conductor who could certainly make the Philharmonia play with great refinement. Verdi's *Force of Destiny* Overture was electrifying, while the five Mahler *Wunderhorn* songs, sung by Thomas Allen, had great transparency. The Schumann symphony, a difficult piece to hold together, sounded lively and at times abrasive. The critics felt it was an out-of-the-rut concert, with some strange speeds, either just too slow or too fast, but from a man who was clearly an enthusiastic champion of the composer rather than being a showman.

After the concert Christopher Bishop and Martin Jones put the proposition to Sinopoli: would he be interested in the Principal Conductorship of the Philharmonia if everyone was in agreement? The answer was an immediate 'Yes.' The orchestra voted on the appointment and not one player was against the proposal. A verbal offer was made to Sinopoli within a week and a draft contract was drawn up on 5 March.

The enthusiasm of the Council rested on their feeling that Sinopoli was willing to take a full part in the life of the Philharmonia. He had a wide range of interesting projects with the orchestra in mind, including the promotion of children's concerts and local tours, and was willing to take part in some social functions. He was an established conductor and had just signed an exclusive four-year recording contract with Deutsche Grammophon in December 1982. A quick appointment was in everyone's interest and paralleled that of Muti just ten years before.

Not all was to be plain sailing even before the contract was signed. At a stage before a formal offer had been made to Sinopoli, and before the orchestra had voted on the appointment, Ashkenazy's agent, Jasper Parrott, discovered that Sinopoli had been approached, and immediately informed Ashkenazy, who felt slighted that he had not been kept informed.

The Management of the Orchestra were in a difficult position. It would have been courteous in due course to inform Ashkenazy, but since Parrott had made it clear that he wanted Ashkenazy to be considered for the post of Principal Conductor, they felt it was hardly ethical to discuss one candidate for the post with another at this juncture.

Although he soon withdrew from the post of Principal Guest Conductor, Ashkenazy remained loyal to the Philharmonia, continuing the very close relationship already established and conducting two extremely successful extended tours in 1984.

The appointment of Sinopoli was to take effect from 1 January 1984 but there were plans already to do at least one recording and a couple of concerts before then. Meanwhile, the season continued with the older generation of conductors, Sanderling conducting the Philharmonia in three concerts. At the rehearsal for the second of these the players were saddened to hear of the death of Sir Adrian Boult. A great favourite with the profession, he had courtesy, wit and an economy of word and gesture that would be greatly missed. The following evening, 24 February, the Philharmonia dedicated their performance of Brahms's beautiful *Nänie* to his memory. In asking the audience not to applaud, as a gesture of respect, Christopher Bishop reminded them that Sir Adrian had championed the orchestra in its darkest hours in 1964 when they faced extinction and had pleaded with the public not to allow the Philharmonia 'to be snuffed out like a candle'.

Neville Marriner conducted a concert and recording of Mendelssohn's *Midsummer Night's Dream* in mid-March. He had early memories of the orchestra. He had played at the back of the second violins for Toscanini in 1952 and as an extra on other occasions. His own Academy of St Martin in the Fields had grown out of a desire to found a string orchestra of the same quality as the Philharmonia, and he now brought over twenty-five years of experience as well as great personal charm. Rehearsals with Marriner are a model of how to get the best from players without rubbing anyone up the wrong way, and in performance he allows the occasional smile of warm encouragement to lift the atmosphere.

A novelty came in the engagement of the Philharmonia for a classic rock disc, the *Best of the Alan Parsons Project*. Recorded at EMI's Abbey Road studios, it was arranged, produced and conducted by Andrew Powell, a member of the *Project*. All the numbers came from the pens of Powell himself and his colleague, Eric Woolfson, a former engineer on EMI's own staff. The whole idea was an interesting departure and one to which the orchestra took well.

April saw the beginning of another du Maurier series of concerts, and 13 April produced a very fine performance of Elgar's First Symphony by Bernard Haitink, recorded a week later for EMI.

Ashkenazy returned in May to conduct and record Sibelius's Third Symphony and Matačić, who was scheduled to go with the orchestra to Barcelona, conducted a Wagner concert. Soloist was Anne Evans, the chosen Brünahilde for the next season's Welsh National Opera *Ring*. She gave real promise of things to come in the closing scene of *Götterdämmerung*, rising strongly above the full orchestra. *The Flying Dutchman* Overture appeared on the second of the Barcelona concert programmes which Matačić conducted on 8 and 9 June in the Palau.

In June the orchestra had the opportunity to make their first recording with Sinopoli. Schubert's *Unfinished* Symphony and Mendelssohn's *Italian* Symphony were scheduled to be recorded by Deutsche Grammophon in Kingsway Hall on 24 and 25 June. Both are very well-known works but the Philharmonia had the chance to become familiar with Sinopoli's view of the Mendelssohn at least from two concerts he was conducting just a week earlier. It was to the Mendelssohn, too, that he gave most of his own interpretation, the inner movements in particular having a flow and steadiness of rhythm that were distinctive. On 21 June he conducted just one work, Mahler's Ninth Symphony. It is a work that needs some savagery but the critics found that it was there too often for their taste and gave him rather a rough ride for it. They claimed it was over-aggressive, but Sinopoli had intended that the second movement's waltzes, for example, were to clash harshly against one another, explaining in rehearsal that this section of the work was 'not nice'.

The summer recording programme, for once, had no complete operas, but more than adequate compensation came in a whole batch of film and television sessions which paid well and were to prove highly successful. For Handmade Films the orchestra recorded the soundtrack of *Bullshot*, conducted by John du Prez. Then at CTS studios Carl Davis conducted the music for the film *Champions* and for a major Channel 4 Television serial, *The Far Pavilions*, a good example of the bonuses to be gained from this new aspect of the Philharmonia's work, for the serial was highly acclaimed when it was first screened in January 1984 and Chrysalis issued a record of the music from the soundtrack just a month later, an extra source of income without a single note of music having to be played.

Matačić made his Prom début on 23 July with the Philharmonia and had as soloist in Beethoven's First Piano Concerto Cecile Ousset. The major work in the concert was Bruckner's Third Symphony, a work seldom heard but entirely suited to Matačić, whose career had been closely associated with Bruckner's music in the past. A week later, a second Prom shifted the emphasis to the twentieth century with Britten's Cello Symphony, Rachmaninov's Second Symphony and the Prelude to Janáček's *From the House of the Dead*, all conducted by Simon Rattle.

The theme of the 1983 Edinburgh Festival was Vienna 1900, and it was wholly appropriate that the Philharmonia should begin the opening concert of the Festival with Berg's *Three Orchestral Pieces*.

Perhaps the most exciting concerts of September were on the 12th and 13th, when the orchestra were due to give two performances of Bach's B minor Mass with Muti in Italy. The performance on 12 September was in the Sala Nervi in Rome and was to be a special occasion, in the presence of His Holiness the Pope. The soloists were Margaret Marshall, Ortrun Wenkel, Francisco Araiza and Gwynne Howell, with the Swedish Radio Chorus. The orchestra flew out on the afternoon of 10 September and were delighted at the reunion with Muti after nearly a year's absence. The rehearsals were intense but happy occasions.

The Pope was not able to attend, as he was in Austria, but seven thousand people were packed in the vast hangar-like hall of the Sala Nervi. For the Press the concert was a triumph. *L'Europeo* described the Philharmonia as making 'a stupendous sound even at the back of the sections' and spoke of the outstanding virtuosity of the soloists, 'the baroque trumpet, the oboes, the infallible hunting horn'. The infallible hunting horn was of course Michael Thompson who did not crack a note at rehearsal or performance. The difficulty of the solo is not helped by having to wait some ten numbers and about an hour's music before launching 'cold' into the treacherous *obbligato*. The lack of an interval was not appreciated by the orchestra or choir, for whom it was a very long evening. For Muti it was, in his own words, 'the climax of ten years'. The triumph was repeated in the lovely old Teatro Morlacchi in Perugïa next day.

Back in London the preparations began for Bruckner's Eighth Symphony with Giulini which would open the orchestra's Festival Hall season. Much had been made in the press of falling audience numbers but in fact for the other three London orchestras their numbers had dropped by only one per cent, to an average of sixty per cent houses, whereas the Philharmonia attendances averaged seventy-eight per cent, the same as the previous season. The eighteen per cent difference could be accounted for by the subscription scheme, the numbers for which were also rising very steadily.

The third Festival Hall concert of the season, on Thursday 29 September, brought an unexpected but exciting début for a new young conductor. The planned programme was Mahler's Third Symphony with Tilson Thomas, but he had to withdraw at a late stage with shoulder trouble, and there seemed to be no one available but a twenty-five-year-old Finnish conductor, Esa-Pekka Salonen, who had conducted every leading Scandinavian orchestra but never abroad. Bishop knew nothing about him except that the Swedish Chorus in Rome had spoken highly of him and the agent, Joeske van Walsum, had a video of him conducting which he could let him see.

Salonen seemed very good on film and to be absolutely sure, Martin Jones was invited round to see it from the players' point of view. They rang Salonen: he wanted the weekend to think about it as he did not know Mahler Third Symphony. By Monday he had learned the work and accepted the engagement.

The Thursday performance was a triumph for the young Finn. There were some signs of inexperience and some loss of tension but the overall command and authority were unnervingly apparent, together with his total grasp of the score. The results did not end with the glowing Press tributes. The Philharmonia immediately signed him up exclusively from the 1984–5 season, beginning with the 1984 Edinburgh Festival, and the success of his work that season culminated in his appointment as Principal Guest Conductor from January 1985.

Sinopoli's Venetian background had resulted in an invitation to conduct the Philharmonia at the Biennale Festival in Venice during the first few days of October. Sinopoli had wanted three dates, but in the end only 1 October was possible and even that meant flying out on the day of the concert. The success of his Mahler Ninth in June made him anxious to repeat the work in Venice, together with three Webern works, the *Five Pieces* for orchestra, *Passacaglia* and *Variations*. Shortage of rehearsal time and travel delays reduced this to just the *Passacaglia* and the *Variations*. With the difficult acoustics of the Teatro la Fenice the players had difficulty hearing each other, and the experience of playing surrounded by the audience on three sides was uncomfortable, but the results for the audience seemed to be very impressive. *Corriere della Sera* commented that, 'With a rare and disciplined orchestra like the Philharmonia, Sinopoli gave us a dialectic Webern, always very authentic and true.'

After a month of concerts, chiefly with Matačić and Ashkenazy, the orchestra were joined by Muti in London for a series of three concerts. On the last day of October, Radu Lupu joined him for a performance of Schumann's Piano Concerto and then Muti directed the rarely heard First Symphony of Bruckner. It made a welcome change from the preponderance of late Bruckner symphonies currently in the London concert calendar – Matačić's concert had included the Ninth.

The last Muti concert featured John Wallace, making his Festival Hall solo début with the Philharmonia in Hummel's Trumpet Concerto. In Leeds a month later another Philharmonia principal, oboist Gordon Hunt, gave a virtuoso performance on the Vaughan Williams Concerto. The conductor was Paavo Berglund, a native of Finland like Sibelius whose Second Symphony he conducted in the same concert. Berglund was beginning to work more regularly with the Philharmonia. With his own Bournemouth Symphony Orchestra he had been used to a lot of rehearsal but he was adapting well to the conditions in the London orchestras. Audiences soon overcame the strangeness of seeing his baton held in his left hand, and the success of his performances brought bookings far into the next season, including a major tour in October 1984.

Leader Christopher Warren-Green extended his activities to leading a reduced Philharmonia Orchestra in a concert in Aylesbury's Civic Centre on 1 December. Two Mozart symphonies framed two Haydn concertos, John Wallace in the Trumpet Concerto and Michael Thompson in a Horn Concerto. The second of the Mozart symphonies was the 'Linz', and Warren-Green was thought to be taking a big risk in trying to direct such a difficult work from his leader's chair, but it worked. Further experience was gained in this field with a recording for Nimbus on 19 and 20 December of the Trumpet Concerto and both Horn Concertos. It was issued in July 1984, the first Compact Disc to be pressed in Britain.

The year ended with the Philharmonia's first major recording with Sinopoli. It was of Puccini's *Manon Lescaut* which he had conducted at Covent Garden in May 1983 and which BBC2 viewers had seen on television. It would be a critical test of the conductor-orchestra relationship. *Manon Lescaut* is a work that a symphony orchestra finds difficult just to pick up and play, unlike *Tosca* or *La Bohème*, for example. It needs learning, and here Sinopoli was very careful with his orchestral rehearsal. His English was still not very good, especially in front of over eighty people, but the rapport that existed allowed him to ask for specific phrasing or bowing and for the players to ask for a change of beat here, a clearer intention there. Sinopoli also got on exceedingly well with the singers and was rewarded with some outstanding performances.

Less happily, the Manon Lescaut sessions were the last to be made in Kingsway Hall. Built in 1913 and used as one of the world's finest recording halls for forty years, it had been bought by the Greater London Council in March 1983 for £975,000. EMI and Decca who leased the hall had been offered it for £1 million but the offer was not taken up as both companies were involved in mergers at the time. The Women's Committee of the GLC wanted to start the process of rebuilding and refurbishing and so no more recording sessions could be allowed. Even when completed, around April 1985, recording might not be permitted or even possible, as the rebuilding was likely to affect the unique acoustics. It was sadly appropriate that the Philharmonia should be the last orchestra to play in Kingsway Hall as it had been the venue for its very first public concert in October 1945.

January 1984 saw not only Sinopoli's appointment as Principal Conductor confirmed for a five-year period but also the announcement of Oliver Knussen as the Philharmonia's Composer in Residence. Knussen had established a fine rapport with the Philharmonia, especially through the du Maurier *Music of Today* concerts and had already had his own Third Symphony recorded by them in 1981. His Fourth Symphony would be his first composition under his new title, commissioned by the orchestra for the 1985–6 season.

By far the most adventurous undertaking of the first months of 1984 was a major tour with Ashkenazy. From mid-February to mid-March he conducted the Philharmonia in Canada, the United States and Australia, the highlight a complete cycle of the Beethoven symphonies and piano concertos at the Adelaide Festival. The players voted it one of the most enjoyable tours ever undertaken by the Philharmonia, and the Beethoven cycle was hailed as a unique milestone in Adelaide's musical history. Administrator Jane Moss had planned everything superbly and this was her last tour before she left the Philharmonia. The successful co-operation of this extended spell of work with the seemingly tireless Ashkenazy was repeated in a hectic tour at the end of May. Concerts in Italy, Germany, Austria, Switzerland and France were followed by two concerts in Reykjavik, the second of which featured Ashkenazy's son as solo pianist.

Between these two major tours, Simon Rattle conducted a series of concerts in April 1984 entitled 'Mahler, Strauss and their influence', and which were sponsored by Toshiba. Rattle had been offered a concentrated period of work, and Christopher Bishop suggested that he choose a linking theme. Works by Mahler and Richard Strauss were combined with pieces from the Second Viennese School of composers in a highly enterprising programme. Integrated with the six concerts was a showing of Ken Russell's film *Mahler*, in the Queen Elizabeth Hall, a talk by Hans Keller in the Purcell Room and an exhibition of photographs. Not all the concerts were full, but they were generally well attended by 1984 standards.

In May the London public saw Sinopoli conduct the Philharmonia for the first time since his appointment as Principal Conductor had taken effect. Two performances of the Verdi *Requiem* brought him before the Philharmonia Chorus for the first time. Following in the footsteps of Giulini and Muti made it even more of a challenge for Sinopoli to justify himself to the critics, a challenge that was not made any easier by last-minute problems of illness of the soloists and their last-minute replacements.

The last concerts of the 1983–4 season were conducted by Muti and included some interested works. Cherubini's *Coronation* Mass was one such work, and it was recorded by EMI. Muti's 6 July concert marked the end of the four-year sponsorship by the House of du Maurier. Their help in allowing more rehearsal time, the engagement of the best artists and the selling of more seats by funding the administration of the subscription scheme had been incalculable, and there were other more permanent reminders of their service to the Philharmonia in the boxed sets of Beethoven symphonies and Tchaikovsky ballets. The orchestra had also now adopted the familiar du Maurier red as its 'house colour' permanently.

For its 1984–5 season the orchestra would certainly need to look for major new sponsorship. Some of the season's concerts were already supported by Nissan, Condé Nast and NCR, but more needed to be found. Ideally, three sponsors, each contributing £100,000, would be better, to spread the risk in future seasons. One worrying aspect of future work was a falling-off in the recording industry: sixty-six sessions were played in the 1983–4 season, eighty-two the season before. Considerable compensation was being found in an increase in film work. Just one example came in June 1984 when eight sessions for a major Warner Brothers film, *Ladyhawke*, were squeezed into one of the busiest weeks in the year. The orchestra could ill afford to turn them down in the light of the very high fees such sessions offered.

A glance at the programmes for 1984–5 shows that the Philharmonia was 'in excellent health', to use Chairman Martin Jones' favourite phrase in Philharmonia Trust meeting reports. The list of conductors contained many of the names with which the orchestra had already made history – Giulini, Sawallisch, Sanderling – and a continuation of the highly successful work with Muti and Ashkenazy. After two Proms and young Esa-Pekka Salonen's Edinburgh Festival début with two concerts of works by Brahms, Sibelius and Lutoslawski, Giulini opened the autumn 1984 Festival Hall season with a Brahms cycle. Sawallisch would be in London in February 1985 and then take the orchestra on a tour to Spain, Ashkenazy had a Swiss tour also in February 1985 and there were concerts with Andrew Davis. Berglund framed the season with a tour to Sweden, Denmark and Finland in September 1984 and to Finland again in July 1985. The major tour of the season was undoubtedly a visit to Japan in March 1985 with Simon Rattle and Neville Marriner.

The 1984–5 season would also be the first full one for Sinopoli as Principal Conductor. Concerts were planned for October and November 1984 and again in January 1985, with works as diverse as Elgar's *Caractacus* March and Mahler's Second Symphony. Sinopoli would also tour with the Philharmonia, to Lille in November 1984, Sicily in April and Italy in June 1985, May 1985 marked the centenary of the birth of Otto Klemperer, and Giulini would conduct two performances of Beethoven's *Missa Solemnis*. It would be a tribute to the memory of a great era in the Philharmonia's past and a fitting reminder that the wheel had indeed turned full circle in a return to the quality of standards associated with that era.

The artistic health of the Philharmonia has scarcely, if ever, been better. Financially, the position in the summer of 1984 looked decidedly less healthy. Not only was there the removal of the du Maurier lifeline but in March 1984 the Arts Council published its report *The Glory of the Garden* in which it threatened severe cuts in grant aid to many musical organizations. By far the most radical of its suggestions was that one of the London orchestras should be uprooted and moved to somewhere in the Midlands, probably Nottingham. The Philharmonia did not feel itself to be in any danger but they were disappointed that no decision had yet been taken on a plan it had submitted in March 1983, jointly with the London Philharmonic Orchestra, suggesting that the current free-for-all at the Royal Festival Hall was artistically unsatisfactory. With the intended demise of the Greater London Council, there was a unique opportunity to establish a Board, on which the orchestras would be represented, which would oversee the planning of the London concert season and which would engage the Philharmonia and London Philharmonic Orchestras for their Festival Hall appearances. These two orchestras would thus be the resident; the London Symphony Orchestra, who were established at the Barbican, would give a small number of concerts at the Festival Hall, while the Royal Philharmonic Orchestra concentrated on touring and concerts at the Fairfield Hall and a number of Festival Hall dates. This idea was re-submitted by the Philharmonia and London Philharmonic Orchestras in response to an official request for plans from the Arts Council in November 1983 and had appeared to meet with their approval.

After the appearance of *The Glory of the Garden*, the Arts Council certainly did not hurry to make up its mind. It spent the rest of 1984 waiting in vain for one orchestra to offer to leave London, and it appointed Neil Duncan as 'special adviser' to report on the four orchestras with a clear decision on which of the four was to be axed. The growing feeling that it had put itself in an almost impossible situation was confirmed on 20 December when the Council announced to the Press that it would not be publishing the special adviser's report and that the £280,000 cuts promised in April would be spread over all four orchestras.

The Philharmonia learned of this officially in a letter dated 17 January 1985. The letter, from the Secretary-General of the Arts Council, also informed the orchestra that direct funding would be based on assessment of its estimates and plans and would be withdrawn if there was any marked fall in standards or efficiency. Two further conditions were that the four orchestras would be required to repeat at least one third of their London programmes in the regions and that a minimum of one third of the members of the governing body of each orchestra would have to be chosen from outside the playing members of that orchestra.

There were mixed feelings in the orchestra at the appointment in December 1984 of Ronald Grierson of the Arts Council to head a working party that would look at the running of the South Bank by the Arts Council after the GLC's presumed demise in April 1986. It meant the loss of an indefatigable Chairman of the Philharmonia Trust and an honorary member of the orchestra (since 1981) but the appointment of someone who knew so much about the London orchestral scene to such a position after ten years work with the Philharmonia was reassuring indeed.

At long last, on 8 February 1985, Christopher Bishop received a letter from the Arts Council expressing its concern over the delay in coming to a decision about the plan for the Festival Hall. To the great relief of the Philharmonia and the London Philharmonic Orchestras the plan would be given the full support and funding of the Arts Council. Further relief soon followed with the announcement, on the day that the orchestra flew to japan, of the offer of new major sponsorship from Nissan UK Limited. Nissan had been very supportive in recent years of individual concerts: now they were providing a very generous lifeline of £100, 000 per year for four years.

A further indication of the upturn in the Philharmonia's fortunes was their appointment on 1 April 1985 of a President, Monsieur Vincent Meyer. A young Swiss philanthropist, passionately interested in music and with a deep personal enthusiasm for the Philharmonia, Vincent Meyer had been introduced to the orchestra in 1984 by Daniel Salem, Vice-Chairman and later Grierson's successor as Chairman of the Trust. At that stage Meyer's help was a generous donation but now his enthusiasm lay in helping to raise money abroad for the Philharmonia in addition to taking an intense personal interest in the orchestra's affairs. Like the Philharmonia's first President, the Maharaja of Mysore, Vincent Meyer has the challenge of providing the orchestra with a secure foundation on which it can flourish and move forward and outward in the perilous world of the Arts.

All British orchestras exist in a jungle that offers poor financial pickings and little shelter from political games and artistic philistinism and the Philharmonia has been prey to all three in its time. It survived the first nine months of its life with only two public concerts and no recording contract; it survived Walter Legge's withdrawal of his personal financial support in 1964; it survived near-collapse and absorption in 1972 and it struggled into the 1980s through recession and financial cutbacks. In its fortieth year it receives consistent praise from public and Press alike for its adventurous and constructive programmes. This, coupled with the renowned artistic excellence with which the word

'Philharmonia' has always been synonymous, its distinguished conductors and artists, and consistently high attendances at the Festival Hall, gives the orchestra absolute confidence that it will flourish for another forty years.

Appendix A: The Council of Management

The constitution of a London self-governing orchestra is not always clearly understood, and it may be helpful here to outline it as it applies to the Philharmonia Orchestra in particular.

The orchestra is a registered charity limited by guarantee and became such in 1964 when Walter Legge suspended the old Philharmonia. The Council is, in fact, a working board of directors. Its members are elected from the orchestral membership for a period of three years, and one third of the Council must stand for re-election each year, thus ensuring a healthy flow of new ideas and some degree of continuity. It has to deal with every aspect of the orchestra's life from the financial statement given by the accountant at every meeting to personnel matters, conductors, repertoire, tours, fund-raising and the endless minor crises that all such organizations experience.

The Council employs a staff of seventeen to run its affairs – Managing Director, Administrator, Finance Officer, Personnel Manager and so on – a small number when one looks at the Los Angeles Philharmonic's staff of over fifty, for example. Making music on a world-class level is both time-consuming and costly, and so the two halves of the management team must pull together. The final decision on any matter rests with the Council.

Election to the Council is a serious and considered decision by candidate and electors alike. The work is hard, with some thirty meetings every year and no financial reward or special privileges. Relations with colleagues can suffer, and sometimes unpopular decisions have to be taken, so members must be both impartial and sensitive to the players.

Informal meetings can and do take place at any time and are useful for dealing with minor matters and consulting with the players. For the formal meetings an agenda is drawn up by the Chairman and the Managing Director. The most frequent problems are those concerning personnel and can vary from a member having turned up in brown socks for the second concert in a week to the seating in the viola section. With the Managing Director in attendance the Council is the meeting-ground between the players and the administration.

Appendix B: Recordings

For an orchestra that has spent much of its working life in a recording studio, a complete discography would here be both appropriate and helpful but because of its very size there just is not space to include it in this volume. The author has compiled a complete discography covering the period July 1945 to December 1984, and it is hoped that it will be available separately during the latter part of 1985. However, it may be helpful for readers to have a list of Philharmonia and New Philharmonia recordings currently available and one is set out below.

Although an outline of the Philharmonia's recording history are to be found in the main text of the book, it is worth giving just a brief summary here:

July 1945 to June 1946:
 Casual recordings booked by letter agreement with Columbia and HMV (EMI Records)

June 1946 to July 1972:
 The Philharmonia had an exclusive contract with Columbia until 1964 which also allowed it to record for the other EMI companies HMV, Parlophone and Capitol. From March 1964 the contract was non-exclusive, i.e. the orchestra could also record for other companies.

March 1964 to date:
 In addition to EMI, the Philharmonia has recorded for nearly all the major record companies, usually by letter agreement. The contract arrangement with EMI was unusual, and from 1972 EMI also engaged the orchestra on a 'per job' basis.

The Philharmonia claims to be 'the world's most recorded orchestra'.

Philharmonia Recordings

The list below is of Philharmonia and New Philharmonia recordings available in April 1985. The author is grateful for the help provided by the *Gramophone Classical Catalogue* in compiling this list. The information is as accurate and up-to-date as possible but readers should bear in mind that the record market is constantly changing and any catalogue dates rapidly.

Recordings are set out under conductor heading, in alphabetical order. Catalogue numbers are of long-play records only, tapes and compact discs have not been listed to avoid complication.

Conductor:	**ABBADO**	
Tchaikovsky:	*Symphony 2*	2542 113
	Romeo and Juliet	
Conductor:	**ACKERMANN**	
	Operetta excerpts (Schwarzkopf)	ASD2807
R. Strauss:	*Four Last Songs*	RLS751
	Closing Scene from Capriccio	
Conductor:	**ANSERMET**	
Stravinsky:	*Firebird Suite*	CC7500
Conductor: (and soloist)	**ASHKENAZY**	
Beethoven:	*Symphony 5*	SXDL7540
	Symphony 6	SXDL7578
	Symphony 7	411941-1DH
	Coriolan Overture	
	Egmont Overture	
	Leonora No. 3 Overture	SXDL7540
Bruch:	*Kol Nidrei*	SXDL7678
Dvořák:	*Cello Concerto* (Harrell)	
Borodin:	*Prince Igor-Dances*	410121-1
Mozart:	*Piano Concertos 11/13*	SXDL7556
	Piano Concertos 15/16	SXL7010
	Piano Concertos 17/21	SXL6881

	Piano Concertos 19/24	SXL6947
	Piano Concertos 22	SXL6982
	Piano Concertos 23/27	SXDL7530
	Piano Concertos 25/26	411810-1DH
	Concert Rondo K382	SXL6982
Mussorgsky:	*Pictures at an Exhibition*	410121-1
Sibelius:	*Symphony 2*	SXDL7513
	Symphony 5	SXDL7541
	Symphony 7	SXDL7580
	En Saga	SXDL7541
	Tapiola	SXDL7580
	Symphony 4	SXDL7517
	Finlandia	
	Luonnatar (Söderstrom)	
Tchaikovsky:	*Violin Concerto*	SXL6854
	Valse-Scherzo (Belkin)	
Conductor:	**ATHERTON**	
Bennett:	*Aubade*	ZRG907
Conductor:	**ATZMON**	
Liszt:	*Piano Concertos 1/2* (Ohlsson)	CFP4402
Conductor:	**BARBIROLLI**	
Berlioz:	*Nuits d'été* (Baker)	ASD2444
Brahms:	*Piano Concerto 1* (Barenboim)	SXLP30283
Elgar:	*Symphony 1*	SXLP30268
Mahler:	*Symphony 5*	SLS785
	Symphony 6	
	Rückert Lieder	SLS785/ASD2721/
		CEP4144243
	(Baker)	ASD4409
Ravel:	*Scheherazade* (Baker)	ASD2444
Tchaikovsky:	*Piano Concerto 1* (Ogdon)	SXLP30552
Elgar:	*Enigma Variations*	ESD7169
	Cockaigne Overture	
Verdi:	*Requiem*	CFP4144283
Elgar:	*Pomp and Circumstance 1-5*	SXLP30456
	Elegy for Strings	
	Froissart Overture	
	Sospiri	
Conductor:	**BARTOLETTI**	
Puccini:	*Manon Lescaut*	SLS962
Conductor:	**BARZIN**	
Bruch:	*Violin Concerto 1*	*CFP40374*
Mendelssohn:	*Violin Concerto* (Milstein)	
Conductor:	**BOETTCHER**	
Cherubini:	*Symphony in D*	*6500 154*

Weber	*Symphony 1*	
Conductor:	**BÖHM**	
Mozart:	*Così fan tutte*	*SLS5028*
Conductor:	**BONYNGE**	
Meyerbeer:	*Les Huguenots*	*SET460*
	Popular Songs (Sutherland)	*SXL6619*
Conductor:	**BOULEZ**	
Debussy:	*La Mer*	60143
	Prélude à l'àprès-midi	
	Jeux	
Conductor:	**BOULT**	
Beethoven:	*Coriolan Overture*	CFP4144091
	Violin Concerto (Suk)	
Elgar:	*Dream of Gerontius*	SLS987
Holst:	*The Planets*	ESD7135
Moeran:	*Symphony*	SRCS70
Vaughan Williams:	*Symphony 3*	ASD2393
	Symphony 4	ASD2375
	Symphony 6	ASD2329
	In the Fen Country	ASD2393
	Norfolk Rhapsody	ASD2375
	Lark Ascending (Bean)	ASD2329
Elgar:	*Violin Concerto* (Menuhin)	SXLP2900001
Howells:	*Merry Eve*	SRCS69
	Elegy	
	Corydon's Dance	
	Scherzo in Arden	
Vaughan Williams:	*Wasps – March of Kitchen Utensils*	SRCS71
Delius:	*Marche Caprice*	
Conductor:	**BRAITHWAITE**	
Berkeley:	*Piano Concerto* (Wilde)	SRCS94
Moeran:	*Rhapsody 3* (McCabe)	SRCS91
Leigh:	*Agincourt*	SRCS95
Conductor:	**BRITTEN**	
Britten:	*Sinfonia da Requiem*	SXL6641
Conductor:	**CANTELLI**	
Brahms:	*Symphony 1*	SH314
	Symphony 3	
Debussy:	*La Mer*	SH374
	Martyre de St Sebastian	
Mendelssohn:	*Symphony 4*	SH290
Mozart:	*Musical Joke*	RLS7701
Schubert:	*Symphony 8*	SH290
Schumann:	*Symphony 4*	SH315

Tchaikovsky:	*Symphony 6*	SHB52
Conductor:	**COBOS**	
Bruch:	*Violin Concerto 2*	ASD3310
	Scottish Fantasy (Perlman)	
Donizetti:	*Lucia*	6703 080
Rossini:	*Otello*	6769 023
Conductor:	**COPLAND**	
Copland:	*Symphony 3*	61869
	Film music	61672
Conductor:	**A. DAVIS**	
Duruflé:	*Requiem*	76633
	Danse Lente	
Dvořák:	*Symphony 6*	36708
Faure:	*Pavane*	76734
	Requiem	
	Pelléas et Mélisande	76526
Greig:	*Peer Gynt*	76527
	Songs (Söderstrom)	
Fauré:	*Ballade*	PAD173
	Fantasie	
Ravel:	*Piano Concerto in G* (Varsano)	
Tchaikovsky:	*Piano Concerto 1* (Vered)	VIV16
Conductor:	**C. DAVIS**	
Berlioz:	*Harold in Italy* (Menuhin)	SXLP30314
Brahms:	*Violin Concerto* (Grumiaux)	6527 197
Conductor:	**DEL MAR**	
Bax:	*Symphony 6*	SRCS35
Blake:	*Violin Concerto* (Iona Brown)	ZRG922
Rubbra:	*Symphony 6*	SRCS127
	Symphony 8	
Conductor:	**DOBROWEN**	
Brahms:	*Violin Concerto*	RLS739
Chausson:	*Poeme* (Neveu)	
Brahms:	*Piano Concerto 2* (Solomon)	SLS5094
Tchaikovsky:	*Piano Concerto 1* (Solomon)	
Conductor:	**DORATI**	
Bartók:	*Violin Concertos 1/2* (Menuhin)	SXLP30533
Tchaikovsky:	*Suites 1-4*	6768 035
Conductor:	**DOWNES**	
Lloyd:	*Symphony 4*	SRCS129
	Symphony 5	SRCS124
	Symphony 8	SRCS113

Conductor:	**DUTOIT**	
Caplet:	*Epiphanie*	STU71368
Lalo:	*Cello Concerto* (Lodeon)	
Buendia:	*Suite Concertante*	411738-IDH
Rodrigo:	*Concierto di Aranjuez* (Robles)	
Saint-Saëns:	*Piano Concerto 4*	SXL7008
	Paino Concertos 1-4 (Roge)	D244D3
Tchaikovsky:	*Violin Concerto*	STU71452
	Serénade Mélancolique	
	Valse-Scherzo (Amoyal)	
Saint-Saëns:	*Tone Poems*	SXL6975
Conductor:	**FRANCIS**	
Donizetti:	*Ugo, Conte di Parigi*	OR1
Finzi:	*Clarinet Concerto*	A6601
Stanford:	*Clarinet Concerto* (King)	
Conductor:	**FREMAUX**	
Rodrigo:	*Concierto di Aranjuex*	IM37848
	Fantasia para un gentilhombre (Williams)	
Conductor:	**FRÜHBECK DE BURGOS**	
Falla:	*Amor Brujo and other pieces*	JB50
Haydn:	*Creation*	SLS5125
Mendelssohn:	*Elijah*	SLS935
	Midsummer Night's Dream	JB72
Orff:	*Carmina Burana*	ESD7177
Rossini:	*Introduction and Variations*	ASD2455
Weber:	*Clarinet Concerto 1* (de Peyer)	
Ravel:	*Bolero*	ESD7019
Chabrier:	*España*	
Prokofiev:	*Classical Symphony*	
Stravinsky:	*Fireworks*	
	Circus Polka	
Mozart:	*D minor Requiem*	CFP4399
Conductor:	**FURTWÄNGLER**	
Beethoven:	*Piano Concerto 5* (Edwin Fischer)	RLS2900013
Wagner:	*Tristan und Isolde*	RLS684
Conductor:	**GALLIERA**	
Beethoven:	*Violin Concerto* (Grumiaux)	CBR1024
Grieg:	*Piano Concerto* (Lipatti)	HLM7046
Rossini:	*Il Barbiere*	SLS853
R. Strauss	*Horn Concerto 1* (Brain)	RLS7701
Conductor:	**GAMBA**	
	Operatic arias (Pavarotti)	SXL7013
Conductor:	**GARDELLI**	

Verdi:	*Il Corsara*	6700 098
	Il Masnadieri	6703 064
Conductor:	**GIBSON**	
Mozart:	*Complete music for Violin and Orchestra* (Szeryng)	6747 376
Conductor:	**GIULINI**	
Beethoven:	*Violin Concerto* (Perlman)	ASD4059
Britten:	*Variations and Fugue*	SXLP30240
	Les Illuminations	2531 199
	Four Sea Interludes	SXLP30240
Debussy:	*La Mer*	SXLP30146
	Nocturnes	
Dvořák:	*Symphony 9*	SXLP30163
	Carnival Overture	
Mozart:	*Symphonies 40/41*	JB8
	Don Giovanni	SLS5083
	Nozze di Figaro	SLS5152
	Mass in D minor	ASD3723
Rossini:	*Stabat Mater*	2532 046
	Overtures	CFP40379
Verdi:	*Requiem*	SLS909
	Four Sacred Pieces	SXLP30508
Conductor:	**GRACIS**	
Rachmaninov:	*Piano Concerto 4*	SXLP30169
Ravel:	*Piano Concerto in G* (Michelangeli)	
Conductor:	**GROVES**	
Hoddinott:	*Sinfonia fidei*	RHD401
	Noctures and Cadenzas	
	Jack Straw Overture	
Conductor:	**HAITINK**	
Elgar:	*Symphony 1*	ASD1077941
	Symphony 2	EL270147-1
Walton	*Symphony 1*	ASD4091
Conductor:	**HANDLEY**	
Dvořák:	*Symphony 9*	ABM759
Finzi:	*Grand Fantasia and Toccata*	SRCS92
	Eclogue (Katin)	
	Clarinet Concerto (Denman)	
	Let us Garlands Bring	SRCS93
	2 Milton Sonnets	
	Farewell to Arms	
	In Terra Pax	
G. Bush:	*Yorick*	SRCS95
Delius:	*Cello Concerto*	RS9010
Holst:	Invocation	

Vaughan Williams:	*Fantasia on Sussex Folk Tunes* (Lloyd Webber)	
Conductor:	**HINDEMITH**	
Hindemith:	*Horn Concerto* (Brain)	RLS7701
Conductor:	**HOPKINS**	
Hopkins:	*John and the Magic Music Man*	RHS360
Conductor:	**HORENSTEIN**	
Beethoven:	*Violin Concerto* (Gruenberg)	CBR1024
Nielsen:	*Symphony 5*	RHS300
	Saga-Drom	
Conductor:	**HOWARTH**	
Xenakis:	*Aroura*	HEAD13
	Antikthon	
	Synaphai(Madge)	
Conductor:	**JOO**	
R. Strauss:	*Der Rosenkavalier-Suite*	—
	Die Frau ohne Schatten-Suite	—
Wagner:	*Opera arias* (Marton)	SEFD5024
Conductor:	**JUDD**	
Donizetti:	*Ne m'oubliez pas (exc.)*	OR4
Meyerbeer:	*Dinorah*	OR5
Conductor:	**KARAJAN**	
Beethoven:	*Egmont Overture*	SLS5053
	Coriolan Overture	
	Leonora 3 Overture	
	Fidelio-Abscheulicher	RLS7715
	Ah, perfido (Schwarzkopf)	
Balakirev:	*Symphony 1*	
Berlioz:	*Symphonie fantastique*	
Bizet:	*L'Arlésienne Suite*	EMX2028
	Carmen Suite	
Britten:	*Bridge Variations*	XLP60002
Mozart:	*Horn Concertos 1-4* (Brain)	ASD1140
	Sinfonia Concertante (Sutcliffe, Walton, James, Brain)	RLS7715
Schubert:	*Symphony 8*	SXLP30513
Schumann:	*Piano Concerto* (Lipatti)	HLM7046
Sibelius:	*Symphony 5*	SXLP30430
	Symphony 7	
R. Strauss:	*Don Juan*	RLS7715
	Till Eulenspiegel	
	Ariadne auf Naxos	RLS760
	Der Rosenkavalier	SLS810
	Tod und Verklärung	RLS7715

Rossini:	*Overtures*	SXLP30203
Vaughan Williams:	*Fantasia*	XLP60002
Verdi:	*Falstaff*	SLS5211
Conductor:	**KLEMPERER**	
Bach:	*Mass in B minor*	SLS930
	St Matthew Passion	SLS827
Beethoven:	*Missa Solemnis*	SLS922
	Fantasia Op 80	SLS5180
	Piano Concertos 1-5 (Barenboim)	
	Symphonies 1-9	SLS788
	Symphony 7	—
	Fidelio	SLS5006
Berlioz:	*Symphonie Fantastique*	EMX2030
Brahms:	*Symphony 1*	SXLP30217
	Symphony 3	SXLP30255
	Academic Festival Overture	
	Ein Deutsches Requiem	SLS821
	Alto Rhapsody	
	Tragic Overture	SXLP30255
Bruckner:	*Symphony 4*	SXLP30167
	Symphony 6	SXLP30448
Mahler:	*Symphony 2*	SLS806
	Symphony 7	IC163 01931-2
	Symphony 9	SXDW3021
	Lied von der Erde	SAN179
	Des Knaben Wunderhorn 5/9	SXLP2700001
	Rückert Lieder 1/4/5 (Ludwig)	
Mendelssohn:	*Midsummer Night's Dream*	SXLP30196
Mozart:	*Don Giovanni*	SLS1434623
	Die Zauberflöte	SLS912
	Symphonies 25/29/31	SLS5048
	Symphonies 33-36	
	Symphonies 38-41	
	Overture Così	
	Overture Zauberflöte	
	Overture Tito	
	Overture Seraglio	
	Overture Don Giovanni	
	Overture Nozze di Figaro	
	Adagio and Fugue C minor	
	Serenade in G	
	Masonic Funeral Music	
Wagner:	*Opera excerpts*	SXLP30436
		SXLP30525
		SXLP30528
	Wesendonck Lieder	SXLP2700001
	Tristan und Isolde (exc) (Ludwig)	SXLP30525

Also for release during 1985 – Klemperer Edition (EMI)

Beethoven:	*Symphonies 1-9, Egmont music, Grosse Fuge, Coriolan, Fidelio* and *Consecration of House Overtures*	
	Symphonies 3/5/7 (mono)	
	Overtures (unspecified)	
	Violin Concerto (Menuhin)	
Bruckner:	*Symphony 7*	
Haydn:	*Symphonies 100/104*	
Klemperer:	*Symphony 2*	
Mendelssohn:	*Symphonies 3/4*	
Mozart:	*Symphonies* (unspecified)	
Schubert:	*Symphonies 5/8/9*	
R. Strauss:	*Till Eulenspiegel*	
	Don Juan	
	Tod und Verklärung	
Tchaikovsky:	*Symphonies 4/5/6*	
Conductor:	**KLETZKI**	
Chopin:	*Piano Concerto 1* (Pollini)	SXLP30160
Rimsky-Korsakov	*Scheherazade*	CFP40341
Tchaikovsky:	*Symphony 6*	CFP40220
Mendelssohn:	*Midsummer Night's Dream* (Nocturne)	RLS7701
Tchaikovsky:	*Capriccio Italien*	CFP40341
Conductor:	**KOIZUMI**	
Dohnányi:	*Nursery Variations*	ASD3197
Rachmnaninov:	*Paganini Rhapsody* (Ortiz)	
Conductor:	**KORD**	
Sibelius:	*Tone Poems*	SPA549
Conductor:	**KUBELIK**	
Brahms:	*Piano Concerto 1* (Solomon)	SLS5094
Conductor:	**KURTZ**	
Bruch:	*Violin Concerto*	ASD334
Mendelssohn:	*Violin Concerto* (Menuhin)	
Prokofiev:	*Romeo and Juliet* (exc)	ESD7151
Tchaikovsky:	*Swan Lake* (exc)	CFP40296
	Excerpts – Swan Lake	SLS859
	Excerpts – Nutcracker	
	Excerpts – Sleeping Beauty	
Saint-Saëns:	*Carnival of the Animals*	ESD7114
Prokofiev:	*Peter and the Wolf (H. Menuhin/Simon)*	
Conductor:	**LANCHBERY**	
Tchaikovsky:	*Swan Lake*	SLS5271
	Sleeping Beauty	SLS5272
	Nutcracker	SLS5270

Ketelby:	*Misc. pieces*	ASD3542
Conductor:	**LEDGER**	
Elgar:	*Coronation Ide*	ASD3345
Parry:	*I Was Glad*	
Conductor:	**LEINSDORF**	
Stravinsky:	*Petrushka*	VIV42
Conductor:	**LEPPARD**	
Britten:	*Young Person's Guide*	CFP185
Grieg:	*Four Symphonic Dancers*	6514203
	Old Norwegian Romance	
Mozart:	*Clarinet Concerto* (McCaw)	UNS239
	C minor Mass	ASD2959
Nielsen:	*Clarinet Concerto* (McCaw)	UNS239
Prokofiev:	*Peter and the Wolf*	CFP185
Conductor:	**LEVI**	
Rachmaninov:	*Piano Concerto 2*	CFP4383
	Paganini Rhapsody (Tirimo)	
Conductor:	**LEVINE**	
Cilea:	*Adriana Lecouvreur*	79310
Puccini:	*Tosca*	SLS5213
Conductor:	**LUDWIG**	
Wagner:	*Operatic excerpts*	SXLP30557
	(Nilsson, Hotter)	
Conductor:	**MAAZEL**	
Ravel:	*Orchestral works*	EMX2007
Debussy:	*Prélude à l'après-midi*	EMX2008
Mussorgsky:	*Pictures at an Exhibition*	
Puccini:	*Suor Angelica*	79312
	Il Tabarro	
Tchaikovsky:	*Piano Concertos 1/3* (Gilels)	EMX2001
Conductor:	**MACKERRAS**	
Sullivan:	*Pineapple Poll*	SXDL7619
	Overture di Ballo	
Meyerbeer:	*Les Patineurs*	ESD7115
Ponchielli:	*Dance of the Hours*	
Conductor:	**MALKO**	
Rachmaninov:	*Piano Concertos 1/2* (Lympany)	IMP5
Tchaikovsky:	*Nutcracker* (exc)	ESD7115
Prokofiev:	*Classical Symphony*	SXLP30437
	Symphony 7	
	Love of Three Oranges	

Conductor:	**MARKEVICH**	
Stravinsky:	*Rite of Spring*	PM116272-1
Conductor:	**MARRINER**	
Mendelssohn:	*Midsummer Night's Dream*	411 106-1
Gershwin:	*Rhapsody in Blue*	411 123-1PH
Litolff:	*Scherzo*	
Addinsell:	*Warsaw Concerto*	
Chopin:	*Fantasia*	
Weber:	*Polacca brillante* (Dichter)	
Offenbach:	*Overtures*	6514 089
Conductor:	**MATA**	
Rodrigo:	*Concierto pastoral*	RL25193
	Fantasia para un gentilhombre (Galway)	
Conductor:	**MATAČIĆ**	
Lehar:	*Lustige Witwe*	SLS823
R. Strauss	*Arabella* (exc)	RLS751
Conductor:	**MEASHAM**	
Kabalevsky:	*Symphony 2*	RHS346
Miaskovsky:	*Symphony 2*	
Conductor:	**MEHTA**	
Puccini:	*Tosca*	GL20105
Conductor:	**MENGES**	
Grieg:	*Piano Concerto*	SLS5094
Schumann:	*Piano Concerto* (Solomon)	
Grieg:	*Piano Concerto* (Lympany)	IMP5
Conductor:	**MORRIS**	
Mahler:	*Symphony 1*	GSGC2045
Conductor:	**MUTI**	
Cherubini:	*Requiem in C minor*	ASD4071
	Requiem in D minor	ASD3073
Donizetti:	*Don Pasquale*	SLS1434363
Gluck:	*Orfeo ed Euridice*	SLS5255
Mendelssohn:	*Symphony 5*	ASD3781
Mozart:	*Symphony 24*	ASD1435281
	Symphony 25	ASD3326
	Symphony 29	
	Piano Concerto 22 (Richter)	ADS1435281
	Violin Concertos 2/4 (Mutter)	ASD4185
Orff:	*Carmina Burana*	ASD3900
Schumann:	*Symphony 1*	SLS5199
	Symphony 2	
	Symphony 3	

	Symphony 4	
	Bride of Messina Overture	
	Hermann and Dorothea Overture	
	Violin Concerto (Kremer)	ASD1435191
Sibelius:	*Violin Concerto* (Kremer)	
Tchaikovsky:	*Symphonies 1-6*	SLS1545303
	Manfred Symphony	
	Romeo and Juliet	
Verdi:	*Requiem*	SLS5185
	La Traviata	SLS5240
	Aïda	SLS977
	Un ballo in maschera	SLS984
Vivaldi:	*Gloria*	ASD3418
	Magnificat	
Verdi:	*Opera Choruses*	ASD3979
	(Ambrosian Singers)	
Conductor:	**NAVARRO**	
Rodrigo:	*Concierto di Aranjuez*	2531208
	Concierto madrigal (Yepes, Monden)	
Conductor:	**PRÊTRE**	
Poulenc:	*Misc. pieces*	ASD4067
Conductor:	**PRITCHARD**	
Dohnányi:	*Piano Concerto 1* (Vazsonyi)	GSGC2052
Liszt:	*Piano Concerto 1* (Rosen)	—
Rachmaninov:	*Piano Concerto 2* (Ogdon)	SXLP30552
Conductor:	**RATTLE**	
Holst:	*The Planets*	ASD4047
Janácek:	*Sinfonietta*	ASD1435221
	Taras Bulba	
Maxwell Davies:	*Symphony*	HEAD21
Sibelius:	*Symphony 5*	ASD4168
	Night Ride and Sunrise	
Conductor:	**RESCIGNO**	
Verdi:	*Operatic arias* (Callas)	ASD3817
Puccini:	*Operatic arias* (Schwarzkopf)	SXDW3049
Conductor:	**RUDEL**	
Massenet:	*Cendrillon*	79323
Verdi:	*Rigoletto*	SLS5193
Conductor:	**SANDERLING**	
Schubert/Liszt:	*Wanderer Fantasia*	RHS367
Schumann:	*Piano Concerto* (Rogoff)	
Beethoven:	*Symphonies 1-9*	SLS5239
	Fidelio Overture	
	Coriolan Overture	

	Prometheus Overture	
Conductor:	**SANTI**	
Verdi:	*Operatic arias* (Bergonzi)	6570045
Conductor:	**SARGENT**	
Coleridge-Taylor:	*Hiawatha's Wedding Feast*	ESD7161
Elgar:	*Serenade*	SXLP30126
Bartók:	*Piano Concerto 3* (Ogdon)	SXLP30514
Conductor:	**SAWALLISCH**	
Beethoven:	*Piano Concerto 5* (Egorov)	ASD1434331
Mendelssohn:	*Symphony 4*	412008-IPS
	Symphony 5	
Mozart:	*Piano Concertos 21/22*	SXLP30124
	(Annie Fischer)	
Orff:	*Die Kluge*	IC13743291-3
	Der Mond	
R. Strauss:	*Capriccio*	1435243
	Horn Concerto 2 (Brain)	RLS7701
Conductor:	**SCIMONE**	
Clementi:	*Symphonies 1-4*	STU71174
Puccini:	*Messa di Gloria*	NUM75090
Rossini:	*Edipo a Colonna*	ITL70054
	Mose in Egitto	6769081
	Overtures	STU71178
Conductor:	**SEGAL**	
Beethoven:	*Piano Concerto 5* (Firkušny)	PFS4291
Conductor:	**SERAFIN**	
Donizetti:	*Lucia*	SLS5166
Puccini:	*Opera arias* (Callas)	ALP3799
	Opera excerpts (Callas)	ALP3824
	Opera arias (Callas)	SLS869
Conductor:	**M. SHOSTAKOVICH**	
Shostakovich:	*Violin Concerto 1*(D. Oistrakh)	ASD4046
Conductor:	**SILVESTRI**	
Franck:	*Symphony*	CFP40090
Liszt:	*Piano Concertos 1/2* (François)	CFP40057
Conductor:	**SIMON**	
Respighi:	*Brazilian Impressions*	ABRD1098
	Vetrate di Chiesa	
	French Ballet Music of 1920s	ABRD1119
Conductor:	**SINOPOLI**	
Mendelssohn:	*Symphony 4*	410862-1

Puccini:	*Manon Lescaut*	413893-1GH3
Schubert:	*Symphony 8*	410862-1
Conductor:	**STOKOWSKI**	
Dvořák:	*Symphony 9*	VICS2038
Tchaikovsky:	*Nutcracker/Swan Lake*	VIV10
Conductor:	**SÜSSKIND**	
Grieg:	*Peer Gynt*	SXLP30105
	Symphonic Dances	
Liszt:	*Hungarian Fantasia* (Solomon)	SLS5094
Mozart:	*Horn Concerto 2* (Brain)	RLS7701
	Piano Concertos (Schnabel)	EX290072-3
Franck:	*Symphonic Variations*	IMP5
Litolff:	*Scherzo* (Lympany)	
Sibelius:	*Violin Concerto* (Neveu)	RLS739
	Operaticrias: (Schwarzkopf)	SXDW3049
Conductor:	**SVETLANOV**	
Glazunov:	*The Seasons*	ASD3601
	Valses de Concert 1/2	
Conductor:	**TILSON THOMAS**	
Debussy:	*La Mer*	D37832
	Nocturnes	
Mendelssohn:	*Violin Concerto*	39007
Saint-Saëns:	*Violin Concerto 3* (Lin)	
Tchaikovsky:	*Suites 2/4*	36702
Knussen:	*Symphony 3*	RHD400
Stravinsky:	*Petrushka*	D37271
	Scherzo à la Russe (Troon)	
Conductor:	**TUNG**	
Berlioz:	*Symphonie Fantastique*	ABM754
Rachmaninov:	*Symphony No. 2*	ACM2016
Conductor:	**DE WAART**	
Mozart:	*Oboe Concerto*	6500174
R. Strauss:	*Oboe Concerto* (Holliger)	
Conductor:	**WALTON**	
Walton:	*Façade*	SLS5246
	Partita –	SLS5246
		SXLP30234
	Belshazzar's Feast	
	Symphony 1	SLS5246
	Crown Imperial	
	Orb and Sceptre	
	Johannesburg Festival Overture	
	Portsmouth Point	
	Spitfire Prelude and Fugue	

	Henry V Suite	SXLP30139
	Hamlet (Funeral March)	
	Richard III Suite	
	Violin Concerto (Menuhin)	ASD2542
Conductor:	**WARREN-GREEN**	
Haydn:	*Trumpet Concerto* (Wallace)	NIM214
	Horn Concertos 1/2 (Thompson)	
Conductor:	**WELDON**	
Coleridge-Taylor:	*Petite Suite de Concert*	ESD7161
Grieg:	*Homage March*	ESD7156
Conductor:	**WILLCOCKS**	
Bennett:	*Spells*	ZRG907
Vaughan Williams	*Five Tudor Portraits*	SLS5082
Fauré:	*Requiem*	ASD2358
	Pavane	
Howells:	*Hymnus Paradisi*	ESD1020662

Index

Please note throughout that
Bean, Hugh
–, Mary
indicates that the two are related.
Bean, Hugh
Bean, T.E.,
indicates that they are not related.